THE CONVENTION PARLIAMENT

1689:

A Biographical Study
of Its Members

THE
CONVENTION
PARLIAMENT
1689:

*A Biographical Study
of Its Members*

by

GEORGE L. CHERRY

BOOKMAN ASSOCIATES, INC.
New York 3

PREFACE

During the preparation of *Early English Liberalism* (New York, 1962), as well as articles on the Revolution of 1688, much time was consumed to determine the identity, political significance, economic status, and social position of participants of the Convention Parliament of 1689. Not all of the effort, however, was without value since considerable material was accumulated on the active membership in the process of identification.

Upon the completion of the study of the early phase of English Liberalism, attention has been devoted to a comprehensive study of the members of the House of Commons of 1688. The decision to undertake this research was enhanced by an expression of the need for a study of this type by David Ogg in his *England in the Reigns of James II and William III* (Oxford, 1955).

Through the application of the biographical technique in the study of history, an attempt has been made to collect as much information about the members as possible. They consisted of a formidable array of men each unique in personality, background, and experience. In order to understand and to classify them, the student of the period should have information about each member's age, social status, residence, political experience and outlook, family background and connections, education, economic interests and activities, and marital status. This material has been assembled from a wide variety of sources in a single volume for the first time. Although no attempt has been made to exhaust the reserve of potential sources in England, sufficient information has been assembled to provide a more complete understanding of the men who served in the Convention Parliament of 1689.

The preparation of this book was made possible in part through a research grant to the writer from Southern Illinois University.

THE CONVENTION PARLIAMENT

1689:

A Biographical Study

of Its Members

Acton, Sir Edward (1650-1716), baronet, of Aldenham Hall and Acton Scott, Shropshire, sheriff of Shropshire, 1684-85; recorder of Bridgenorth, 1701; and Member of Parliament (Tory) for Bridgenorth Borough, Shropshire, 1689-90, 1690-95, 1695-98, 1698-1700, and 1701. Descended from the Civil War royalist, Edward Acton, he was the eldest son and heir of Sir Walter Acton, second baronet, whose family owned 6,321 acres of land in Salop. He succeeded to the baronetcy in 1665. In May, 1666, he matriculated at Queen's College, Oxford, and received an M.A. in 1667. Later, after completing his studies at the Inner Temple, he was called to the Bar. Sir Edward married Mary Walter, an heiress, and died in 1716.

Alford, John (1645-1691), esquire, of Offington, Sussex, Member of Parliament (Tory) from Midhurst Borough, Sussex, 1679, 1679-81, and Bramber Borough, Sussex, 1689. He was the son of Edward Alford, a former Member of Parliament. Alford matriculated at Christ Church College, Oxford, in November, 1664, at age seventeen. His wife, Sarah, lived until 1734 while he died in May, 1691.

Amherst, Geoffrey (1649-1713), esquire, of Riverhead, Kent, Member of Parliament for Bletchingly Borough, Kent, 1689-90. The son and heir of John Amherst of Amherst, a bencher at Gray's Inn, he was the first of the family to live at Riverhead in Kent. Amherst matriculated at Christ's College, Cambridge, in March, 1667, at age seventeen. After completion of his studies at Gray's Inn, which he entered in 1666, he was called to the Bar in February, 1670. Like his father, he became a bencher at the Inn. He married, first, Elizabeth Yates and then, Dorothy Amherst of Penbury. Their son was Jeffrey Amherst, the illustrious general. He died in 1713.

Andrew, Thomas (c. 1647-1722), esquire, of Harlston, Northamptonshire, Member of Parliament for Higham Ferrers Borough, Northamptonshire, 1689-90, 1690-95, 1695-98, and for Northampton County, 1701, and 1701-02. He was the son of William Andrew of Staffordshire. Andrew was admitted to Emmanuel College, Cambridge, in June, 1662. He married Ann Kynnesman and died in October, 1722.

Andrewes, Sir Matthew (d. 1711), knight, of Ashley, Surrey, Member of Parliament (Whig) from Shaftesbury Borough,

Dorsetshire 1679-81, 1681, 1689-90, and sheriff of Surrey County in 1674. He was knighted on board an East India Company ship in 1675 and his wife, Anne, died in 1709. He died in 1711.

Appleyard, Matthew (b. 1661), esquire, of Burstwick Hall, Garth, East Riding, Yorkshire, Member of Parliament (Tory) for Heyden Borough, Yorkshire, 1661-70 and 1689-95. The son of Sir Matthew Appleyard, a prominent royalist Member of Parliament and military commander in the Civil War who was knighted on the field near Leicester and was appointed governor of that city, he was in politics a strong adherent to the church and state. After attending a private school at Beverly, he was admitted to St. John's College, Cambridge, where his tutor was Mr. Johnston. Appleyard died in London.

Arnold, John (b. 1654), esquire, of Westminster, the king's brewer; sheriff of Monmouth County, 1669; and Member of Parliament (Whig) for Monmouth Borough, Monmouth County, 1680-81 and 1695-98, and for Southwark Borough, Surrey County, 1689-95. In January, 1689, he was elected Member of Parliament for both Monmouth and Southwark boroughs, but chose to represent Southwark in the Convention Parliament. He was the son and heir of Michael Arnold of Westminster. Arnold matriculated at St. John's College, Cambridge, in June, 1670, at age sixteen and received a B.A. in 1674. He entered Gray's Inn in November, 1678. In 1683 the Duke of Bedford brought charges of *de scandalis magnatum* in court against Sir Trevor Williams and John Arnold for false and scandalous words spoken against him and was awarded damages in the amount of ƒ10,000. On January 28, 1689, Arnold seconded Gilbert Dolben's motion in a state of the nation speech "That king James 2. having voluntarily forsaken the kingdom, it is a voluntary demise in him."[1]

Ashburnham, John (1656-1710), baron, of Sussex, custos rotulorum in Brecon County, 1702-10, and Member of Parliament (Tory) for Hastings, a Cinque Port, 1679-81, 1685-87, and 1689. A Tory in politics, he was the son and heir of William Ashburnham, Member of Parliament in the Restoration, and the grandson of John Ashburnham, a staunch royalist, groom of the bedchamber, Member of Parliament and a close friend of Charles II, who spent much of his lifetime attempting to rebuild the family holdings which his father had dissipated through his generosity to his friends. The grandfather had vast economic interests which included 24,489 acres of land in the counties of Sussex, Suffolk, Brecon, and Carmarthen as well as land speculation, money lending, and tapestry manufacturing. In May, 1689, the grandson was created Baron Ashburnham of Ashburnham. After spending two years at Eton, he was admitted to Peterhouse College, Cambridge, at age fourteen in May, 1670, and was granted an M.A. in 1671. In 1677 he married Bridget, the daughter and heiress of Walter Vaughn of Brecknockshire, Wales. He died in January, 1710.

Ashe, William (1647-1713), esquire, of Heytesbury, Wiltshire, Member of Parliament for Heytesbury Borough Wiltshire, 1668-1701, 1708-13, and for Wiltshire, 1701-02. He was the son and heir of Edward Ashe, citizen and draper of London, a former Member of Parliament from Heytesbury in the reign of Charles I who purchased the manor of Heytesbury in Wiltshire which his descendants held for 150 years. In November, 1664, Ashe matriculated at St. Edmund Hall, Oxford, at age seventeen; he also studied law at the Inner Temple. He married Anna, the daughter of Alexander Popham, and was the father of Alexander and Edward Ashe. He died in 1713.

Ashurst, Sir Henry (1645-1711), baronet, of Waterstock, Oxfordshire, commissioner for duties on hackney coaches in 1694, and Member of Parliament (Whig) for Turo Borough, Cornwall County, 1681-95, and for Wilton Borough, Wiltshire, 1698-1702. A London merchant engaged in the West Indian trade, he was the son of Henry Ashurst, a wealthy and generous London merchant, who supported the parliamentary and Presbyterian causes and who served as a London alderman. Henry, his son, was a friend of the Presbyterian leader, Richard Baxter. His uncle, Colonel William Ashurst, was Member of Parliament for Lancaster and his brother, Sir William Ashurst, was lord mayor and Member of Parliament for London. He was created first baronet in July, 1688. Although Henry Ashhurst founded the family of Ashhurst of Woodstock, Sir Henry built the manor house there. He married Dyana, the daughter of William, Lord Paget, and died in 1711.

Ashurst, Sir William (1647-1720), knight, of London, alderman and lord mayor of London, 1693-94; a commissioner for taking subscriptions to the Bank of England and for excise, 1695-99, 1714-20, and Member of Parliament (Whig) for London City, Middlesex, 1689-90, 1695-1702, and 1705-10. A London banker and bank director, he was the second son of Henry Ashurst, a London mercer and the brother of Sir Henry Ashurst. He was knighted in 1689. He married Elizabeth, daughter of Robert Thompson, governor of the Old East India Company, and died in 1720.

Astley, Sir Jacob (1639-1729), baronet, of Hill Morton, Warwickshire, sheriff of Norfolkshire, 1663-64, a commissioner of trade, 1714-17, and Member of Parliament for Norfolk County, 1685-87, 1689-90, 1695-1701, 1702-05, and 1710-22. The third son of Edward Astley, knight, he inherited the estates of his uncle, Sir Isaac Astley, as well as the entailed lands of his grandfather, Lord Astley. He was created a baronet in June, 1660. After entering King's College, Cambridge, at Easter-time in 1657, he matriculated at Christ Church, Oxford, in July, 1659. Astley married Blanche Wodehouse, the daughter of Sir Philip Wodehouse, baronet, of Kimberley, and died in 1729, at age 90.

Austen, Sir John (c. 1640-1698), baronet, of Bexley, Kent, a commissioner of customs, 1697-98, and Member of Parliament for Rye, a Cinque Port, 1669-79, 1689-90, and 1695-98. He was the eldest son of Robert Austen of Bexley, Kent, who was created baronet in 1660 by Charles II and who was sheriff of Kent, 1660-61, and entered Gray's Inn in 1657. Austen married Rose, the daughter and heiress of Sir John Hale, a knight from Stagenhoe in Hertfordshire. He died in 1698.

Austen, Robert (b. 1657), esquire, of Tenterden, Kent, army officer and Member of Parliament (Whig) from Winchelsea, a Cinque Port in 1689. The second son of Robert Austen, esquire, of Holland, Kent, he was the brother of Sir John Austen. After service in the Cinque Port militia, he was commissioned a lieutenant in Captain Robert Austen's company stationed at Tenterden, Kent. Following duty with several military units, he received an assignment as first lieutenant in the First Marine Regiment in 1691. His wife was Elizabeth Stowell.

Ayscoghe, Sir Edward (1650-1699), knight, of South Kelsey, Lincoln County, captain of horse, 1680; deputy lieutenant, 1680-

81; sheriff of Lincolnshire, 1683-84; high steward of Grimsby, 1686; a commissioner of the prize office; and Member of Parliament for Grimsby, 1685-99. He was the son and heir of Sir Edward Ayscoghe, knight of South Kelsey, Lincolnshire. After attending Lincoln School in Melton, he matriculated at Sidney College, Cambridge, in September, 1667, and entered Gray's Inn in June, 1671. He was knighted in 1672. Twice married, his first wife was Mary Skinner and his second, the daughter of William Harbord of Northampton.

Babington, Philip (b. 1635), esquire, of Ogle Castle, Northumberland, Parliamentary Army officer; governor of Berwick; and Member of Parliament from Berwick-on-Tweed Borough, Northumberland, 1689-90. He was the son of William Babington of Ogle Castle, who had been a colonel in the parliamentary Army and governor of Berwick for Charles II. Babington entered Christ Church College, Oxford, in 1650 and Gray's Inn in 1661. His military career was distinguished. In 1654, while a captain in the Parliamentary Army, he was with Colonel Morgan's forces when the latter routed the troops of General Middleton in Scotland. In the Restoration he was promoted to the rank of major. As a colonel Babington was the commander of the garrison at Berwick, 1688-93.

Babington, Thomas (1635-1708), esquire, of Rothley Temple, Leicestershire, sheriff of Leicestershire, 1677, and Member of Parliament (Tory) from Leicester Borough, Leicestershire, 1685-89. He was the son and heir of Matthew Babington whose lineage could be traced to Henry III's reign and who had been a Member of Parliament for Leicester in 1660 at the restoration of Charles II and succeeded him in 1669. In 1688 he refused to support the king's proposal to repeal the Test Act, but he supported James II the following year and declined to vote for the motion offering the crown to William and Mary. Babington married Elizabeth Jesson of Coventry and, after her death in 1669, Margaret Hall of Gretford, Leicestershire. At his death in 1708, he was succeeded by his son, Thomas.

Bagot, Sir Walter (1644-1704), baronet, of Blithfield, Staffordshire, justice of peace and deputy lord lieutenant of Staffordshire, 1677-1704, and Member of Parliament from the same county, 1679-81, 1685-87, 1688-90, and 1693-95. He was the eldest son of Sir Edward Bagot, second baronet, a Member of Parliament for Stafford County during the Restoration, whose family held 22,381 acres of land in the counties of Stafford, Denbigh, and Merioneth. Sir Walter succeeded to the baronetcy in 1673. In November, 1662, he matriculated at Christ Church College, Oxford, at age seventeen and entered the Middle Temple in 1666. His intellectual interests continued after his school career, for he was the sponsor of Dr. Plott's *History of Staffordshire*. Bagot married Jane, the daughter and sole heiress of Charles Salusbury, who had bought vast estates in Wales. By the marriage, Sir Walter acquired the estate of Pool Park in Denbigh County. He died in February, 1704.

Baldwyn, Charles (1651-1706), esquire, of Stoke Castle, Shropshire, chancellor of Hereford Castle and Member of Parliament for Ludlow Borough, Shropshire, 1681, 1689, and 1690-98. The Baldwyn family had long been involved in parliamentary affairs since Charles's grandfather was a royalist member of the Long Parliament and his father, Samuel Baldwyn, a serjeant-at-law, represented Ludlow Borough during the Restoration. Baldwyn was well educated. After attending Shrewsbury School, he matriculated at Queen's College, Oxford, in December 1667, at age fifteen. Later, he attended the Inner Temple from which school he was called to the Bar as a barrister. In 1684 he received an LL. B. degree from Cambridge University. He married Elizabeth, daughter and heiress of Nicholas Acton, and died in January, 1706.

Bale, Christopher, esquire, mayor of Exeter, Member of Parliament (Tory) for Exeter City, Devonshire, 1689.

Banks, Caleb (1659-1696), esquire, of Maidstone, Kent, served as deputy lieutenant of Kent, 1683, army officer, and Member of Parliament (Tory) for Maidstone Borough, Kent, 1689, for Queenborough, Kent, 1685, 1695-96, and for Rochester Borough, Kent, 1691. His father was Sir John Banks, baronet, of Maidstone, Kent. Banks was admitted at Queen's College, Cambridge, April, 1675, and attended Gray's Inn. For two years he toured Europe with John Locke as his tutor. Although he was a barrister, he spent most of his time managing his father's estates in Kent. He married Elizabeth, the daughter of Samuel

Fortrey, a merchant. He refused to sign the Association of 1696. He died in September, 1696, at age thirty-seven.

Banks, Sir John (1627-1699), baronet, of London and after 1681 of Fryers, Aylesford, Kent, justice of peace, deputy lieutenant, mayor of Maidstone, and Member of Parliament (Tory) for Maidstone Borough, Kent, 1654, 1656, 1659, 1695, for Rochester City, Kent, 1679, 1681, 1685, 1689, and for Queensborough Borough, Kent, 1690. The son of Caleb Banks, who had inherited a woolen drapery business in London, John continued the business after serving his apprenticeship as a merchant. He enlarged his operations by investments in the East Indian and Mediterranean trade as well as in Kentish estates. Besides his role as victualler of the navy, he helped finance the governments of Cromwell and three successive kings. At his death his gross wealth was estimated at £180,000. Although he was a member of Cromwell's Parliaments, he favored the restoration of Charles II and was created a baronet in 1661. While he was a friend of John Locke, who was a tutor of his son Caleb, and a member of the Royal Society, he was a moderate Tory with marriage ties to the Finch family. During the Exclusion crisis he was accused of Papist leanings because of his support of the Duke of York, and he voted against the Exclusion Bill. When James requested the deputy lieutenants to ask the three questions about the Test and penal acts, Banks replied that "he cannot agree to the two first questions. (But he) agrees to the last."[2] His moderate Tory, anti-James attitude was an advantage to him at the Revolution. Although the Prince of Orange recommended him as candidate for Parliament, Banks voted against declaring the throne vacant and offering the crown to William and Mary. However, he helped the king finance the French war. Banks married Elizabeth, the daughter of John Dethick, a merchant with interests in the Mediterranean and India and lord mayor of London. He died in 1699.

Banks, William (1658-1690), esquire, of Winstanley Hall, Lancashire, 1679 and 1689-90. The eldest son of William Banks, he inherited the manor of Winstanley in 1676 which had originally been purchased by an ancestor, James Banks, a London goldsmith. His father had been vice-admiral of Lancashire and

Cheshire and Member of Parliament for Liverpool. Banks was admitted to Gray's Inn in June, 1676. He married Lettice, a cousin, the daughter of Richard Legh of Lyme Regis, and died without heirs in 1690.

Barker, Sir John (1656-1696), baronet, of Grimston Hall, in the parish of Trinley St. Martin, near Ipswich, Suffolk, Member of Parliament (Tory) from Ipswich Borough, Suffolk, 1680-81, 1685-87, and 1689-96. His father was Sir John Barker, second baronet of Grimston Hall. At the death of his brother, Sir John succeeded to the baronetcy in 1665 and returned to Ipswich to make Grimston Hall his home. In February, 1674, he was admitted to Merton College, Oxford, at age eighteen. Barker married Bridget, the daughter of Sir Nicholas Bacon of Shrubland, and died in 1696.

Barnardiston, Sir Thomas (1646-1698), baronet, of Ketton, Suffolk County, Member of Parliament from Great Grimsby Borough, Lincoln County, 1685, 1689-90, and Sudbury Borough, Suffolk, 1690, 1695-98. The Barnardiston family was one of the oldest in England with a direct line of descent for thirty generations. Its name was derived from the town of Barnardiston which the family had controlled since the time of the Conquest. Besides their estates, the Barnardistons had important commercial interests. The first baronet, also Sir Thomas, was assessor for Suffolk in the Civil War and was a member of the committee of the Eastern Counties' Association. During the Protectorate, he was a member of Cromwell's Parliaments. After the Restoration, he abandoned his republican interests and represented Sudbury in the Cavalier Parliament. He received a baronetcy in 1663. Sir Thomas, his son, attended St. Catherine's College, Cambridge, being admitted in 1664, and Gray's Inn where he enrolled in 1667. He succeeded to the baronetcy in 1669. In 1670 he married Elizabeth King and died in October, 1698, at age fifty-two.

Bassett, Sir William, knight, of Claverton, Somerset, Member of Parliament (Tory) for Bath City, Somerset County, 1678-1689, and knighted in 1660.

Bayntun, Nicholas (b. 1649), esquire, of Bromham, Wiltshire, Member of Parliament for New Woodstock Borough, Oxfordshire, 1678-79, 1679-81, 1681, and for Chippenham Borough,

Wiltshire, 1689-90. His family could trace its ancestry to Sir Henry Bayntun, who had been Knight Marshall to Henry II and who owned a vast estate, Bromham, in Wiltshire. Members of the family had served in almost every Parliament since the mid-sixteenth century, representing the boroughs of Calne, Chippenham, and Devizes, all of which were near the estate of Bromham. Sir Edward Bayntun, the father of Nicholas, who had been a colonel of horse in the Parliamentary Army, was a Member of Parliament from Devizes during the Civil War, but he was suspended and placed on the list of secluded members because of his part in the army's attack upon the House of Commons. Yet, he sat in the first Protectorate Parliament and returned with the secluded members to the Rump Parliament at the action of General Monck. Later, he was returned as Member of Parliament from Calne to the Convention and Cavalier Parliaments. His second son, Nicholas, was admitted to St. John's College, Oxford, in June, 1664, at age fifteen.

Beake, Thomas (d. 1733), esquire, clerk of the council and director of the Charitable Corporation and Member of Parliament for Aylesbury Borough, Buckinghamshire, 1689. He died in March, 1733.

Beaumont, John (1636-1701), esquire, of Burton, Leicestershire, army officer; governor of Dover Castle; commander of the garrison at the Cinque Ports; and Member of Parliament (Whig) for Nottingham Borough, Nottinghamshire, 1685-87, and for Hastings, a Cinque Port, 1689-93. His father was Sapcote Beaumont, Viscount Beaumont of Swords, Ireland, who had suffered deeply for the royal cause during the Civil War when his home was sacked and burned by the parliamentary forces. John, his second son, attended Market School at Bosworth, Leicestershire, and was admitted as a nobleman at Christ's College, Cambridge, in November, 1653, at age seventeen. After attending Charles II in exile, he was commissioned a captain in Our Holland Regiment and rose to the rank of lieutenant colonel by 1685. In September, 1688, Beaumont was on duty with the King's Regiment quartered at Portsmouth where the Duke of Berwick was governor when James II decided to enroll Irish Catholic recruits in the regiment. The king's order required that five Irish recruits be enlisted in each of the companies under the command of the Duke of Berwick. Beaumont and four other officers, known as the "Portsmouth Captains" refused to accept the recruits declaring that they were "raw, undisciplined Irishmen" and that if untrained troopers were to be recruited "they had all of them credit enough to raise Englishmen." All of the captains signed the complaint which was not accepted by James II and, subsequently, the officers were ordered to induct the Irish recruits. Rather than comply with the king's command, the captains attempted to resign, but James, angered to an extent that "he could not control his passion," ordered them to appear before a council of war. During its proceedings, the officers were offered a reprieve if they would receive the recruits. When they refused, they were stripped of their rank and declared "incapable to serve the King anymore." [3] The opposition of the army was so strong, however, that no further attempts were made to use Irish recruits. After joining the Prince of Orange at Torbay, Beaumont was appointed colonel of a regiment in December, 1688, and was given command of the regiment from which he had been dismissed earlier at the coronation. Later, he served William in Ireland, Flanders, and Scotland and as governor of Dover Castle. He retained his commission until 1695. Although he was twice married, he left no children and died in July, 1701.

Bennet, Levinus (1631-1693), baronet, of Babraham, Cambridgeshire, sheriff of Cambridgeshire, 1652-53, and Member of Parliament (Whig) from Cambridge County, 1679-93. He was the son and heir of Sir Thomas, baronet of St. Andrews, Holborn. Levinus succeeded to the baronetcy in 1667. Although Bennet had attended Gray's Inn in 1644, he was not admitted to the Bar, and his principal interests were mercantile. He was an enthusiastic proponent of William III and the revolutionary settlement. He married Judith, the daughter of William Boenerg of London, and died in 1693.

Berkeley, Maurice (1628-1690), Viscount FitzHarding, of Berehaven, Ireland, army officer; Irish privy councilor, 1663; lord lieutenant of Somerset, 1689-90; and Member of Parliament (Tory) for Wells Borough, Somerset, 1661-79, Bath City, Somerset, 1681, 1685-87, and 1689-90. He was the brother of the first Viscount FitzHarding and was created baronet of Bruton, Somerset County. In 1685 he was commissioned captain of an independent cavalry troop. He succeeded his brother as third viscount. FitzHarding married Anne, daughter of Sir Henry Lee, first baronet of Quarendon, and died in June, 1690.

Berkley, Edward (1644-1700), esquire, of Pylle, Somersetshire, Member of Parliament (Tory) from Wells City, Somerset County, 1679-80, 1685-87, and 1689-1700. He was the son of Edward Berkley whose family had for generations been the greatest electoral power in Somersetshire. Berkley was admitted to Wadham College, Oxford, in July, 1661, at age seventeen and entered Lincoln's Inn in 1665. His death occurred in 1700.

Bernard, Sir Robert (1670-1703), baronet, of Brampton, Huntingdonshire, sheriff of the counties of Cambridge and Huntingdon, 1688 (but did not take office), and 1691-92, and Member of Parliament for Huntingdon County, 1689-92. His father was Sir John Bernard, who had been the Member of Parliament for Huntingdon County in the Long and Cavalier Parliaments. Sir Robert succeeded to the baronetcy in 1679. He married Anne, the daughter of Robert Weldon of London, and died in 1703.

Bertie, Charles (1634-1711), honorable, of Uffington, Lincolnshire, captain in the Coldstream Guards, 1668-73; secretary to the lord treasurer, 1673; treasurer of the ordinance, 1684; and Member of Parliament (Tory) from Stamford Borough, Lincolnshire, 1678-79, 1685-87, and 1689-1711. He was the fifth son of Montagu Bertie, the second Earl of Lindsey by his first wife, Martha, Dowager Countess of Holderness, daughter of Sir William Cokayne, knight, lord mayor of London. After studying under Richard Busby at Westminster School, Bertie was admitted to the Middle Temple in 1658. He was granted an M.A. by Oxford in September, 1665, and incorporated as an M.A. at Cambridge from Oxford in 1667. He married Mary, the widow of Sir Samuel Jones, and the daughter of Peter Tryon of Northampton, and died in March, 1711.

Bertie, Henry (d. 1734), esquire, of Chesterton, Cambridgeshire, cavalry captain, 1678-79, 1681, and 1685; deputy lord lieutenant of Oxfordshire, 1689; and Member of Parliament (Tory) for Westbury, 1678-79, 1701-02, 1702-1715, New Woodstock Borough, Oxfordshire, 1681, and for Oxford City, 1685-87, and 1689-95. He was the third son of Montagu Bertie, the Earl of Lindsey, and his second wife, Bridget Wray, and the uncle of the Earl of Abingdon. Bertie had extensive military experience. After serving as a captain in Lord Gerard's regiment of horse, he commanded a troop of horse in the Oxford militia in 1681 and 1685. In the invasion crisis of 1685, he was captain of an independent troop of horse until it was mustered out of service in June, 1685. During November, 1685, his commission was revoked because he had not been "forward in the parliament to vote up the popish officers." He was one of those who early joined the Prince of Orange. His estate was considerably enhanced by his marriage to Philadelphia, the daughter of Sir Edward Norreys. By this union, he acquired Weston-on-the-Green. Later, he married Catherine Fetherstone and died in December, 1734.

Bertie, Montagu (1668-1743), esquire, captain of the Oxford University volunteers, 1685; lord lieutenant and custos rotulorum of Berkshire, 1701-02; a member of the privy council, 1702, 1714; constable and lord lieutenant of the Tower of London, 1702-15; lord lieutenant of Oxfordshire, 1702-05 and 1712-15; chief justice in Eyre South of the Trent, 1702-06 and 1711-15; recorder and high steward of Oxford, 1699-1743; one of the lord justices of England, 1714; and Member of Parliament (Tory) from Berkshire, 1689-90 and for Oxfordshire, 1690-99. He was the son and heir of James Bertie, first Earl of Abingdon by his first wife, Eleanor, daughter and heiress of Sir Henry Lee. The Earl was an early supporter of the invasion of William of Orange and contributed £30,000 to support the expedition but in the Convention Parliament he objected to awarding the crown to William and used his influence against the declaration of the vacancy of the throne. Montagu succeeded to the earldom in 1699. Bertie first married Anne, the daughter and heiress of Peter Venables, the Baron of Kinderton of Chester County, who was lady of the bedchamber to Queen Anne during her entire reign. In 1717 he married Mary Gould, the widow of General Charles Churchill. He died in June, 1743.

Bertie, Peregrine (d. 1711), esquire, of Georgestreet in York Buildings, Middlesex, an army officer in Europe, vice chamberlain and teller of the Exchequer under Queen Anne, and Member of Parliament (Tory) for Westbury Borough, Wiltshire, 1689 and 1690. He was the fifth son of James, the Earl of Abingdon and the cousin of Charles Montagu, the Earl of Manchester, whom he accompanied to Europe. They were in Venice in February, 1687. Bertie saw military action as a volunteer at the siege of Arras under the noted French general, Turenne. In England he was on military duty with several cavalry units between 1666 and 1676. In 1685 he was an officer in an independent troop of horse.

Bertie, Robert (1660-1723), Lord Willoughby of Eresby, baron, army officer, and Member of Parliament for Boston Borough, Lincolnshire 1685-87 and 1689-90. The son and heir of Robert, the third Earl of Lindsey, he was styled Lord Willoughby, 1666-90; he was summoned to the House of Lords in his father's barony in 1690. He succeeded his father as Earl of Lindsey and lord great chamberlain in 1701. He was created Marquis of Lindsey in 1706 and Duke of Ancaster in 1715. Under Queen Anne he served as lord lieutenant and custos rotulorum for Lincoln County, privy councilor and lord justice of Great Britain. Willoughby married Mary, the daughter of Sir Richard Wynn, from whom he acquired a considerable estate in Carnarvon County, and Albina Farrington. He died in July, 1723.

Bickerstaffe, Philip, esquire, of Clinton, Northumberland County, Member of Parliament (Tory) from Berwick-on-Tweed Borough, Northumberlandshire, 1685-87 and for Northumberland County, 1689. A merchant, he was the brother of Sir Charles Bickerstaffe, knight. He was commissioned an ensign in the Lord High Admiral's Regiment in 1664 and by 1672 had risen to the rank of lieutenant.

Biddulph, Sir Michael (1652-1718), baronet, of Elmhurst and Westcombe, Kent, Member of Parliament (Whig) for Litchfield City, Stafford County, 1679-81, 1689-90, 1695-1705, and 1708-10. His father was Theophilus Biddulph, baronet, a London mercer and a Member of Parliament. The family fortune had been built on the commercial activity of his parents' forebearers. Sir Michael succeeded to the baronetcy in 1683. After attending St. Paul's School, he entered Christ's College, Cambridge, in 1671, at age seventeen. Active in politics, Biddulph was the leader of the Whig party in Litchfield and his interests, principles, and votes in Parliament were Whig. As late as 1696, he subscribed to the Association in support of William III. His estates were considerably enhanced by the marriage, first, to Henrietta, the daughter of Colonel Roger Whitley Chesne, who brought him a fortune of £8,000 and, second, to Elizabeth, the daughter of William D'Oyly, a milliner. He died in April, 1718.

Bigg, John (b. 1644), esquire, of Graffham, Huntingdonshire, was elected Member of Parliament (Tory) from Huntingdon Borough, Huntingdon County, 1689. He was admitted to Trinity College, Cambridge, in April, 1661, and was granted a B.A. in 1664. Bigg married Francis, the daughter of Sir Nicholas Pedley, recorder and a serjeant-at-law.

Bigland, Edward (c. 1620-1704), serjeant-at-law, of Little Leake, Nottingham County, recorder of Nottingham and Member of Parliament from Nottingham Borough, Nottinghamshire, 1689. He was the second son of Edward Leake, clerk. After receiving a B.A. in 1641 and an M.A. in 1644 from Queen's College, Cambridge, he entered Gray's Inn in June, 1648. Bigland became a barrister in 1655, a bencher in 1677, and a serjeant-at-law in 1680. He died in 1704.

Bilson, Thomas, esquire, of Mapledurham, Southampton County, Member of Parliament for Petersfield Borough, Southamptonshire, 1685-87, and 1689.

Birch, John (1616-1691), esquire, of Bristol, served as a distinguished parliamentary officer during the Civil War; a commissioner of excise in the Protectorate; a teller for the counties in Richard Cromwell's Parliament; a member of General Monck's council of state; auditor of the Exchequer in the Restoration; chairman of the committee of elections and privilege, 1689; Member of Parliament (Whig) for Leominster Borough, Hereford, 1646-48, 1654-55, 1656-58, 1659, 1660, Penryn Borough, Cornwall, 1661-79, Weobley Borough, Hereford, 1679-81 and 1689-91. A man of undistinguished origin, he was the eldest son of Samuel Birch of Ardwick, Lancashire. His humble background often gave rise to disparaging comments by his colleagues. During the Commonwealth he was described as "Once a carrier, now a colonel" and, later, Burnet wrote of him: "He was the roughest and boldest speaker in the house and talked in the language of a carrier. . . ."[4] Although his beginnings were inauspicious, he had, through his determination, energy, and skill, risen to the top of the English business world. Early in his life he was apprenticed to Thomas Selfe, a Bristol grocer, and Birch established a lucrative business after his marriage to his master's widow. During the Civil War, his economic activities broadened. In order to protect his property, he entered the Parliamentary Army. When the conflict forced a suspension of his grocery business, he loaned money to the parliamentary government at 8% interest, and he speculated in church property while governor of Hereford. His purchases included half of the Palace of Hereford and six of the bishop's manors. The Civil War provided an opportunity for him to use his qualities and talents to rise into prominence. He entered military service as a captain of volunteers and saw action at the siege of Bristol. In the assault on Arundel, he was severely wounded and was left on the field as dead. Later, he served as a lieutenant colonel under Sir Arthur Hesilrige and as the colonel of a regiment under Cromwell in the west. He led successful assaults on Bridgewater and Ludlow Castle and held Hertfordshire for the parliamentary government. For this achievement, he received the thanks of Parliament and a grant of £6,000. A staunch, pious Presbyterian, whose religious views spilled over into his political life, he often opposed the government for its transgression of rights and privileges and supported policies and measures that would limit royal prerogative and advance parliamentary power as well as individual freedom. During the Commonwealth, Birch was imprisoned twenty-one times for opposing Cromwell's measures, and when he was excluded from the 1656 Parliament, he, together with eighty others, protested the action. Yet, as a member of Monck's council of state, he played an important role in the restoration of Charles Stuart. In the Restoration Parliaments, Birch spoke frequently on constitutional questions. Although he expressed belief that the power of the state was vested in the king, Lords, and Commons, he offered motions that would limit the power of the king and enhance the power of Parliament. During the Exclusion debate, he stated that "Our legislative power is unbounded." He agitated for a policy of

religious toleration initiated by parliamentary action.[5] Birch
made substantial contributions to the revolutionary settlement.
Not only did he welcome the invasion of the Prince of Orange
but he also provided the leadership that molded the religious
limitations of the Crown. In fact, he saw deep religious implications in the events and circumstances of the revolutionary
developments. In the debate on William's letter to the Convention, he asserted his reluctance to express appreciation to the
Prince for his deliverance of England unless the clause, "that
God has done it by his means," was added. Then, he said:
"I could never have believed, some months since, what God,
by his hand, hath wrought for this kingdom." Furthermore, he
believed that the flight of James had been effected by the
"hand of God." In his speech on the state of the nation, he
emphasized the past troubles and future perils of Catholicism.
This menace, Birch said, had been intermittent but persistent
since the reign of James I.[6] His predilection for the Catholic
cause produced the loss of Palatinate and the invasion of parliamentary rights. After his marriage to Henrietta, Charles had,
with the establishment of Catholicism as his objective, attempted to reign without Parliament by constructing an abso-
lute form of government. An arbitrary type of government
seemed to Birch to be required for the extension of the Catholic
religion. By his marriage to Mary of Modena, James II had
revived the trend toward absolutism and Catholicism. Birch
believed that many of England's ills during the seventeenth
century arose from agreements with Catholic powers, marriages
with Catholic princesses, and the Catholic proclivity of the
reigning sovereigns, and that, although a bitter, half-century
struggle had been waged against the threat, little had been
accomplished for the security of religion.[7] At the conclusion of
his speech, Birch offered a motion, modified by Sir Robert
Sawyer, that it "was found inconsistent for a Protestant king
to be governed by a popish prince." [8] Without a dissenting
voice, Commons approved the resolution. Since the House of
Lords immediately concurred when the resolution was received,
the Convention, motivated by Birch's leadership, had assumed
authority to place limitations on the executive.[9] Later, after the

motion had been offered that conditions be required before the crown was offered to William, he supported the proposal that stipulations should be drafted to keep England from being engulfed by "Slavery and Popery." He too favored taking only "a day's time" to complete the task since he was "as much afraid of losing time as anyone" and urged the members to "prepare what you would have repealed, and present it." [10] These ideas were the essence of the motion that initiated the action of the Somers Committee.

Blackett, Sir Edward (1649-1718), baronet, of Newby, Yorkshire, magistrate for West and North Ridings; alderman and mayor of Newcastle-on-Tyne; sheriff of Northumberland, 1679-80; and Member of Parliament for Ripon Borough, Yorkshire, 1689-90 and Northumberland County, 1690-1700. He was the eldest son of Sir William Blackett, first baronet, who had amassed considerable wealth through his mining and colliery activities and who had been a Member of Parliament for Newcastle, 1673-80. Blackett, who lived at Motfen Hall when he succeeded to the baronetcy, in 1673 purchased Newby Park, York. He married Mary Norton, Mary Yorke, and Diana, the daughter of Baron Delamere, and died in 1718.

Blackett, Sir William (1657-1705), baronet, of Newcastle-on-Tyne, Northumberland, alderman and mayor, 1683 and 1698; sheriff of Northumberland, 1688-89; and a Member of Parliament for Newcastle-on-Tyne, 1685-90, 1695-1700, and 1705. The third son of Sir William Blackett, first baronet, he built the mansion house at Wallington and was created first baronet in 1685. Blackett was a Newcastle businessman, who had been governor of the Hostmen's Company in 1684 and was highly regarded in the county for his honesty. In Parliament he was recognized as a popular and distinguished orator. Although he was offered an appointment after the Revolution by William III, he refused to accept it. He married Julia, the daughter of Christopher Conyers, and died in 1705.

Blake, Francis (b. 1664), knight, of Foordcaster, Northumberland County, Member of Parliament (Whig) for Berwick-on-Tweed, Northumberland County, 1689-95 and for Northumberland County, 1701-05. He was the son of William Blake of

Oxfordshire and was later knighted. Blake had been a student at St. Edmund Hall, Oxford, where he received a B.A. in 1680 and at the Middle Temple.

Blofeild, Thomas (1629-1708), esquire, merchant of Norwich, Norfolk County, alderman and mayor of Norwich, justice of peace, deputy lieutenant sheriff, 1695, and Member of Parliament for Norwich City, Norfolk, 1689. He was the son of Thomas Blofeild of Warham and Briston, Norfolk, and married Elizabeth Negus, also of Norwich City. Blofeild died in 1708.

Blois, Sir Charles (1657-1738), baronet, of Grundesbury, Suffolk County, Member of Parliament from Ipswich Borough, Suffolk County, May 1689-1695 and Dunwick Borough, Suffolk County, 1706-09. He was elected May 28, 1689, to fill the vacancy created by Peyton Ventries, who had been appointed puisne justice of the court of common pleas. The son of Sir William Blois, whose family had owned an 5,800 acre estate since the reign of Henry VII, Sir Charles added to the holdings by inheriting Cocksfield Hall from his aunt. He was married twice; first, to Mary Kemp and, second, to Ann Hawtrey. He died in 1738.

Blount, Sir Thomas Pope (1649-1697), baronet, of Tittenhanger (Blount's Hall), Hertfordshire, distinguished writer; commissioner of public accounts, 1694-97; and Member of Parliament (Whig) for St. Albans Borough, Hertfordshire, 1679-81, and Hertford County, 1689-97. A descendant from an old Staffordshire family, the Blounts of Blount Hall, he was the eldest son of Sir Henry Blount, knight, a famous traveler, and author of *A Voyage to the Levant*. Before he studied at Lincoln's Inn, he had received a careful private education under the supervision of his father. Early in life, he acquired a reputation for the extent and variety of his learning and was appraised as a learned and judicious man. His most important works were *Censura Celebriorum Authorum*, 1690; *A Natural History*, 1693; *Remarks on Poetry*, 1694; and *Essays on Several Subjects*, 1692. His intellectual tastes revealed a preference for literature and criticism. He was a proponent of liberal policies and a patron of learning, although he spoke disparagingly of scholars when he said: "There is not a simpler animal and more superfluous member of the state than a mere scholar." In 1678 Blount inherited the estate of Blount Hall during his father's lifetime upon the death of his mother since the land had been previously granted to her. He was created first baronet in 1680. He married Jane, daughter of Sir Henry Caesar. To this union were born fourteen children. He died in 1697.

Bocland, Maurice (1647-1698), esquire, of Standlich, Wiltshire, Member of Parliament (Whig) for Downton Borough, Wiltshire, 1678-81, 1685-87, 1689-95, and 1698. The son of Walter Bocland, he attended Magdalen College, Oxford, and the Middle Temple. He died in 1698.

Boone, Charles, esquire, of Mountboone, Member of Parliament for Hardness Borough, Devonshire, 1689.

Borlase, Sir John (1640-1689), baronet, of Bockmer, Buckinghamshire, Member of Parliament (Tory) for Chipping Wycombe Borough, Buckinghamshire, 1673-81, Great Marlow Borough, Buckinghamshire, 1685-87 and 1689. He was the son and heir of Sir John Borlase, a staunch loyalist in the Civil War, a lord justice of Ireland, who owned vast estates in Buckingham and Oxford which produced an income of £2,500 yearly. After attending Oriel College, Oxford, he inherited the estates at which he entertained Charles II and Nell Gwynn, and succeeded to the baronetcy in 1672. In Parliament, Sir John was affiliated with the court party although he had supported the Earl of Essex. He died in February, 1689.

Boscawen, Charles (1630-1689), esquire, of Nansonallen, Cornwall, Member of Parliament for Tregony Borough, Cornwall, January, 1689. He was the member of an unambitious, wealthy Cornish family that acquired estates on the Fal River. The Boscawen family had marriage ties with the Arundels, Bassetts, St. Aubyns, Lowers, and Godolphins. Charles attended the Middle Temple and died in 1689.

Boscawen, Hugh (d. 1701), esquire, Member of Parliament (Whig) for Cornwall County, 1646, 1659, 1660, 1689, 1690, 1695, 1698, and 1701, and for Tregony Borough, Cornwall 1661, 1679-81. Owner of the estate of Tregothnan on the banks of the Fal River, Boscawen helped restore Charles II as well as exile James II. At the Convention Parliament he staunchly supported William and urged in his speeches the implementation of Whig principles. In the debate on the state of the nation, he defended the authority of Parliament as a representative body to act for the preservation of English "Laws and Religion." Speaking in support of Sir Henry Capel's motion that the throne was vacant, he asserted that if James's departure was a demise, the Convention should proceed to fill the throne. To fail to take action immediately would create difficulty because of the claim of James and his son on the throne. This problem could be solved by awarding the crown to William. He added: "We must not fight a bulrush: therefore declare that the throne is void." [11] After the throne had been declared vacant, the attention of the Convention was directed to the means to secure English "Religion, Laws, and Liberties" before the throne would be filled. The foundations of the principles used were Prince's Declaration and the speeches of the Convention members. Boscawen urged that the assertions of William's Declaration as well as other manifestations of arbitrary government by kings, their ministers, and harsh laws should be circumscribed by limitations. He particularly stressed the necessity for a "redress of Grievances." Without this right, he said, it would be "better to have no law at all." Following his speech the Convention resolved "That, before the Committee proceed to fill the Throne, now vacant, they will proceed to secure our Religion, Laws, and Liberties." [12] His powerful parliamentary career of over fifty years ended with his death in 1701.

Boyle, Henry (c. 1670-1725), esquire, of Lanesborough, Yorkshire, a lord of the treasury, 1699-1701; privy councilor, 1701; chancellor of the Exchequer, 1701-08; lord lieutenant of West Riding, York, 1704-15; lord treasurer of Ireland, 1704-15; Secretary of State for the Northern Department, 1708-10; Lord President of the Council, 1721-25; and Member of Parliament (Whig) for Tamworth Borough, Staffordshire, 1689-90, Aldborough, Yorkshire, 1690, Cambridge University, 1692-1705, and Westminster, 1705-10. The second son of Charles Boyle, Lord Clifford, Henry was the younger brother of the Earl of Burlington and the first cousin of the Duke of Somerset. In 1714 he was raised to the peerage by George I as Baron Carleton, of Carleton, Yorkshire. After receiving an M.A. from Trinity College, Cambridge, Boyle continued his intellectual interests and patronized the arts. After the Battle of Blenheim, upon finding

Addison living in modest circumstances, he encouraged him, through promises, to write a poem *The Campaign*, commemorating Marlborough's great victory. For this favor Addison dedicated the third volume to Boyle with the compliment that among the English leaders none had "made himself more friends and fewer enemies." [13] Jonathon Swift, however, was less generous in his evaluation when he wrote that Boyle "had some very scurvy qualities, particularly avarice." [14] Besides Addison, he also encouraged and aided the dramatist, Southern. In this age of turbulent politics, Boyle with strong Whig views was highly respected for his ability, wisdom, integrity, and tact. Dying unmarried in 1725, he willed his residence, Carleton House, to the Prince of Wales.

Brereton, Edward (c. 1642-1725), esquire, of Burras, Wales, alderman and council member of the city of Denbigh; sheriff of Denbigh County, 1678; and Member of Parliament (Tory) for Denbigh Borough, Wales, 1689-1705. He was the third son of Sir John Brereton, knight, and the brother of Lord Brereton. Brereton had been a student at Oriel College, Oxford, and at Lincoln's Inn (1660). In 1678 he was commissioned an ensign in the Duchess of York's infantry regiment. He died in 1725.

Brett, Richard, esquire, of Marwell, Southampton County, after being elected to represent Southampton Borough in January, 1689, died and was replaced by Sir Charles Windham. He had been commissioned an ensign in the Earl of Peterborough's infantry regiment in 1673.

Brewer, John (1654-1724), esquire, of West Farley, Kent, army officer, 1674; receiver of prizes, 1707; an official of the Escheat Office, 1713; and Member of Parliament for New Romney, a Cinque Port, 1689-1710. He entered Wadham College, Oxford, in 1669 and Gray's Inn two years later. Called to the Bar in 1678, he became a bencher in 1706. In 1674 he received a commission as ensign in Buckingham's regiment. Brewer died in 1724.

Bridger, Richard, esquire, of Godalming, Surrey, Member of Parliament for Lewes Borough, Sussex, 1678-89. He was admitted to Gray's Inn in 1651 as the fourth son of George Bridger.

Brodrep, Richard, (d. 1706), esquire, of Bandrip, a village near Bridgewater, Somerset, Member of Parliament for Bridport Borough, Dorsetshire in 1689. He was the son of Christopher Brodrep, a member of a landowning family in Somerset and he died in 1706.

Bromley, William (1656-1707), esquire, of Holt in Worcester County, Member of Parliament (Whig) for Worcester City, Worcestershire, 1685-87, 1689-1700, and for Worcester County, 1701-2, 1705-07. He was the son and heir of Henry Bromley who had represented Worcester County in the Cavalier Parliament. Bromley entered Christ Church College, Oxford, in July, 1673, at age seventeen and the Middle Temple in 1674. He married Margaret, the daughter of Sir Rowland Berkeley, and died in August, 1707.

Brownlow, Sir John (1659-1697), baronet, of Belton, Lincolnshire, sheriff of Lincolnshire, 1688-89, and Member of Parliament (Tory) for Grantham Borough, Lincolnshire, 1689-90, 1690-95, and 1695-97. The son and heir of Sir Richard Brownlow, he also inherited the estate of his uncle, Sir John Brownlow, in Lincoln County and succeeded to the baronetcy in August, 1688. He attended Westminster School having been admitted in June, 1675. Brownlow married Alice Sherard and died in July, 1697.

Brownlow, William (1665-1701), esquire, of Belton, Lincolnshire, Member of Parliament for Peterborough City, Northamptonshire, 1689-98, and for Bishop's Castle, Shropshire, 1698-1700. He was the son of Sir Richard and the brother and heir of Sir John Brownlow. He succeeded to the fourth baronetcy in 1698. After receiving an education at home under a private tutor, Brownlow enrolled at Sidney College, Cambridge, and entered the Inner Temple in 1684. He married in 1668 (age three) Dorothy, the daughter of Sir Richard Mason, and died in March, 1701.

Bubb, Jeremiah, esquire, army captain; gentleman usher to William III; deputy governor of Carlisle Castle; and Member of Parliament for Carlisle City, Cumberland County, 1689-90 and 1690-95. It seems likely that he was a retainer for the Howards and was appointed deputy governor of Carlisle Castle under the Earl of Carlisle as a reward for services he had rendered.

Bulkeley, Thomas (c. 1636-1705), esquire, of Dinas, Carmarthen County, Wales, infantry captain; and Member of Parliament for Carmarthen County, Wales, 1679-81, 1685-87, 1697-1705, Anglesea County, Wales, 1689-90, and Beaumaris Borough, Anglesa County, 1690-95. The third son of Robert Bulkeley, second Viscount Bulkeley who had been sheriff of Anglesea County and Member of Parliament in Charles II's reign, he owned an estate worth £60 a year in Llaneingan Parish. After attending Jesus College, Oxford University, he was admitted to Gray's Inn in 1654. In 1661 he was granted an M.A. by Dublin University. With a proclivity for military duty, he served as a captain in the Anglesea militia and in Colonel Thomas Erle's infantry regiment which participated in the Irish campaign, although Bulkeley's name did not appear in the army lists after October, 1689. He married Jane, the widow of Griffith Williams, who was the brother of Sir William Williams.

Bull, Henry (c. 1634-1692), esquire, of Shapwick, Somersetshire, Member of Parliament for Wells City, 1660, Milborne Port Borough, 1679-81, and for Bridgeport Borough, 1689-92; all parliamentary constituencies in Somerset County. The son and heir of William Bull of Wells, he entered the Inner Temple in 1650 and was called to the Bar in 1658. He died in 1692.

Buller, John, esquire, of Morval and Isle of Thanet, Cornwall, Member of Parliament for Liskeard Borough, Cornwall County, 1678-81, and 1689. He was the son of John Buller, a large landowner in the counties of Cornwall and Devon, who had been a Member of Parliament for East Looe during the Protectorate and who had acquired the manor and estates of Morval through his marriage to Anne, the daughter of John Coode. He married Mary, the daughter and co-heir of Sir Henry Pollexfen, Lord Chief Justice of the Court of Common Pleas.

Burdett, Robert (1640-1716), esquire, of Forwark, Derby County, Member of Parliament (Tory) for Warwick County, 1678-79, Litchfield City, Stafford County, 1689-98. The son of Francis Burdett, who had Whiggish and anti-Catholic views, he gradually accepted the Tory position on church and state policies. In 1689 he voted against the vacancy of the throne, and in 1695 he was one of those who initially refused to sign the Protestant Association. Burdett matriculated at Queen's College,

Oxford, in 1659 and entered Gray's Inn in 1662. He married Mary Pigot, Magdalen Ashton, and Mary Brome, and died in January, 1716.

Burrard, John (1646-1698), esquire, of Barby Manor, Northamptonshire, lieutenant colonel of infantry; vice-admiral of the seas; deputy lieutenant of Hampshire; riding forester of New Forest; and Member of Parliament for Limington Borough, Southampton, 1679-98. He was the son of Thomas Burrard of Old Palace Yard, Westminister, who acquired Barby Manor through his marriage to Elizabeth Isham. Burrard, after inheriting Barby Manor from his mother, sold it in 1683. He married, first, Elizabeth Button and, second, Alicia, the daughter of Lord Herbert of Cherbury. He died in 1698.

Burridge, John (1651-1733), esquire, of Lyme Regis, Dorset, lord mayor of Lyme Regis, and Member of Parliament (Whig) for the same borough, 1689-95, and 1701-1710. He was the son of Robert Burridge and entered Wadham College, Oxford, 1668. He died in September, 1733.

Byde, Sir Thomas (c. 1630-1704), knight, of Ware Park, Hertfordshire, sheriff of Hertfordshire, 1669, and Member of Parliament (Whig) for Hertford Borough, Hertfordshire, 1660, 1679, 1685, and 1689. His father, John Byde, who was a London alderman and a brewer in Shoreditch, purchased Ware Park for his residence. Sir Thomas was admitted to Merchant Taylors' School in 1642 and was knighted in 1661. He married Mary Skinner and died in 1704.

Byerley, Robert (1661-1714), esquire, of Mitheridge Grange, Durham County, a commissioner for keeping the queen's privy seal; an army officer; and a Member of Parliament (Tory) for Durham County, 1685-90, and for Knaresborough, Yorkshire, 1695-1713. The son of Anthony Byerley of Denton, Durham County, a regimental colonel under the Marquis of Newcastle in the Civil War, he continued the military tradition of the family. In 1685, as a captain, he raised and commanded an independent troop of horse at Doncaster, York. By 1689 he had risen to the rank of regimental colonel and was given command of the late Lord Hewitt's regiment of horse. He attended Queen's College, Oxford, in 1677 and died in May, 1714.

Campion, William (1639-1700), esquire, of Combwell, army

officer, and Member of Parliament for Seaford, a Cinque Port, 1689-98. He was the son of Sir William Campion, knight, a distinguished royalist during the Civil War, who had skillfully defended Barstoll House in Buckinghamshire against the attacks of the parliamentary forces and who was killed at the siege of Colchester in 1648 at age thirty-four. Although an attorney, Campion held a commission as an ensign in Princess Anne's infantry regiment before the Revolution and saw action at Dundalk as a captain in the same unit in 1689. He married Francis, the daughter of Sir John Glynne, knight and serjeant-at-law under Charles II.

Capel, Sir Henry (1638-1696), knight, of Kew, Surrey, privy councilor of Ireland, 1673-85 and 1693, and England, 1679-80, 1689; first lord of the admiralty, 1679-80; lord treasurer, 1689-90; a lord justice (1693) and lord lieutenant of Ireland, 1695; and Member of Parliament (Whig) for Tewkesbury, Gloucestershire, 1661-81 and 1690-92, and for Cockermouth, Cumberland County, 1689-92. The Capel family had long been important in public affairs. In the sixteenth century Sir William Capel, a merchant, had purchased the family estate at Hadham and had been lord mayor of London. The Capels prospered and became prominent in the country. Arthur, the father of Sir Henry, was created a baron in 1641 and served as Member of Parliament in the Long Parliament where he, at first, opposed Charles I but, later, became a staunch royalist and was exempted in 1649 for his role in the Civil War. Sir Henry's brother, the Earl of Essex, supported the Whigs and, after being charged as an accessory to the Rye House Plot, was committed to the Tower where he was found with his throat slashed. A landowner through inheritance from his grandmother, Sir Henry was active in politics and was a vigorous opponent of court interest in Parliament during the reign of Charles II. When the king decided not to call a meeting of Parliament in 1680, Capel, then a member of the council, asked, along with three other councilors, to be excused from further attendance of the council. Later in the year, he was one of the strongest proponents of the Exclusion Bill in the House of Commons. Because of the strong opposition to the hereditary rights of the Duke of York, Capel found himself *persona non grata* at the court and retired to his country estate for a time. By his strong liberal views on religion and politics, he continued his role as Whig leader in opposition with Lord Wharton and made valuable contributions to the Revolution and the settlement. His attitude was lucidly expressed in his will as follows: "I have preserved this estate, and for the contrivance of it in our family have steadily endeavoured to preserve the true Protestant Religion, the rights of the Crown and those of the people, giving entirely my assistance and consent to this revolution." [15] In the Convention debates he supported the granting of caretaker powers to William while Parliament was forging the settlement. Religion was an important aspect of his proposals. He believed that the Protestants were the prime movers in bringing William to England and that European Protestants anticipated a settlement that would buttress their cause. A Protestant government established by members of parliament who were freely elected would meet the requirements at home[16] and abroad while "Popery and Protestant government" were incompatible. Capel then offered the motion "that the Crown is vacant" in order that a satisfactory political settlement could be made.[17] After the Lords and Commons had disagreed on the Commons resolution, he was selected as a member of the conference committee to consider the words "vacancy" and "abdicated." While he had been a knight since the coronation of Charles II, he acquired further honors when he was created Baron Capel of Tewkesbury and was appointed to several offices following the Revolution. Capel married Dorothy, the daughter of Sir Richard Bennett of Kew Green, Survey, and lived there in an "old timber house" where Sir John Evelyn was a frequent visitor. He died of convulsions in May, 1696.

Carew, Sir John (1633-1692), baronet, of Anthony, Cornwall, sheriff of Cornwall in November, 1688; Member of Parliament for Cornwall County, 1660; Bodmin Borough, Cornwall, 1661-79; Lostwithiel Borough, Cornwall, 1679-81; Cornwall County, 1689-90; and Saltash Borough, Cornwall, 1690-92. He was the eldest son of Sir Alexander Carew, a large landowner in Cornwall, who, although he had espoused the parliamentary cause in the Civil War, was executed for treason in 1644 in spite of the petition of his wife that he be spared because he was distracted. Upon the execution of his father, Sir John succeeded as third baronet and entered the Inner Temple in 1651. He married, first, Sarah, the daughter of Anthony Hungerford, and the sister of Sir Edward Hungerford; second, Elizabeth Norton; and, third, Mary, the daughter of Sir William Morice. He died in August, 1692.

Carr, Sir Ralph (1633-1709), knight, of Coken, Durham County, governor of the Hostman's Company, 1677-83; mayor of Newcastle, 1676, 1693, and 1705; and Member of Parliament (Tory) for Newcastle-on-Tyne, Northumberland, 1679-81, and 1689-90. The son of William Carr, a Newcastle merchant, he followed a business career and purchased the estates of Coken, Durham County, in 1665. After attending school at Houghton-in-the-Spring in Durham, he entered St. John's College, Cambridge, in 1652 and Gray's Inn in 1654. He was knighted in 1676. Carr married Jane Anderson and Isabella D'Arcy and died in March, 1709.

Carter, Lawrence, esquire, of Newarke near Leicester, receiver general for the Duchy of Lancaster; deputy recorder of Leicester; and Member of Parliament (Whig) for Leicester Borough, Leicester County, in 1689 and in several Parliaments during the reign of William III. He was a barrister of the Inner Temple and had married Mary, the daughter of Thomas Wodeland, the solicitor to whom he was articled. In 1685 Carter was the architect and engineer of the water system that was constructed for the city of Leicester. He was a staunch supporter of William of Orange and the Revolution although he was reported to have High Church and royalist beliefs.

Cary, Anthony (1656-1694), Viscount of Falkland, of Great Tew, Oxfordshire, lord to the bedchamber of Prince George, 1689-90; treasurer of the navy, 1681-89; deputy lieutenant of Oxfordshire, 1689, first lord of the admiralty, 1693-94; and Member of Parliament (Tory) for Oxfordshire, 1685-87, Great Marlow, Buckinghamshire, 1689-90, and Great Bedwin, Wiltshire, 1690-94. The only son and heir of Henry, Viscount of Falkland, who had been a Member of Parliament in 1659, he succeeded his father as fourth viscount in 1663 and entered Christ Church College, Oxford, in May, 1672. Although an official of the government, Falkland concurred in the Revolution because he feared the threats of Catholicism and arbitrary government from the policies of James II. His sympathy for the moment was aroused by the dispensing of laws, the creation of the ecclesiastical commission, and the annulment of charters. His position was expressed in his frequent participation in the Convention debates in which he expressed his strong support of William and his desire for a type of settlement that would preclude "the danger of Popery and Arbitrary Power." [18] In making the settlement he supported the vacancy motion, urged that the resolution on a Catholic prince be approved, and proposed that the Prince's Declaration be used as the basis for the formulation of a "lasting foundation of government." [19] In spite of his powerful position in William's government, he was voted guilty of high misdemeanor and breach of trust by the House of Commons in January, 1694, for requesting and accepting £2000 from the king and was committed to the Tower. His marriage to Rebecca, the daughter of Sir Rowland Lytton, brought him a great fortune. He died of smallpox in May, 1694.

Cary, William (1662-c. 1710), esquire, of Clovelly, Devonshire, Member of Parliament (Tory) for Okehampton Borough, Devonshire, 1689-95, and for Launceston Borough, Cornwall County, 1695-1710. The son of George Cary, dean of Exeter, he was admitted to Queen's College, Oxford, in March, 1678, and entered the Middle Temple in 1679.

Catlyn, Sir Neville (1633-1702), knight, of Kirby Cane, Norfolk, Member of Parliament (Tory) for Norfolk County, 1679, Norwich City, Norfolk, 1685-87, 1689-90. The Catlyn family, originally from Suffolk, changed its residence to Norfolk when Richard, the father of Sir Neville, inherited the estate of Kirby Cane. Sir Neville's mother was the sister of Henry Neville, Member of Parliament from Abingdon in 1650 and an adherent to Harrington's republican group. Nevertheless, his father supported the royalist cause in the Civil War. He matriculated at King's College, Cambridge, at Easter in 1650 and was knighted in 1662. Following his father's political inclinations, he was a Tory in outlook and was first elected to Parliament from Norfolk in 1679 when he campaigned against the Whigs. Upon his death in July, 1702, the male line of the family became extinct.

Cave, Sir Roger (1651-1703), baronet, of Stanford, North-amptonshire, sheriff of Northampton, 1679-80, and Member of Parliament (Tory) for Coventry City, Warwickshire, 1685-87, and 1689-90. The son of Sir Thomas Cave, baronet, he succeeded to the baronetcy in 1671. He was admitted to Christ's College, Cambridge, in June, 1671. Cave married Martha Browne and Mary, the daughter of William Bromley, speaker of the House of Commons and secretary to Queen Anne. He died in October, 1703.

Cesar, Sir Charles (c. 1655-1694), knight, of Bennington, Hertfordshire, justice of peace and deputy lieutenant for Hertfordshire, and Member of Parliament (Whig) for the same county in 1680 and 1689. The son of Henry Cesar, a London merchant, he attended Cambridge University where he studied for a master of arts degree and where he was knighted in 1671. He was punctual and orderly in the conduct of his activities and was exacting in his demands of others. He was intolerant toward those who favored Catholicism and arbitrary government. Neither would he associate with people of questionable conduct nor those who would bargain away the people's rights for personal advantage. Cesar married Susanna, the daughter of Thomas Bonfoy, a London merchant, and died in 1694.

Chadwick, James, esquire, Member of Parliament (Whig) for New Romney, a Cinque Port in Kent, 1689.

Chafin, Thomas (1651-1691), esquire, of Chetell, Dorsetshire, Member of Parliament for Poole Borough, Dorset, 1679-81, 1685-87, Dorchester Borough, Dorset, 1689-90, and Hindon Borough, Wiltshire, 1690-1691. The son of Thomas Chafin, he entered Magdalen College, Oxford in May, 1666 and died in 1691.

Chetwynd, John (1643-1702), esquire, of Newcastle-under-Lyme, Staffordshire, judge; sheriff of Staffordshire, 1695-96; and Member of Parliament (Tory) for Stafford Borough, 1689-90, 1690-95, Tamworth Borough, Staffordshire, 1698-99, and Stafford, 1701, 1702. The eldest son and heir of John Chetwynd, he inherited the estate of Ingestre, Staffordshire, from his third cousin, Walter Chetwynd, the antiquary who encouraged the preparation of Robert Plott's *Natural History of Staffordshire*. He married Lucy Roane of Surrey and died in December, 1702.

Cheyne, William (1657-1738), esquire, of Drayton Beauchamp, Buckinghamshire, lord lieutenant of Buckinghamshire, 1712-14; and Member of Parliament (Whig) for Amersham Borough, Buckinghamshire, 1681, 1685-87, 1701-02, 1705-08; Appleby Borough, Westmorland, 1689-95; and Buckinghamshire, 1696-1701, 1702-05. He was the eldest son of Charles Cheyne, Viscount Newhaven, whom he succeeded in 1698, and entered Brasenose College, Oxford, July, 1671. In politics he was a Whig under the sponsorship of Lord Wharton, but after a disagreement in 1699 they fought a duel. Cheyne was married twice and died in May, 1738.

Chicheley, Sir John (c. 1641-1691), knight, of Bloomsbury, Middlesex County, naval officer; a commissioner of the navy, 1675-80; a commissioner of ordinance, 1679-81; a lord of the admiralty, 1681-84 and 1690; a Member of Parliament from Newton Borough, Lancastershire, 1679-81, 1685-87, and 1689-90. The second son of Sir Thomas, knight, Member of Parliament from Cambridgeshire, he entered the navy early in the Restoration and had risen to the rank of captain in command of the *Milford* by 1663. Soon after participating in naval action off the Trexel during the Second Dutch War, he was knighted. He was promoted to the rank of vice-admiral in the Mediterranean in 1670 and to rear admiral of the red flag in 1673. Following the Third Dutch War he held several administrative posts in the navy until removed from the admiralty board in May, 1690. Chicheley was admitted to the Inner Temple in November, 1657. He died in May, 1691, leaving a son, John.

Chicheley, Sir Thomas (1618-1699), knight, of Wimpole, Cambridgeshire, sheriff of Cambridgeshire, 1640-42, 1661; an army officer; master general of ordnance, 1670-74; a privy councilor; and Member of Parliament from Cambridgeshire, 1640-42, 1661-79, and from Cambridge Borough, 1679, 1685, and 1689. The son of Sir Thomas Chicheley, knight, he was the younger brother of Henry Chicheley, the Archbishop of Canterbury and the founder of All Souls College, Oxford. The family possessed rich estates in Cambridgeshire and was considered one of the wealthiest in eastern England. Many of its members had been active in the political life of the times as sheriffs or as Members of Parliament. Sir Thomas, a staunch royalist in the Long Par-

liament, was disabled in 1642 for his support of the king and
the Earl of Strafford. His efforts on behalf of the Crown in the
Civil War were costly since he was forced to compound his
estate by heavy payment. After the Restoration, however, he
was restored to favor and given many government employments
as well as a knighthood. Because of his opulent existence at
home in Covent Garden, he was forced to sell the family estate
of Wimpole to Sir John Cutler, a wealthy London grocer in
1686. He was admitted to the Inner Temple in November,
1633, and was given an M.A. by Oxford University in 1636.
Chicheley married Sarah, the daughter of Sir William Russell,
baronet, Member of Parliament for Cambridgeshire in 1640 and
1661 and died in February, 1699.

Chichester, Sir Arthur (d. 1718), baronet, of Youlston, Devonshire, served as Member of Parliament (Tory) for Barnstaple
Borough, Devonshire, 1685-90 and 1713-18. He was the second
son of Sir John Chichester of Raleigh, who had been Member
of Parliament for Barnstaple in the Cavalier Parliament and the
brother of John, whom he succeeded as third baronet in 1680.
The family estate consisted of over 7,000 acres of land in
Devonshire. Sir Arthur married Elizabeth Drew of Grange,
Devon, and died in February, 1718.

Chisnall, Sir Edward (1646-1718), knight, of Chisnall, Lancashire, Member of Parliament (Tory) for Wigon Borough, Lancashire, 1689-90, and for Preston Borough, Lancashire, 1690-95.
The eldest son of Edward Chisnall, esquire, a royalist colonel
in the Civil War who had seen action with Prince Rupert at
Marston Moor and who had assisted the Countess of Derby in
the defense of Latham House, he succeeded his father in 1652
and was knighted in April, 1671. Although he studied at Gray's
Inn, he was not called to the Bar. Twice married, he left no
male heirs and died in 1718.

Chivers, Henry (d. 1720), esquire, of Calne, Wiltshire, served
as an army officer, 1685-90, and as Member of Parliament
(Tory) for Calne Borough, Wiltshire, 1689, 1690, 1698, 1701,
and 1702. A member of a draper company, he served as a
captain in the Duke of Beaufort's infantry regiment during the
Monmouth invasion and later was an officer in Colonel Kirke's
regiment. He was the only Wiltshire Member of Parliament who

replied favorably to James II's questions about the repeal of
the Test and penal laws.

Cholmondeley, Francis, esquire, of Vale Royal, Cheshire, Member of Parliament for Newton Borough, Lancaster, 1689-90. He
was the third son of Thomas Cholmondeley, who held over
30,000 acres of land in the counties of Cheshire, Norfolk, and
Devon, and the brother of Thomas, Member of Parliament for
Cheshire, 1670-78 and 1685. Francis was granted an M.A. degree
by Oxford University in July, 1669.

Christie, Thomas, esquire, Member of Parliament (Tory) for
Bedford Borough, Bedfordshire, 1685-87 and 1689. He had been
elected at Bedford in 1685 through a packed burgess roll.
Although he was not an ultra-royalist, he had consented to
surrender the town charter and agreed to reply favorably to the
three questions insofar as his conscience would permit.

Churchill, George (1653-1710), esquire, of Mintern, Devonshire, officer in the army as well as the navy; a vice-admiral;
a lord of the bedchamber to Prince George; a lord of the
admiralty; a member of the council of the lord high admiral;
and Member of Parliament from St. Albans Borough, Hertfordshire, 1685-1710. The third son of Sir Winston Churchill, a
country gentleman who enhanced the status of his family as a
court politician under Charles II, he was the brother of the
Duke of Marlborough and Arbella Churchill, the mistress of the
Duke of York and mother of Marshall Berwick. Although he
made his reputation as an admiral, he saw service as an army
officer. In this capacity he entered the Duke of York's infantry
regiment as an ensign in 1676 under the command of his
brother, John, then a lieutenant colonel. Churchill had advanced
to the rank of captain by the time of Monmouth's invasion. His
naval career began as a volunteer in the Second Dutch War.
Soon after the Third Dutch War, in which he served as a
lieutenant, he was placed in command of a convoy aboard the
Falcon. While in command of the *Newcastle* in 1688, he agreed,
upon the encouragement of his brother, to abandon James II
and was one of the first naval officers to offer his services to
William of Orange. During the war of the League of Augsburg,
he fought with distinction at the Battle of La Hogue in 1692.
After leaving the service for a time because of the promotion

of a junior officer, Captain Aylmer, to flag rank, he returned as a lord of the admiralty in 1699 and was appointed to the lord high admiral's council upon the accession of Anne. Through his influence on Prince George, the lord high admiral, Churchill directed naval affairs as his brother managed military matters although with considerably less success. Complaints of inefficiency and mismanagement brought discredit to Churchill who was characterized as "ignorant, incapable, and overbearing." [20] Upon the death of Prince George, he retired to his estate in Windsor Park where he lived on the huge fortune which he had accumulated from the perquisites of his office. Since he was unmarried, his fortune was inherited by a natural son upon his death in May, 1710.

Clarges, Sir Thomas (d. 1695), knight, of Westminster, commissary general of musters for General Monck, 1660, privy councilor for Ireland, and Member of Parliament (Tory) for Tregony Borough, Cornwall County, 1660, Westminster Borough, Middlesex County, 1660, Southwark Borough, Surrey County, 1666-78, Christchurch Borough, Southampton County, 1678-81, 1685-87, and Oxford University, 1689-95. The son of John de Clarges, a blacksmith of Flemish extraction, he was the brother-in-law of General George Monck, who married his sister, Anne. Early in his career Clarges was an apothecary and a physician, holding a medical degree from Oxford University and having attended Gray's Inn. At the time of the Revolution he was a seasoned politician, who had begun his political career during the Protectorate as an agent of Richard Cromwell, carrying messages to General Monck in Scotland. Because of his assistance in the Restoration he was knighted by Charles II and appointed to the Irish privy council. For his service to the Crown he was viewed as a friend of the court and on many issues, particularly in his support of the Anglican Church, he was Tory. Yet, he exerted his influence in opposition to the king's revenue policies, the undue use of the prerogative, and the encroachment of the Crown on individual rights. Before the Revolution he had helped pass the Habeas Corpus Act, asserted the principle of parliamentary freedom of speech in the attack upon the speaker, and actively supported the Revolution before the Convention met. He was among the former

Members of Parliament who met with William of Orange in December, 1688, to prepare for the meeting of the Convention and was a member of the committee which prepared the address to the Prince, asking him to assume caretaker powers in England. In the debates of the Convention Parliament Clarges supported the ideas of the hereditary monarchy and a powerful representative Parliament. He believed that the elements of the settlement should be created out of the principles asserted in the Prince's Declaration. In his analysis of the status of the government because of the departure of James II, he doubted if the Convention would assert "that the crown is void" because of the possibility of transforming the type of government. He was also dubious about using the term "abdicated" and believed "deserted" was the proper word to apply to the king's action. Citing the precedent in the case of Edward II, who had committed "all manner of irregularities and oppressions, by the advice of wicked counselors," he called attention to the action of the magnates at Bristol who had chosen the Duke of Aquitaine *custos regni* when they were informed that the king had "forsaken the kingdom." A similar decision in regard to James was appropriate and urged that the Commons accept the word, "desertion," approved by the lords.[21] Nevertheless, he asserted that under the circumstances the Convention, which resembled a Parliament, freely elected and representative of the people, had the power to make the settlement according to the principles of William's Declaration. This power, however, should not be exerted to destroy the hereditary monarchy.[22] Because of these interpretations he would not support the vacancy of the throne, the proclamation of William and Mary as the new sovereigns, the bill for declaring the Convention a lawful Parliament, and the bill for the suspension of the *writ of habeas corpus*. Yet, he supported the measures for frequent Parliaments and for religious indulgence and comprehension. He married Mary Proctor of Nottingham and died in 1695.

Clayton, Sir Robert (1629-1707), knight, of London, London alderman; sheriff of London, 1671; lord mayor of London 1679-80; commissioner of customs, 1689-97; director of the Bank of England; and Member of Parliament (Whig) for London, 1678-

81, 1689-90, 1701-02, 1705-07, and for Bletchingly Borough, Surrey, 1690-95, 1698-1700, 1701. A member of the Clayton or Cleeton family of Bulwich, Northamptonshire, he was the son of a small farmer. As a young man he was apprenticed to his uncle, Robert Abbott, a scrivner. A fellow apprentice in this business was John Morris, who, upon dying in 1682, left his valuable estates to Clayton. The latter became one of the weathiest men in London with his widespread economic interests. Besides being a member of the Scrivner's and Draper's Companies, he was a director of the Bank of England. Much of his wealth was used for elegant living. In 1672 he built a magnificent town house in the Old Jewery at an excessive cost. Here he entertained lavishly with dinners and banquets which rivaled those of the king in magnificence. In addition he purchased from Sir John Evelyn the manor of Bletchingly, a villa among the Surrey Hills. The house at Marden, with its exquisite landscaping, was the object of envy from all visitors. The magnitude of Clayton's wealth was revealed when he loaned William III £30,000 to meet the army payroll in 1697. A Member of Parliament for three decades, he was one of the leading proponents of the Whig interests. As a representative of London in the Oxford Parliament, he and his supporters arrived in the city wearing hat bands with the slogan "no popery, no slavery." In response to the requests of his London constituents, he introduced the motion for the introduction of the Exclusion Bill which received a second from Lord Russell. Later in the year he was a member of a delegation from the city council which was sent to request that Charles summon a Parliament. In the conference with the king at Hampton Court, he was harshly rebuked by Charles for his efforts. This rebuff did not restrain further action against arbitrary royal policies. When the writ of *quo warranto* was issued against London, Clayton was appointed to a committee that was charged with the preparation of the defense against the legal action. Because of his opposition to royal policies, he was continuously harassed by court officials. But Clayton continued his support of Whig policies, and when James fled to France, he was one of the council delegates sent to confer with William of Orange. His devoted service won him election to the Convention Parliament by acclamation and appointment as a commissioner of customs in 1689. He had been knighted at Guildhall in 1671 while sheriff of Middlesex. Clayton married Martha, the daughter of Perient Trott, a London merchant, but his forty-six-year union produced no heirs and his wealth was inherited, upon his death in 1707, by his nephew, William Clayton.

Coke, John (1654-1692), esquire, of Melbourne, Derbyshire, an army colonel, and Member of Parliament (Tory) for Derby Borough, Derbyshire, 1685-87 and 1689-90. He succeeded his father, Thomas Coke in 1656, an ardent royalist, who had paid a £2,200 assessment on his estate for supporting Charles I in the Civil War. After studying at Christ Church College, Oxford, Coke was admitted to Gray's Inn in 1669. As early as 1685 he held a commission as a captain in Princess Anne's infantry regiment and raised a troop of cavalry in 1688. Elected to James II's Parliament, Coke opposed the royal policy of appointing Catholic officers in the army. When in a vigorous manner the king insisted that his appointive power be given parliamentary sanction, Coke replied: "I hope we are all Englishmen, and not to be frightened with a few hard words." [23] For his frank exhortation Coke was imprisoned in the Tower. He died in Geneva in 1692.

Colchester, Sir Dunscomb (1629-1696), knight, of Abbenhall, army officer; alderman, 1672; mayor of Gloucester, 1674; venderer of Dean Forest; and Member of Parliament for Gloucester City, Gloucester, 1689-90. He was the son of Richard Colchester, lord of the manor of Westbury-on-Severn and one of the Curitors-in-Chancery. Although he entered one of the inns of court, he was not called to the Bar. He was knighted at Whitehall while serving as lord mayor of Gloucester. Colchester married Elizabeth, the daughter of Sir John Maynard, and died in May, 1696.

Coleman, William, esquire, Member of Parliament (Tory) from Tiverton Borough, Devonshire, 1689.

Colemore, William (1649-1722), esquire, of Warwick City, Warwickshire, Member of Parliament (Tory) for Warwick City, 1689-95. He was the son of William Colemore of Warwick and he attended Magdalen College, Oxford, as well as the Middle Temple. He died in November, 1722.

Colleton, Sir Peter (1635-1694), baronet, of Exmouth, Devonshire, proprietor of the Bahamas, 1667; governor of Barbados, 1673-74; commissioner of public accounts; Fellow of the Royal Society; and Member of Parliament for Bossiney, Cornwall County, 1689-94. The son of John Colleton, baronet, who was one of the proprietors of Georgia and the Carolinas, he inherited the baronetcy as well as the proprietorship of the Carolinas. Later he acquired five additional proprietorships and a charter for the Bahamas. He married Elizabeth Johnson, the sister of Colonel John Leslie of the Barbados, and died in March, 1694.

Colt, John Dutton (1643-1722), esquire, of Leominster, Herefordshire, bailiff of Leominster, 1680, and Member of Parliament (Whig) for Leominster, 1679-81, 1689-98 and 1701. He was the eldest son of George Colt who, after commanding troops in the abortive Battle of Worcester, was drowned off the coast of Holland while fleeing to exile. John Dutton was rescued by servants and taken to Breda where he developed a friendship with Prince Charles. Upon his return to England in 1660 Colt acquired Dutton House and large estates through his marriage to Mary, the daughter of John Booth. Not long afterwards he became a capital burgess and then bailiff of Leominster. In his capacity as town official and Member of Parliament, he was a vigorous proponent of urban privileges. His defense of individual rights and Protestantism created conflict with the Crown in spite of his friendship with Charles. Although the king offered him £20,000 for the surrender of the Leominster Charter, Colt would not relinquish the document. Continued refusals, together with a derogatory remark about the Duke of York, led to a charge of treason against him. Upon finding Colt guilty in 1684 Judge Jeffreys fined him £100,000 and committed him to King's Bench Prison. Charles then issued a new charter for Leominster. Released from prison through the influence of Lord Preston, Colt expressed his appreciation to James II and requested that he be given no further employments. Although an active participant in the Revolution, his support of charter rights was an annoyance to William III. When Cold implemented the old charter in Leominster, William asked him by what law he had the authority for his action. He replied: "By the same law by which your majesty wears the crown." [24] After the death of his first wife, Colt married Margaret Cooke and died in 1722.

Coningsby, Thomas (1656-1729), esquire, of Hampton Court, Herefordshire, army officer; a commissioner of appeals in excise, Ireland, 1689-90; joint paymaster of forces, Ireland, 1690-98; a lord justice, Ireland, 1690-92; vice-treasurer, Ireland, 1692-1710; a privy councilor, Ireland, 1693; lord lieutenant and custos rotulorum of the counties of Hereford and Radnor 1714-21; and Member of Parliament (Whig) for Leominster Borough, Herefordshire, 1679-81, 1685-87, 1689-1710, and 1715-16. A member of an influential parliamentary family, he was the great-grandson of Sir Thomas Coningsby and the son of Humphrey Coningsby. His mother was the sister and co-heir of Adam, Viscount Lilburne. At nineteen Coningsby married Barbara, the daughter of Ferdanindo Gorges, a Barbados merchant, whose misdeeds caused him losses from which he could not recover. After the death of his first wife, he married Frances, the daughter of the Earl of Ranelagh. Elected to Parliament from Leominster, Coningsby represented the borough almost without interruption until his elevation to a peerage in 1719. As a Whig politician he actively supported the Revolution of 1688 and fought against Jacobitism during his political career. During William's reign he served the king in both military and civil capacities. Although he was accused of corruption and irregularities by his opponents, his political career was not damaged as long as William was king. His influence was slight, however, under Queen Anne, but Coningsby regained his former prestige under George I until he was committed to the Tower for his remarks about Lord Harcourt. He was created Baron Coningsby in 1692 and granted an earldom in 1719. He died in May, 1729, after a long illness.

Cooke, William (1621-1695), esquire, of Highnam, Gloucestershire, sheriff of Gloucestershire, 1663; justice of peace, 1670 and 1683; alderman, 1672; mayor, 1673, 1688; and Member of Parliament for Gloucester City, Gloustershire, 1678-79 and 1689-95. The eldest son of Sir Robert Cooke, he was the lord of the manor of Highnam. Early in the Civil War he fought with the Cavalier forces and during this time his manor house, Highnam, was burned by the parliamentary troops. Later in the conflict he supported the Roundhead cause. After the war he rebuilt his manor house from plans drafted by Inigo Jones. He married Anne Rolle of Devon and died in 1695.

Cooke, Sir William (1630-1708), baronet, of Brome Hall, Norfolk, Member of Parliament (Tory) for Yarmouth Borough, 1685-87 and Norfolk County, 1689-90, 1690-95, and 1698-1700. He was the son and heir of Sir William Cooke, baronet, whom he succeeded in 1682, and married Jane Steward. Cooke was admitted to Gray's Inn in 1648. He died in 1708.

Coote, Richard (1636-1701), baron, of Castle Cuffe, Queen's County, Ireland, governor of Leitrim county, Ireland; treasurer to Queen Mary; governor of Massachusetts, 1695, and New York, 1697-1701; and Member of Parliament for Droitwich Borough, Worcestershire, 1689-95. He was second son and heir of Sir Charles Coote, Lord Coloony of Ireland, and succeeded his father as second baron in 1683. His large estates in Cavan and Monaghan counties in Ireland were enhanced by his marriage to Catherine Nanfan of Worcestershire and through a grant by William III of 77,000 acres of forfeited Irish land when he was created Earl of Bellamont in 1689. The many rewards that he received were compensation for his initial and continued support of William of Orange both in Parliament and in Ireland. For this support, however, he was attainted in his absence by James II's Irish Parliament in May, 1689. Besides his involvement in English and Irish affairs, he was instrumental in shaping colonial policy. In 1695 he was appointed governor of Massachusetts with special instructions to suppress piracy which was widely practiced in the colonies. Colonel Robert Livingston suggested that Captain William Kidd, with a warship and special authority, could eliminate freebooting in American waters, but the plans were vetoed by the king. Persistent in the pursuit of their project, Livingston and Coote persuaded Shrewsbury, Somers, Oxford, and Romney to advance £6,000 to equip the *Adventure* for assignment to Captain Kidd. Armed with special powers to arrest pirates, he became the terror of all merchants by his own piratical acts. Upon his arrival in New York, the colony of which he had been appointed governor in 1697, he was disturbed by the reports of Captain Kidd's irregular activities and concluded that he was required to apprehend him.

In an exchange of letters, Kidd wrote that he was innocent of the charges to which Coote replied that if this claim were true, Kidd could safely come to Boston to confer with him. Upon Kidd's arrival in Boston harbor in June, 1699, he was arrested for piracy and sent to England for trial while his illegal cargo was seized by Coote. When the incident was debated in Parliament the irregular fitting of Kidd's ship, the *Adventure*, and the legality of Coote's possession of Kidd's seizures were discussed. Parliament decided that the governor could retain the goods. Coote died in New York in March, 1701.

Cope, Sir John (1634-1721), baronet, of Hanwell, army officer; justice of peace, 1685; deputy lieutenant, 1689; and Member of Parliament (Whig) for Oxfordshire, 1679-81, and 1689-90, and from Banbury Borough, Oxfordshire, 1699-1700. The third son of Sir John Cope, baronet, he succeeded his brother Sir Anthony as fifth baronet in 1675. In 1699 he purchased the estate of Bromhill Park, Hampshire. His estates consisted of over 3,000 acres in four English counties. He entered Queen's College, Oxford, in November, 1651, and then traveled extensively in Europe. At the Restoration, Cope was given command of a detachment of troops at Dunkirk and was in charge of the port when it was transferred to France in 1662. While in France he married Anne Booth, an innkeeper at Dunkirk, but the estate of Hanwell was willed away from their children. In 1695 Cope was on a committee chosen by the proprietors of the Bank of England to draft laws and ordinances governing the operation of the institution. He died in January, 1721.

Cordell, Sir John (1646-1704), baronet, of Melford Hall, Suffolk, sheriff of Suffolk, 1684, Member of Parliament (Tory) for Sudbury, 1685-87, and Suffolk County, 1689-90. The son and heir of Sir Robert Cordell, baronet, he succeeded as third baronet in 1680. In 1674 he married Elizabeth Waldegrave and died in May, 1704.

Cornwall, Henry (1653-1717), esquire, of Brewardine Castle, Herefordshire, page to the Duke of York; master of horse to Princess Mary; army officer; and Member of Parliament (Tory) from Weobly Borough, Herefordshire, 1685-87, 1701, 1702-08, Hereford City, 1689-95, and Herefordshire, 1698-1700. He was the son of Edward Cornwall and a half-brother to Captain

Roger Vaughn. Cornwall entered military service as an ensign in John Churchill's admiralty regiment in June, 1672, and after service in a number of military commands, he was appointed colonel of a Norfolk infantry regiment which he had raised during the Monmouth Rebellion. When he was superseded in this command by Colonel Oliver Nicholas, he was appointed master of horse to Prince Mary and remained at the Dutch court until the flight of James II. Because he could not in conscience fight against the king, he resigned from the army and, although his sympathy was with William of Orange, he did not support the Revolution nor accept a position in the new government. Cornwall was twice married, first, to Margarita Huyssen and, second, to Susanna, the daughter of Sir John Williams. He died in February, 1717.

Coryton, Sir John (1648-1690), baronet, of West Newton Ferrers, Cornwall, sheriff of Cornwall County, 1683-84, and Member of Parliament for Newport Borough, Cornwall County, 1679, and Callington Borough, Cornwall County, 1685 (until unseated), 1689-90. The son and heir of Sir John Coryton, baronet, of Coryton, who had represented Cornwall in Parliament for several years, he succeeded to the baronetcy in 1680. In November, 1666, he entered Exeter College, Oxford. He married Elizabeth, the daughter of Sir Richard Chiverton who had been lord mayor of London, 1657-58. Coryton died without heirs in October, 1690.

Cotton, Sir John (c. 1647-1713), baronet, of Landwade and Madingley, Cambridgeshire, ensign in the Duke of Monmouth's infantry regiment, 1678; recorder of Cambridge; and Member of Parliament for Cambridge Borough, Cambridgeshire, 1689-90, 1690-95, and 1696-1708. He was the son of Sir John Cotton, baronet, of Landwade and succeeded to the baronetcy in 1689. Cotton entered Trinity College, Cambridge, in November, 1663, but did not graduate. He married Elizabeth, the daughter of Sir Joseph Sheldon, lord mayor of London, 1675-76, and died in January, 1713.

Cotton, Sir Robert, knight, of Hatley St. George, Cambridgeshire, Member of Parliament (Whig) for Cambridgeshire, 1679-81, 1685-87, and 1689. The second son of Sir Thomas Cotton, Member of Parliament for Huntingdon County and a grandson of Cotton, the Antiquary, he married Gertrude, the daughter of Sir William Morice, the Secretary of State under Charles II. He was a fervent supporter of William of Orange and the Revolutionary Settlement.

Cotton, Sir Robert (1635-1712), knight and baronet of Combermere, Chester County, Member of Parliament (Whig) for Cheshire, 1679-1702. He was the second son of Thomas Cotton and inherited his grandfather's estate in 1649 following his elder brother's death. He was knighted in 1660 and created first baronet in 1677. Cotton married Hester, the daughter of Sir John Salusbury, baronet, and died in December, 1712.

Courtenay, Francis (1650-1699), esquire, of Powderham Castle, Devonshire, Member of Parliament from Devonshire, 1689-99. He was the son and heir apparent of Sir William Courtenay, a royalist in the Civil War, who had converted Devonshire to the support of Charles II before the Restoration. Courtenay married Mary, the daughter of William Bovey, a London merchant, and died in 1699 before the death of his father.

Courtenay, Humphrey (1643-1696), esquire, of Tremere, Cornwall County, Member of Parliament for Michael Borough, Cornwall County, 1689-96. He had attended Balliol College, Oxford, in 1659 and was called to the Bar from the Inner Temple in 1677. Courtenay died in March, 1696.

Courtenay, Richard, esquire, of Colyton, Devonshire, army officer and Member of Parliament from Honiton Borough, Devonshire, 1689. The fourth son of Sir William Courtenay, a Devonshire royalist in the Civil War, he was the brother of Francis Courtenay, Member of Parliament from Devon County. He held a commission as captain in Lord Berkeley's regiment of marines. Twice married, his second wife was Catherine, the daughter of Sir William Waller. Courtenay was drowned along with his son in a shipwreck off the Italian coast.

Cowper, Sir William (1665-1706), baronet, of Hertford Castle, Hertfordshire, recorder of Colchester; king's counsel, 1694; clerk of Parliament; privy councilor, 1705; lord keeper of the great seal, 1705; a commissioner for the union of England and Scotland, 1706; lord chancellor, 1704; and Member of Parliament (Whig) for Hertford Borough, Hertfordshire, 1679-1700. The member of an old Hertfordshire family, he was the grandson of Sir William Cowper and the son of John Cowper. He succeeded his grandfather as second baronet in 1664 and was created Lord Cowper in 1706. He was called to the Bar from Lincoln's Inn in 1688 and developed a high reputation for his knowledge of law. During his legal career he was involved in some of the most noted judicial proceedings of his time. In these cases he displayed his enthusiasm for the principles of political liberty. In 1680 he was associated with the Earl of Shaftesbury in the indictment of the Duke of York as a Catholic recusant. As counsel for the Crown, he prosecuted Sir William Perkins and his associates who were charged with treason for their role in the Assassination Plot of 1696. He acted in the same capacity in the trial of Captain Thomas Vaughn who was charged with treason on the high seas. Although a staunch Whig, Cowper played an important role in Queen Anne's government. Besides holding a position as privy councilor, he was a commissioner for the union of England and Scotland and lord high chancellor of Great Britain. On several occasions he wrote speeches for the Queen. He was a Fellow in the Royal Society. Cowper married Sarah, the daughter of Samuel Holled, a London merchant, and died in December, 1706.

Crawford, Robert (16----1706), esquire, army officer 1673-1706; governor of Sheerness, 1690-1706; and Member of Parliament for Queensborough, Kent, 1689-98. A brother of William Crawford, who had been a collector of the hearth tax during the reign of James II, he began his military career as a lieutenant in the Duke of York's infantry regiment in 1673, and, after service with several infantry regiments, he was promoted to the rank of captain and appointed lieutenant governor of Sheerness in 1685. After the Revolution, he was reappointed to his post at Sheerness and succeeded Sir Charles Lyttleton as governor. In April, 1694, he was promoted to the rank of colonel. After the accession of Anne he was recommissioned governor of Sheerness and died in November, 1706.

Cutler, Sir John (1608-1693), knight and baronet of London, alderman of London; sheriff of London and Kent, 1675-76; and Member of Parliament for Taunton Borough, Somersetshire, 1679-80, and for Bodwin Borough, Cornwall County, 1689-93. The son of Thomas Cutler, a London grocer, he became one of London's wealthiest businessmen whose avariciousness and parsimony became legend, although he was generous in his support of philanthropic projects. His contributions to education and charity were many. He was the treasurer of St. Paul's school and a Fellow of the Royal Society. In 1664 he established a lectureship on mechanics at Gresham College with a yearly stipend of £50 under the proviso that the Royal Society should select the topic as well as designate the number of lectures. In 1679 he constructed an anatomical theater for the college of physicians. After he became master warden of the Grocers' Company, he rebuilt the parlor and dining room of its hall and north gallery of his parish church. Upon the approach of the Restoration, Cutler helped solicit funds from the City of London for the use of Charles II. Because of his assistance the king knighted him in 1660 and created him a baronet in 1661. He married twice, first, to Elizabeth, the daughter of Sir Thomas Foote, lord mayor of London, 1649-50, and second, to Elisha Tipping. Cutler died in April, 1693, leaving an estate of £300,000.

Darcy, John (1659-1689), honorable, of Yorkshire, army officer; deputy lieutenant of North Riding; and Member of Parliament for Richmond Borough, Yorkshire, 1681, 1685-87, and 1689. He was the eldest son of the second Earl of Holderness, who had seen active duty as a captain during the Civil War in Prince Rupert's cavalry and who had been Member of Parliament for Boroughbridge in 1660 and Yorkshire, 1661-79. After attending Gray's Inn, Darcy was commissioned a major in the Queen's House Guards in 1681 and, as a colonel in 1685, raised a troop of infantry in London. Although he was appointed deputy lieutenant for North Riding, he was removed from his post because of his opposition to James II's policies and forbidden in the king's presence. He married Bridget, the daughter of Robert Sutton, Lord Lexington, and died in January, 1689, during the lifetime of his father.

Darcy, Philip, esquire, of Yorkshire, army officer and Member of Parliament from Richmond Borough, Yorkshire, 1689, after the death of his brother, John. He was the second son of Conyers Darcy, the Earl of Holderness, by his second wife, Lady Frances Howard. In 1680 Darcy was commissioned a major in the Duke of York's House Guards and later served in the Queen's Regiment of cavalry.

Darcy, Sir Thomas (1632-1693), baronet, of St. Osyths, Essex, army officer, 1685, and Member of Parliament for Maldon Borough, Essex, 1679-93. He was the son and heir of Thomas Darcy of Essex County and was created first baronet in June, 1660. After attending Jesus College, Oxford, for a few years, he was admitted to Gray's Inn in 1652. In 1685 he was commissioned a major in the Earl of Feversham's House Guards. Darcy married Cicely, the daughter of Sir Symonds D'Ewes, and Jane Cole and died in 1693.

Darrell, Sir John, Member of Parliament for Rye, a Cinque Port, 1679-80 and 1689.

Dashwood, Sir Robert (1662-1734), knight and baronet, of Northwood, Oxfordshire, sheriff, 1684; deputy lieutenant of Oxon, 1683; and Member of Parliament for Banbury Borough, Oxon, 1689-98, and Oxfordshire, 1699-1700. The son and heir of George Dashwood, a London alderman, who had been a commissioner of excise and a farmer of Irish revenue, he became a London merchant and was knighted at Windsor Castle in 1662 and created a baronet in 1684. After studying at Trinity College, Oxford, he entered the Inner Temple. Dashwood married Penelope, the daughter of Sir Thomas Chamberlayne, and died in July, 1734.

Davers, Sir Robert (1653-1722), baronet, of Rougham, Suffolk, a Barbados planter; colonial official, 1683-84; sheriff of Suffolk (but did not act), 1684; and Member of Parliament (Tory) from Bury St. Edmunds Borough, Suffolk, 1689-1701 1703-05, and Suffolk County, 1705-22. The son and heir of Sir Robert Davers, baronet, he was born in the Barbados and spent some time as a member of the colonial council as well as a baron of the Court of Exchequer and Common Pleas. He succeeded to the baronetcy in 1684. By his marriage to Mary, the daughter of Thomas, Baron of Jermyns, he acquired part of the Jermyns estate at Bury St. Edmunds and purchased the remainder when the male line of the family became extinct. He died in 1722.

Deane, John (b. 1655), esquire, of Mattingly, Hampshire, army officer and Member of Parliament for Great Bedwin Borough, Wiltshire, 1678-79, and for Lugershall Borough, Wiltshire, in 1689. He enrolled at St. John's College, Oxford, and the Inner Temple. Deane entered military service as a captain in King William's Guards and rose to the rank of lieutenant colonel in 1705.

Deedes, Julius, esquire, Member of Parliament (Whig) for Hythe, a Cinque Port, 1678-79, 1685-87, and 1689.

Digby, William (1661-1752), baron, of Coleshill, Warwickshire, Member of Parliament (Tory) for Warwick Borough, Warwickshire, 1685-87, and 1689-98. The Digby estates consisted of 40,000 acres of land in England and Ireland. Having supported Henry Tudor in 1485, the Digbys were rewarded with Coleshill and other grants. Succeeding generations added to the holdings, and by the Civil War the family owned land in the counties of Warwick, Stafford, Buckingham, Leicester, Rutland, Kent, Norfolk, and Dorset. The third son of Kildare Digby, second Baron Digby, he attended Magdalen College, Oxford, receiving his A.B. degree in 1681 and was created D.C.L. in July, 1708. In 1685 he succeeded his brother as the fifth Lord Digby. Because he had supported the Revolution, he was included in the Act of Attainder, enacted by James II's Irish Parliament in 1689. His deep religious views motivated participation in humanitarian activities. Later in his life he was active in the Society for the Propagation of the Gospel and a member of the Common Council for Georgia. Digby married Jane, the daughter of the Earl of Gainsborough. Since he outlived his children, he was succeeded by his grandson, Edward. He died in December, 1752.

Dillington, Edward (b. 1656), esquire, of the Isle of Wight, army officer and a Member of Parliament for Newport Borough, Isle of Wight, June, 1689–February, 1690. The third son of Robert Dillington, baronet, he attended Trinity College and served as a coronet in Lord Gerard's cavalry regiment in 1678.

Dillington, Sir Robert (1665-1689), baronet, of Kinghton, Isle of Wight, Member of Parliament for Newport, Isle of Wight, January, 1689–June, 1689. He was the first son of Sir Robert Dillington, baronet, and the brother of Edward, who replaced him as Member of Parliament from Newport. Robert attended

Queen's College, Oxford, and succeeded to the baronetcy in 1687. He died unmarried in June, 1689.

Dixwell, Sir Basil (1665-1750), baronet, of Brome House, Kent, auditor of excise; governor of Dover Castle, 1696-1702, and Member of Parliament from Dover, a Cinque Port, 1689-90, and 1698-1700. His father was Sir Basil Dixwell, baronet, of Kent. An earlier member of the family, Colonel John Dixwell, was a Member of the Long Parliament from Dover and a regicide, who escaped to New England under an assumed name. The son, Basil, succeeded his father in 1668 and attended Christ Church College, Oxford, as second baronet. He was appointed auditor of excise and governor of Dover Castle but was dismissed from his employments at the succession of Anne in 1702 but had them restored by George I. Dixwell married Dorothy, the daughter of John Temple, paymaster general, and Catherine Longueville. He died in March, 1750.

Dolben, Gilbert (1655-1722), esquire, of Finedon, Northampton, puisne judge of the Irish Court of Common Pleas 1701-20, and Member of Parliament (Tory) for Ripon Borough, Yorkshire, 1685-87, Peterborough City, Northamptonshire, 1689-98, 1700-10, and Yarmouth Borough, Isle of Wight, 1710-14. His father was John Dolben, Archbishop of York, who, before entering the clergy, had performed distinguished military service for the Crown, being severely wounded in the defense of York. Gilbert was well educated and maintained his scholarly interests throughout his life. After attending Westminster School and Christ Church College, Oxford, he studied law at the Inner Temple, being called to the Bar in 1680. Afterwards, he served as a bencher, a reader, and treasurer for the Inn. When Dryden was preparing a translation of Virgil, Dolben helped him with the work and presented him with several editions of the author's works as well as all of the commentaries on these editions. Although his political views were usually Tory, he supported Whig interpretations during the formulation of the revolutionary settlement. Dolben accepted the concept of the contract. Although he stated that the word did not appear in the lawbooks, Sir Edward Coke referred to "what amounts to it." He thought that if the principle did not exist, subjects could not demand that the king live within the law. Dolben agreed with the Whig members that James ceased to be king because "of a voluntary demise in him." He said: "For I lay it down as an undoubted proposition that, when the king does withdraw himself from the administration of government, without any provision to support the commonwealth; when, on the contrary, he stops the use of the great seal, by taking it away with him, this amounts to what law calls demise." [25] After citing precedent in the behavior of four English kings and the opinion of European experts on Civil Law to substantiate his interpretation, he offered a motion which was seconded by John Arnold that the king's action was a demise.[26] In the discussion which followed, Dolben agreed that upon a demise there must be a successor, and the Convention agreed that the term, renunciation, was more nearly applicable to the situation.[27] When the religion of the king was considered, he asserted that a Catholic prince should not occupy the throne. On this issue he said: "There is nothing in statute nor common law against a Popish prince, but it is against the interest of the nation." [28] At the time the lord's refusal to accept the words "abdicated" and "vacancy" was debated, Dolben urged the acceptance of the Commons version of the vacancy resolution. He said: "The lords have so far concurred with your vote, 'That king James has broken the original contract betwixt the king and people.' The premises must agree with the conclusion; ours is the more proper inference, and we must stand by it." [29] Dolben was active in political and judicial affairs during the reigns of William and Anne. He was created a baronet in 1704. He married Anne Mulso in 1683 and died in October, 1722.

Done, Thomas (b. 1655), esquire, of Duddon, Chester County, Member of Parliament (Tory) from Newton Borough, Southampton, 1685-87 and 1689. He was the son of Ralph Done and had attended Gray's Inn in 1672.

Dowdeswell, Richard (1653-1711), esquire, of Bushley, Worcestershire, sheriff of Worcester County, 1689, and Member of Parliament (Whig) for Tewkesbury Borough, Gloucestershire, 1685-87 and 1689-1710. He was the son and heir of William Dowdeswell and entered Christ Church College, Oxford, in 1669. Dowdeswell was active in local politics. Besides serving as sheriff of Worcestershire, he had, in collaboration with Sir Francis Winnington, obtained a charter for Tewkesbury and became one of the principal burgesses. As a Whig Member of Parliament, he was a staunch supporter of a Protestant succession. In 1676 he married Elizabeth, the daughter of Sir Francis Winnington, and died in 1711.

Downay, John (1625-1695), viscount, of Cowick, Yorkshire, member of the Yorkshire militia committee during the Commonwealth, and Member of Parliament (Tory) for Yorkshire, 1660 and for Pontefract Borough, Yorkshire, 1661-81, 1685-87, and 1689-90. The son of John Downay, he succeeded his nephew, Sir Thomas Downay, in the baronetcy in 1642 and in the family estates in 1644. He was knighted in 1660 and created Viscount Downe in 1681. Downay attended Gray's Inn and Jesus College, Cambridge. As an important politician in the North, he, along with Sir Thomas Wharton, was sent to London to present a petition that requested of Monck the return of the excluded members or the summons of a free Parliament. After the Restoration, he was a member of the court party and his close associates were the Musgraves and Secretary Williamson. Although he was a member of the privy council under James II, he refused to reply to the king's questions about future members of Parliament. He married Elizabeth Melton and Dorothy Johnson and died in Octover, 1695.

Doyly, Sir John (1640-1709), baronet, of Chiselhampton, Oxfordshire, captain in the Oxon militia; sheriff of Oxfordshire, 1684-85; and Member of Parliament (Tory) from Woodstock Borough, Oxfordshire, 1689-90. The son and heir of John Doyly, he succeeded his father in 1660 and was created first baronet in 1666. He was admitted to Wadham College, Oxford, in 1657. He was a commissioner for the regulation of Oxford City and, as a captain in the Oxon militia, he was one of the few who remained loyal to James II in 1688. Doyly married Margaret, the daughter of Sir Richard Cholmeley, and died in April, 1709.

Drake, Sir Francis (1642-1718), baronet of Buckland, Devonshire, sheriff of Devonshire, 1662-63, and Member of Parliament (Whig) for Travistock, Borough, Devonshire, 1673-81, and 1689-1700. A descendant of the famous Elizabethan admiral, he was the son and heir of Thomas Drake, who served as a cavalry major for the Parliamentary Army. The Drake family was one of the largest landowners in the southwest, and Sir Francis owned an estate near Buckland. He inherited the baronetcy in June, 1661. He entered Exeter College, Oxford, and was created M.A. in September, 1663. His third wife was Elizabeth, the daughter of Sir Henry Pollexfen. He died in June, 1718.

Drake, Sir William (1651-1690), knight, of Shardeloes, Buckinghamshire, Member of Parliament (Whig) for Agmondesham Borough, Buckinghamshire, 1669-81, 1685-87, and 1689-90. The son of Francis Drake of London, he attended St. John's College, Oxford, and was knighted in 1688. Drake married Elizabeth, the daughter of William Montagu, lord chief baron of the Exchequer, and died in September, 1690.

Duckett, Lionel (1652-1693), esquire, of Box, Wilts County, Member of Parliament for Calne Borough, Wiltshire, 1679-81 and 1689-90. He was the son of William Duckett of Hartham, Wiltshire, and attended St. John's College, Oxford, as well as the Middle Temple. He died in 1693.

Duke, Sir John (1633-1705), baronet, of Benhall, Suffolk, Member of Parliament (Whig) for Oxford Borough, Suffolk County, 1678-80, 1689-90, and 1696-98. The son and heir of Sir Edward Duke, baronet, of Benhall and Brampton, he attended Emmanuel College, Cambridge, and succeeded to the baronetcy in 1671. He married Elizabeth, the daughter of Edward Duke, and died in July, 1705.

Duncomb, William (1661-1706), esquire, of Tangley, Surrey, Member of Parliament (Whig) from Bedford County, 1689. He was the son of Frances Duncomb, baronet, and succeeded him as second baronet. Duncomb attended Eton, Corpus Christi College, Oxford, and the Middle Temple and died in August, 1706.

Dutton, Sir Ralph (d. 1721), baronet, of Sherborne, Gloucestershire, Member of Parliament for Gloucestershire, 1679-81 and 1689-98. He was the youngest son of Sir Ralph Dutton, who had been sheriff of Gloucestershire and a royalist in the Civil War for which his estates were sequestered, and he was forced to flee to Europe. Dutton succeeded his brother in 1675 and was created a baronet in 1678. He married Grizel Poole and Mary, the daughter of Peter Berwick, M.D., a physician to Charles II. He died in 1721.

Dyke, Sir Thomas (1650-1706), baronet, of Horeham, Sussex, commissioner of public accounts, 1696, and Member of Parliament for Sussex County, 1685-87, and East Grinstead, Sussex, 1689-98. In 1684 he was appointed sheriff of Sussex but did not serve. The eldest son of Sir Thomas Dyke, he was created first baronet in March, 1677. He attended Westminster School, Christ Church College, Oxford, as well as the Middle Temple. Dyke married Philadelphia, the daughter of Sir Thomas Nutt, and died in November, 1706.

Edwardes, Sir Francis (c. 1644-1690), baronet, of Shrewsbury, Shropshire, army officer and Member of Parliament for Shrewsbury Borough, Shropshire, 1685-87 and 1689-90. He was the son of Sir Thomas Edwardes, baronet, who had suffered severely during the Civil War and was himself created a baronet in 1678. Edwardes attended Balliol College, Oxford, in 1660 and entered Colonel Henry Cornwall's infantry regiment in 1685. By the time of the Revolution he was an infantry colonel and was killed at the Battle of the Boyne in William III's army. He was married to Eleanor Warburton.

Eldred, John (b. 1638), gentleman, of Stanway, Essex County, Member of Parliament for Harwick Borough, Essex, 1689. The third son of Peter Eldred of St. Christopher's parish, he attended Merchant Taylors' School and St. John's College, Oxford, where he received an A.B. degree in 1654 and an M.A. degree in 1661.

Eliot, Daniel (1646-1702), esquire, of Port Eliot, Cornwall County, Member of Parliament for St. Germains Borough, Cornwall County, 1678-1701. He was the only son of John Eliot, an heir of Sir John Eliot, who had been a bitter antagonist of Charles I. Eliot was educated at Portsmouth School, Suffolk, Christ's College, Cambridge, and Lincoln's Inn. Only one child, Catherine, survived him at his death in October, 1702.

Ellis, Sir William (1654-1727), baronet of Nocton, Lincolnshire, chancellor of the Exchequer, and Member of Parliament (Whig) for Grantham Borough, Lincolnshire, 1679-81 and 1689-1713. The son of Sir Thomas Ellis, baronet of Wyham, he suc-

ceeded to the baronetcy in 1668 and inherited the estate of
Nocton from his uncle. He entered Oxford University in 1670
and was granted an M.A. degree the following year. Ellis married Isabella, the daughter of Richard Hampden, and died in
1727.

Elwill, John (1640-1717), esquire, of Exeter, Devonshire,
receiver general; sheriff of Devon in 1699, and Member of
Parliament (Whig) for Beeralston Borough, Devonshire, 1681,
1689-90, and 1695-98. His father, Sir John Elwill, an Exeter
grocer, sent him to Exeter College, Oxford, for training as a
clergyman, but he became a merchant. Elwill was knighted at
Kensington in 1696 and created a baronet in 1709. He married
Frances Bainfylde and Anne Leigh and died in April, 1717.

England, George (1643-1702), esquire, of Yarmouth, Norfolk,
recorder of Yarmouth, and Member of Parliament for Great
Yarmouth Borough, Norfolk, 1679-1701. The son and heir of
George England, a Yarmouth merchant, he was educated at
Emmanuel College, Cambridge, and Gray's Inn, being called to
the Bar in 1668. He died in 1702.

Erle, Thomas (1650-1720), esquire, of Charborough, Dorset-
shire, a privy councilor; army officer; deputy lieutenant of
Dorsetshire, 1685; and Member of Parliament for Wareham
Borough, Dorsetshire, 1678-81, 1685-87, 1689-98, 1701-18, and
Portsmouth Borough, Hampshire, 1698-1701. He was the son of
Thomas Erle, who had been excluded at Pride's Purge, and the
grandson of Sir Walter Erle, who served the Cavalier cause in
the Civil War and was a member of the Convention Parliament,
1660. Five years later he inherited the estate at Charborough.
After attending Trinity College, Oxford, and the Middle Temple, he became active in local and national politics. In June,
1685, as a militia officer and deputy lieutenant, Erle, along with
two other deputy lieutenants, Colonel Strangeways and Sir
Henry Portman, was ordered to lead the Dorsetshire militia out
of the county to engage the forces of the Duke of Monmouth.
After the defeat of Monmouth, Erle conspired with English
leaders to bring the Prince of Orange to England. One of the
first officers to join the Prince, he raised a regiment soon after
William landed in England and was given command of an
infantry regiment which he led in the Irish campaign. In 1691

he joined the king's forces in Flanders where he fought at Steinkirk, Louden, and Namur. He left his sick bed at Louden to lead his brigade and was badly wounded in the action. In 1694 he was appointed governor of Portsmouth after he had been promoted to the rank of brigadier general. Two years later he became a major general and after Anne's succession was promoted to lieutenant general. Serving under Lord Rivers in the Spanish campaign, he commanded a division at the Battle of Alamanza where he lost his right hand. Later, he was commander-in-chief of an expedition to Ostend. In 1711 he became a full general. He married Elizabeth, the daughter of Sir William Wyndham, and died in July, 1720.

Ernle, Sir John, knight, chancellor of the Exchequer, and Member of Parliament (Tory) for Great Bedwin Borough, Wiltshire, 1681; Calne Borough, Wiltshire, 1685-87, and Marlborough Borough, Wiltshire, 1689.

Ettricke, William (1641-1716), esquire, of Winborne, Dorsetshire, receiver of customs, and Member of Parliament (Tory) for Poole Borough, Dorsetshire, 1685-87, and for Christ Church Borough, Hampshire, 1689-1716. The son of Anthony Ettricke, he was educated at Trinity College, Oxford, and the Middle Temple, being called to the Bar in 1675. In 1679 he became a bencher at the Inn. He died in December, 1716.

Evelyn, George (1616-1699), knight, of Wotton, Surrey, Member of Parliament (Whig) for Reigate Borough, Surrey, 1645-1648 (excluded), Haslemere Borough, Surrey, 1661-78, and Surrey County, 1678-81 and 1688-89. The son of Richard Evelyn, sheriff of Surrey and Sussex, who died in 1640 leaving his estates to his son, he was a recruiter and parliamentarian during the Civil War. He attended Trinity College, Oxford, and the Middle Temple. Charles II knighted him at the Restoration. Evelyn married Mary Caldwell and Mary, the widow of Sir John Cotton, and died in 1699.

Eversfeild, Anthony (1621-1697), esquire, of Steyning, Sussex, Member of Parliament for Horsham Borough, Sussex, 1679-81, 1685-87 and 1689. The son of Nicholas Eversfeild, he matriculated at St. Albans Hall, Oxford, in 1637 and received a B.A. degree in 1640. He refused to give a positive reply to the king's questions on the Test Act.

Eyre, Gyles (1637-1695), esquire, of Brickworth, Wiltshire, recorder for Salisbury 1675; a justice of the Court of King's Bench, May, 1689; and Member of Parliament (Whig) for Salisbury City, Wiltshire, 1689. His father, Gyles, a member of a family that had suffered deeply for its opposition to the policies of Charles I, served on Cromwell's council of state along with his father and two brothers during the Protectorate. He was educated at Exeter College, Oxford, and Lincoln's Inn. After being called to the Bar in 1661, he was active in city politics at Salisbury where he served as recorder and helped secure a charter for the city in 1675. For a time after the surrender of the charter in 1684, he was out of office, but he was reinstated two years later. His fortune was enhanced by his support of the Revolution. Following William's accession he became a serjeant-of-law, a justice of the Court of King's Bench, and a knight. In the Convention Parliament he supported the retention of the words "abdicated" and "vacant" in the Commons resolution. At the conference with the Lords in the Painted Chamber on February 5, Eyre argued that the word "vacant" expressed the proper conclusion for the premises of the Commons resolution. He said: "We declare the late king hath broke the Original Contract, hath violated the fundamental laws, and hath withdrawn himself out of the kingdom, that he hath abdicated, and actually renounced the government." [30] The assertion was superfluous, he said, unless conclusions were to be drawn from "a compendious history of those miseries." Since a conclusion was necessary, the vacancy assertion was an exact statement of the condition: "That we are left without a king; in the words of the Vote, that the throne is thereby vacant." [31] This assertion, however, he noted, referred to the possession of the throne and did not prejudice the right of succession. When he emphasized that the conferees had been called to debate the Lords' amendments and not the consequences of the action, the conference ended and the Lords, after deliberation, voted to approve the Commons resolution without change. He married Dorothy, the daughter of John Ryves, and died in June, 1695.

Fagg, Sir John (c. 1628-1701), baronet, of Wiston, Sussex, and Mystole, Kent, parliamentary colonel in the Civil War; a commissioner to try Charles I; member of the Rump Council of

State; and Member of Parliament for Rye, a Cinque Port, 1645-53, Sussex County, 1654-59, 1681, and Steyning, Sussex County, 1660-81; 1685-1701. The son and heir of John Fagg of Rye, he attended Gray's Inn in 1644 and entered the Long Parliament the following year. As a staunch parliamentarian, he played an important role in military and political affairs. During the Interregnum, besides commanding the Sussex militia, he loaned Parliament £1,000 and was appointed to the commission which tried Charles I, but he did not participate in the proceedings. In 1659 he was imprisoned for his refusal to collaborate with Fleetwood and Lambert, although upon the return of the excluded members to the Rump Parliament, he was voted special thanks. After he was appointed to the Council of State, he exerted his efforts for the restoration of Charles Stuart. For his efforts in the return of the king, he was created first baronet in 1660. After Fagg had purchased the Sherley estate at Wiston, Dr. Thomas Sherley attempted to recover the property on the basis of the settlement made by Sir Thomas Sherley in 1625. When the case was appealed to the House of Lords, Sherley was taken in custody by the Commons for his breach of privilege, since Fagg was a Member of Parliament. As a heated dispute developed between the Houses, the king prorogued Parliament. Fagg married Mary Morley and Anne Hershaw and died in 1701.

Fairfax, Thomas (1657-1710), baron, of Cameron, Scotland, army officer, 1689; governor of Limerick; and Member of Parliament (Tory) for Molton Borough, Yorkshire, 1685-87, and for Yorkshire, 1689-1702. He was the son of the fourth Baron of Fairfax, cousin of Lord Fairfax, the famous commander-in-chief of the parliamentary forces 1645-50. Thomas matriculated in Magdalen College, Oxford, and was awarded a D.C.L. in 1677. He succeeded his father as fifth Baron of Cameron in 1685. Commissioned an infantry captain at the time of Monmouth's invasion, he continued his military career and attained high rank before his death. He became a lieutenant colonel in 1688, a colonel in 1695, and a brigadier general in 1702. Although a Tory in politics, he refused to accept James II's Declaration of Indulgence and was relieved of his army command in 1687. He soon drifted into the anti-royalist party. In preparation for William's invasion Fairfax was given a colonelcy in the third regiment of House Guards in October, 1688. When told of the plans for the revolution, he joined the insurgents with his forces and supported William of Orange. Fairfax married Catherine, the daughter of Thomas, Lord Colpepper, governor of Virginia (1675-82) and the heiress of vast estates in Virginia as well as Leeds Castle. He died in January, 1710.

Fane, Sir Henry (c. 1641-1706), knight, of Aston, Yorkshire, privy councilor, 1690; a commissioner of excise, 1689; army officer, 1667-73; and Member of Parliament (Whig) for Reading Borough, Berkshire, 1689-99. He was the son and heir of Sir George Fane, a younger son of the Earl of Westmoreland. Henry was made Knight of Bath at the restoration of Charles II because of the family's staunch royalism. He was admitted to Gray's Inn in 1657. After being commissioned as an ensign in 1667, he served as a captain in the Duke of Buckingham's and the Queen's regiments. Fane married Elizabeth, the daughter of Francis Sapcote.

Fane, Sir Vere (1645-1693), knight, Mereworth, Kent, lieutenant governor of Dover Castle; lord lieutenant of Kent County; and Member of Parliament (Whig) for Peterborough City, Northamptonshire, 1671-79, and for Kent County, 1679-81 and 1689-91. He was the second son of Mildmay, second Earl of Westmoreland, a staunch royalist during the Civil War and a supporter of Charles II at the Restoration. He succeeded his half brother as fourth Earl of Westmoreland in 1691. As a voting Member of Parliament in 1689, he seconded Lord Wiltshire's motion that Henry Powle be elected speaker of the Convention Parliament. He left the House of Commons in 1691 when he took his seat in the House of Lords. Fane married Rachael, the daughter of John Bence, a London alderman, who had acquired extensive property during the plague. He died in December, 1693, of diabetes.

Fanshaw, Charles (1643-1710), viscount, of Dromore, Ireland, army officer; commissioner of appeals, 1676-89; envoy to Portugal, 1680-84; King's Remembrancer of the Exchequer, 1687-89; and Member of Parliament (Tory), 1689. He was the third son of Thomas, first Viscount Fanshaw, a member of an official family that held the hereditary office of Remembrancer of the

Exchequer. The family's support of Charles I had created heavy debts which required that the estate of Ware be sold in 1668. Thomas, however, inherited the Irish viscountship of Dromore that had been granted to his father as a reward for royalist loyalty. Charles succeeded his nephew as fourth viscount in 1688. Educated at Westminster School, he later attended Christ's College, Cambridge, and the Inner Temple. In the Convention Parliament he questioned the authority of the assembly to depose James II. The sovereign could not be responsible for the charges brought against him because according to law, "the king can do no wrong." If responsibility is to be fixed the "ministers are called to account." Fanshaw, furthermore, doubted if James could be said to have abdicated because he had fled since he had "gone away by compulsion." The king had been heard to say "that he was afraid of being seized by his own subjects." To prove his point Fanshaw emphasized that when James was "at liberty at Feversham he came back." [32] Although the consensus of the House was otherwise, Fanshaw remained loyal to James. When he refused to take the oath of loyalty to William III, he was expelled from the House and committed to the Tower. He died unmarried in March, 1710.

Fawkes, Thomas (b. 1643), esquire, of Farneley, Yorkshire, Member of Parliament from Knaresborough, Yorkshire, 1689. He was the son of Michael Fawkes and entered Gray's Inn in 1659.

Fenwick, Roger (b. 1662), esquire, of Stanton, Northumberland, Member of Parliament for Morpeth, 1689-95. The son of William Fenwick, he attended St. Edmund Hall, Oxford, and Gray's Inn. He was called to the Bar in 1686.

Finch, Heneage (1649-1719), esquire, of Aylesford, Kent, army officer; king's counsel, 1677; solicitor general, 1678-86; privy councilor, 1763-1806; chancellor of the Duchy of Lancaster, 1714-16; and Member of Parliament (Tory) for Oxford University, 1679, 1689-98, 1701-03, and Guildford Borough, Surrey, 1685-87. The second son of Heneage Finch, first Earl of Nottingham, lord keeper and chancellor, he was educated at Westminster School, Christ Church College, Oxford, and the Inner Temple. After being called to the Bar in 1673, he was created D.C.L. in 1683. In the 1680's he held a commission as captain in the Coldstream Guards. After serving both Charles and James as solicitor general, he was removed from his post by the latter in April, 1686. Known as a skillful lawyer, he enhanced his reputation by writing reports of famous trials and legal tracts. In 1688 he was one of several lawyers who defended the seven bishops who were charged with seditious libel for refusing to require the reading of James II's Declaration of Indulgence abrogating the Test and Corporation Acts. In his arguments Finch denied the exercise of royal authority to commit the clergymen to the Tower and the power of the king to dispense laws mentioned in the Declaration. In 1689 he was elected to represent Oxford University in the Convention Parliament. In its meetings Finch played an active role as he was appointed to thirty-one committees. His legal knowledge and his speaking ability were useful in the work of these bodies although his influence was reduced by his earlier association with Stuart absolutism. In his speeches on the settlement Finch favored the cause of William of Orange, but he would not approve the abrogation of certain well-accepted tenets of the constitution. He did accept the contract idea of government and believed the violation of it would produce serious results. The consequent breakdown of government would create almost insurmountable problems. If James were no longer king by his subversion of government and by his flight, Finch believed the throne should be filled with the next in line of succession. It was true that the king could forfeit for himself, but he could not resign or dispose of his inheritance. In the case of James, his escape did not seem a complete renunciation since his departure should be judged a demise and should not be deemed an abdication which would leave the throne vacant. He could not be certain that James's right to the throne was gone. Finch explained: "That the king has lost his title to the crown, and has lost his inheritance, is farther than any gentleman . . . has or will explain himself." [33] Nor did he believe that the right to fill the throne had devolved upon the people because this interpretation would indicate an elective throne. Yet, the English people would endanger their security by sending proposals to James "for the king by going away, etc., and his male-administration ought not to be trusted." [34] Finch believed, however, a satisfactory solution for the preservation of the contract would be the establishment of a regency during the life of the king. This arrangement would preserve the hereditary nature of the crown with descent through an uninterrupted lineal succession. James as king would not be provided with regal powers, for the executive functions would be exercised by the regency. His proposal for a regency brought charges that he was preparing a loophole for the return of James although Finch denied this allegation when he asserted that it would be unwise to return the king to England. His support of the revolutionary principles brought him neither promotion nor office. After Anne's succession he was created Baron Guernsey and George I created him Earl of Aylesford. He married Elizabeth, the daughter of Sir John Banks, merchant and lord mayor of London, through whom Finch acquired an estate at Aylesford, Kent. He died in July, 1719.

Fitz-Williams, Charles (1647-1689), esquire, of London, army officer and Member of Parliament for Peterborough City, Northampton, 1685-87 and 1689. He was the third son of William Fitz-Williams, second baronet, who had served in the Long Parliament and supported the Presbyterian party during the Civil War, although he took no part in the Commonwealth. His mother was Jane, the daughter of Hugh Perry, sheriff and alderman of London. The family acquired considerable land in Ireland as well as England. After studying at Westminster School under Busby, Fitz-Williams entered Magdalen College, Cambridge, from which he received an M.A. degree and studied law at the Middle Temple. He received a captain's commission in Sir Lionel Walden's infantry regiment and later served as a cavalry colonel. He died in 1689.

Fletcher, Sir George (1633-1700), baronet, of Hutton, Cumberland County, justice of peace; deputy lieutenant and sheriff, 1657-58 and 1679-80 for Cumberland County; and Member of Parliament (Tory) for the same shire, 1661-79, 1681, 1689-90, 1690-95, 1695-98, and 1698-1700. His family had served and suffered for the royalist cause in the Civil War. His father, Sir Henry Fletcher, had raised a regiment to support Charles I and was killed in the Battle of Rowton Hill in 1645. At this time George, who succeeded as second baronet, his sisters, and mother were imprisoned in Carlisle Castle. After his release he was fined £2,200 for his father's actions, but the amount was reduced to £714. Earlier he had attended Queen's College, Oxford. Although a Tory, who had supported the Crown, he was dismissed from his position as deputy lieutenant by James II because he would not support the repeal of the Test Act. He married Alice, daughter of the Earl of Coleraine, and Mary, the daughter of the Earl of Hartfell. He died in July, 1700.

Fletcher, Henry (1662-1712), esquire, of Hutton, Cumberland, Member of Parliament (Tory) for Cockermouth, Cumberland County, 1689-90. The son of Sir George Fletcher, he succeeded to the baronetcy in 1700. In June, 1679, he matriculated at Queen's College, Oxford. Fletcher was one of the few Englishmen who promised to support the repeal of the Test Act when asked the three questions by James II. Soon after succeeding to the baronetcy, he settled his estates on his cousin, Thomas Fletcher, and retired to a monastery of English monks at Donay, France, where he died in May, 1712.

Foley, Paul (1645-1699), esquire, of Stoke Edith, Herefordshire, commissioner of public accounts; speaker of the House of Commons, 1695; and 1695-98, Member of Parliament (Tory) for Hereford City, Herefordshire, 1678-81, 1689-99. He was the second son of Thomas Foley of Whitley Court, Worcestershire, who with his father had amassed a fortune in the hardware business. Thomas had inherited great wealth and upon his death left great estates in several counties. Paul purchased the estate of Stoke Edith, Herefordshire, from Alice Lingren in 1697 and two years later demolished the old house and built a new one. He was educated at Magdalen College, Oxford, and the Inner Temple. In 1668 he was called to the Bar and became a bencher in 1683. Although not a practicing lawyer, he was a learned man with an intense interest in precedent. Through his meticulous study of public records, he was able to compose treatises on precedent more profound than either Cotton or Prynne. Although a Tory in politics, he cooperated with the Whigs in making the revolutionary settlement. As one of the managers of the conference with the lords, he helped convince the upper house that the vacancy resolution should be approved. In his speech to the conferees, he assured them that the assumptions were not contrary to England's laws and constitution. He defended the interpretation of a vacant throne by asserting that although the monarchy in England was hereditary in ordinary times, an occasion might occur when a "vacancy may ensue." This occasion would occur when the royal line should fail or when the successor were not known. In either case the power to remedy the deficiency would devolve upon the Lords and Commons. As the representative body of the kingdom and the removing parts of the government, they would remedy the defect by selecting a successor. The Lords subsequently accepted the vacancy resolution and the Convention Parliament proceeded with the settlement.[35] He married Mary, the daughter of John Lane, a London alderman, and died of gangrene of the foot in November, 1699.

Foley, Philip (1653-1735), esquire, of Prestwood, Staffordshire, Member of Parliament (Whig) for Bewdley Borough, Dorcestershire, 1679-81, and Stafford Borough, Staffordshire, 1689. He was the brother of Paul Foley, the speaker of the House of Commons and the youngest son of Thomas Foley, the ironmaster of Stourbridge, who was a lifelong friend of the Presbyterian, Richard Baxter. The family gained control of Stafford Borough in 1689, and returned the Member of Parliament from it until 1738. Although a Whig in the Convention Parliament, he became a Tory about 1692 as did Robert Harley. Yet, he supported the Association in 1695. Foley married Penelope, the daughter of William, Lord Paget, and died in December, 1735.

Foley, Thomas (1651-1702), esquire, of Great Whilley, Worcestershire, Member of Parliament for Worcester County, 1679-81, 1689-98, and Droitwich Borough, Worcestershire, 1699-1701. He was the son of Thomas Foley, who purchased Whitley Court as well as other estates, and the grandson of the wealthy ironmaster of Stourbridge. Foley had attended Pembroke College, Cambridge, and the Inner Temple. He married Elizabeth Ashe, the sister of Lord Keeper North, and owed his seat in Parliament to the court influence he enjoyed through his marriage. He died in February, 1702.

Foote, Samuel, esquire, merchant, of Tiverton, Member of Parliament from Tiverton Borough, Devonshire, 1673-81, and 1689.

Forrester, William (1655-1718), knight, of Apley Castle, Salop County, clerk of the Board of Green Cloth, and Member of Parliament for Wenlock Borough, Salop County, 1678-81 and 1688-1718. He was the son of Francis Forrester of Dothill Park, sheriff of Shropshire, 1652, and owner of over 1,500 acres of land in Shropshire and Staffordshire. Forrester was knighted at Hampton Court in 1689. He married Mary, the daughter of the Earl of Salisbury, and died in February, 1718.

Forster, William (c. 1647-1700), knight, of Bamborough, Northumberland, army officer, and Member of Parliament (Tory) from Northumberland County, 1689-1700. The son and heir of Nicholas Forster, he was knighted in 1660 and received a commission of captain in the Earl of Carlisle's infantry regiment. He attended Gray's Inn. At the Revolution he opposed offering the crown to William and Mary. He died in 1700.

Fortescue, Hugh, esquire, of Penwarne, Cornwall County, Member of Parliament for Tregoney Borough, Cornwall County, 1689. His father was Arthur Fortescue, who owned almost 20,000 acres of land in Cornwall and Buckingham counties and was related to the Boscawen family. Huge married Bridget, the daughter and heir of Hugh Boscawen of Tregothnan, Cornwall, and died in December, 1719.

Fowell, Sir John (1665-1692), baronet, of Fowellscombe, Devonshire, Member of Parliament (Tory) for Totness Borough, Devonshire, 1689-92. He was the son of Sir John Fowell, colonel of parliamentary infantry in the Civil War and governor of Totness. He succeeded his father as third baronet in 1677. Sir John was admitted to King's College, Cambridge, in 1681 and was elected to Parliament from Totness in 1689. He was one of the 151 members of the Convention Parliament who voted against creating the Prince of Orange king of England and for declaring Mary queen. He died unmarried in November, 1692.

Fox, Charles (1659-1713), esquire, of Farley, Wiltshire, army officer; paymaster general of the forces under Charles II, James II, and Anne; vice-treasurer; receiver general; paymaster of revenues in Ireland and treasurer to Queen Dowager under

William III; and Member of Parliament (Whig) for Eye, Suffolk; Calne, Wiltshire; Salisbury, Wiltshire; and Cricklade Borough, Wiltshire, 1685-87 and 1689. His father was Sir Stephen Fox, a Member of Parliament and lord of the treasury under Charles II, who owned extensive estates in Wiltshire. Since the king was his godfather, the youngster was named Charles. After serving as a captain in several infantry regiments, he was promoted to the rank of major in December, 1688. After being relieved of his command by William III, he was reinstated and promoted to the rank of lieutenant colonel in 1692. At the Convention Parliament, Fox supported the Commons resolution that the throne was vacant. He, too, approved the assumption that Catholicism was inconsistent with the English constitution and that Catholics should be excluded from the succession. He favored offering the crown to William and Mary. He married Elizabeth, the daughter of Sir William Trollop of Lincolnshire, and died in 1713.

Frankland, Thomas (1665-1726), esquire, of Thirkelby, Yorkshire, commissioner of excise, 1689; postmaster general, 1690-1715; a commissioner of customs, 1715-18; and Member of Parliament for Thirsk Borough, Yorkshire, 1685-95, 1698-1711, and Hedon, Yorkshire, 1695-98. The son of Sir William Frankland, first baronet, he received a large estate at Chiswick, Middlesex, as a gift from his uncle, the Earl of Fanconberg (Chiswick). He succeeded his father as second baronet in 1697. In 1683 he had been admitted to Lincoln's Inn. Frankland married Elizabeth, the daughter of Sir John Russell and the granddaughter of Oliver Cromwell. He died in October, 1726.

Freke, Thomas, esquire, of Shroton, Dorsetshire, Member of Parliament for Dorsetshire, 1689. He was the son of John Freke and married Creely Hussey of Stour Pagney, Dorset County. Dying without issue, he willed his estates to Thomas Pile.

Freke, Thomas (1660-1714), esquire, of Hannington, Wiltshire, Member of Parliament for Cricklade Borough, Wiltshire, 1685 (until unseated in June), and 1689-90. The son of Thomas Freke, he attended Wadham College, Oxford, and the Middle Temple. He died in 1714.

Frewen, Thomas (1630-1702), barrister, of London, Member of Parliament from Rye, a Cinque Port, 1678-81, 1685-87, 1689

(until disqualified in April), and 1694-98. He was the son of
Stephen Frewen, a member of the Skinner's Company of London. Educated at St. John's College, Oxford, and the Inner
Temple, he received an A.B. and an M.A. from the former and
was admitted to the Bar from the latter. Frewen was married
three times; each wife was a woman of considerable wealth. He
died in September, 1702.

Frownes, Richard, esquire, Member of Parliament for Corfe
Castle Borough, Dorsetshire, 1685-87 and 1689.

Fuller, Samuel, esquire, of Steadham, Sussex, Member of
Parliament for Great Yarmouth Borough, Norfolk, in 1689.

Garraway, William (1616-1701), esquire, of Ford, Sussex
County, gentleman of the privy chamber to Charles II, 1662,
and Member of Parliament (Whig) for Chichester City, Sussex,
1661-79, Arundel Borough, 1679-81, 1685-87, and 1689-90. The
son of Henry Garraway, who had been lord mayor of London,
1639-40, he attended Pembroke College, Cambridge. Garraway
was a supporter of the Revolution of 1688. He was the first
member to speak in the debate on William's letter when the
Convention assembled on January 22. In his comments Garraway recognized the obligation of England to William for his
role in rescuing the nation from "Popery and Slavery" and
proposed that the Convention extend its thanks for his deeds.
He, furthermore, asked that William be requested "to take the
Administration of the Government" until a settlement had been
devised. After the vacancy resolution had been approved, the
state of the nation was further debated. In this discussion the
question of the powers to allocate the crown before the throne
would be filled was explored. Speaking after Lord Falkland,
Garraway emphasized the necessity for limitations in order "to
secure ourselves for the future" and "to do justice to those who
sent us hither." Because of these considerations, he did not
believe William would object to an assertion of conditions for
filling the vacancy. As far as these limitations were concerned,
he believed that they should be listed "under some short Heads"
which would "give security to the government; and let an
oath be administered to him" [the Prince]. In this way the
work of the Convention, he believed, in a few days would be
terminated.[36]

Gee, William (1649-1718), esquire, of Bishop Burton, Yorkshire, Member of Parliament for Kingston Borough, Yorkshire, 1679-81, 1689-90, and Beverley Borough, Yorkshire, 1690-95, 1701-05. He was the son of William Gee and great grandson of a William Gee who had been recorder for Kingston. Gee had attended Westminster School and Christ's College, Cambridge. He married Elizabeth, daughter of Sir John Hotham and Elizabeth Ellerker. He died in 1718.

Gell, Sir John (1613-1689), baronet, of Hopton, Derbyshire, sheriff of Derbyshire, 1673, and Member of Parliament for the same county, 1654-59, and 1689. The family had been established in Derby County during the reign of Edward III. Sir John's father, first baronet, had played an important role for the parliamentary party during the Civil War. He had captured the city of Litchfield and brought the entire county under his control. Later he, because of trouble with the Independents, suffered life imprisonment and confiscation of estates, but was pardoned. His son attended Magdalen College, Oxford, as well as Gray's Inn and inherited the estates and title in 1671. He married Catherine, daughter of John Parker of Berkshire, and died in February, 1689.

Gell, Sir Philip (1655-1719), baronet, of Hopton, Derbyshire, Member of Parliament for Steyning Borough, Sussex County, 1679-81, and Derbyshire, 1689-90, when he was elected to replace Sir John Gell, deceased. The son and heir of Sir John Gell, second baronet, he succeeded to the baronetcy in February, 1689, and married Elizabeth, the daughter of Sir John Fagg of Wiston, Sussex. Dying without children, his estates devolved on John Eyre, a nephew who changed his name. The baronetcy became extinct upon Sir Philip's death in 1719.

Gerard, Sir Charles (1654-1701), baronet, of Harrow-on-the-Hill, Middlesex County, army officer; sheriff of Berkshire, 1681-82; and Member of Parliament for Middlesex County, 1685-95, and Cockermouth Borough, Cumberland County, 1695-98. The son of Sir Francis Gerard of Flamberds, he succeeded to the baronetcy in 1685. In the same year he was commissioned a lieutenant in the Queen Dowager's infantry regiment. Gerard married Honora, the daughter of Lord Seymour and the sister of Charles, Duke of Somerset, and died in 1701.

Gerard, Charles (1659-1701), baron, of Halsall, Lancashire, army officer; custos rotulorum of Montgomery County; recorder of Chester and Bishop's Castle; lord lieutenant of Lancashire; and Member of Parliament (Whig) for Lancashire, 1679-81 and 1689-94. He was the son and heir of Charles Gerard, Viscount Brandon and Earl of Macclesfield, who had been a lieutenant general under Prince Rupert and had seen the execution of Charles I, the Restoration, and the Revolution, and he was the grandson of Gilbert Gerard, who had served as master of the rolls and Member of Parliament under Queen Elizabeth. After his father's elevation to the peerage, he was styled Viscount Brandon through courtesy. He succeeded his father as second earl in 1694. Gerard was educated at Christ Church College, Oxford, and Gray's Inn. After entering military service in his father's regiment in 1679, he served in several military units before he joined the Tangier Regiment for African service. In September, 1688, he was commissioned to raise a cavalry regiment. As a major general he participated in the abortive attack on Brest in 1694 and later was in command of a raid on Dieppe and La Havre. He was in conflict with the court long before the Revolution. In 1680 he was a member of the grand jury that indicted James, Duke of York, as a recusant. Suspected of treasonable activities in 1683, he was committed to the Tower but was released on bail, and, after his trial the next year, was acquitted. Because he had entertained the Duke of Monmouth, he was indicted for high treason and convicted of complicity in the Rye House Plot. Although he was sentenced to death, he received a royal pardon in August, 1687, and the attainder against him was reversed. His marriage with Anne, the daughter of Sir Richard Mason of Salop, was unsuccessful. Although the union had produced two children, he received a separation through an Act of Parliament in 1698 and the children were declared illegitimate. This was the first instance in which a divorce was granted without the prior action of an ecclesiastical court. He died of fever in November, 1701, and was succeeded by his brother, Fitton Gerard.

Gerard, Fitton (1665-1702), esquire, of Lancashire, army officer; a privy councilor, 1689; and Member of Parliament (Whig) for Yarmouth Borough, Isle of Wight, 1689-90; Clitheroe Borough, Lancashire, 1693-95, Lancaster Borough, Lancashire, 1697-98, and Lancashire, 1698-1700. He was the second son of Charles, first Earl of Macclesfield and the brother of Charles, Viscount Brandon, whom he succeeded as Third Earl of Macclesfield. He was educated at Christ Church College, Oxford. Like his brother, he had opposed the policies of the court and had associated with the Duke of Monmouth. During the Whig ascendancy, he had protested against the failure to enact the Exclusion Bill. As Charles's reign drew to a close, he attached himself to the disaffected elements of the Whig party. After he had entertained the Duke of Monmouth in Cheshire, Gerard was presented to the grand jury for treasonable activities, but before action could be taken against him, he fled to Europe. Although he was outlawed, he returned to England at the Revolution and on William's march from Torbay, Gerard commanded a bodyguard of cavalry. He died unmarried in December, 1702.

Glemham, Thomas (1648-1704), esquire, of Glemham Hall, Suffolk County, Member of Parliament for Orford Borough, Suffolk, 1681, 1685-87, and 1689-95. The first son of Sackville Glemham, he attended Trinity College, Oxford, and the Inner Temple. He died at Glemham in September, 1704.

Glyd, John (1652-1689), esquire, of Bletchingly, Surrey County, Member of Parliament for Bletchingly Borough, Surrey, in 1689. The son of Richard Glyd, he attended St. Edmund Hall, Oxford, and Gray's Inn, being called to the Bar in 1674. He died in 1689.

Glynn, Nicholas (1633-1697), esquire, of Glynn, Cornwall County, sheriff of Cornwall County, 1675, and Member of Parliament for Bodwin Borough, Cornwall County, 1678-81, 1685-87, and 1689-95. The son of William Glynn, he attended Exeter College, Oxford, and married Gertrude, the daughter of Anthony Dennis of Devonshire. He died in March, 1697.

Godfrey, Charles (1649-1715), esquire, master of the jewel house; army officer; and Member of Parliament (Whig) for Malmesbury Borough, Wiltshire, in 1689. He was the brother-in-law of the Duke of Marlborough, having married Arbella Churchill, the mistress of the Duke of York. After receiving a commission as captain in Colonel John Russell's regiment in 1674, he served successively as a colonel in cavalry regiments commanded by Lord Gerard and the Duke of Monmouth. Although closely associated with Marlborough, he was a follower of Lord Wharton in politics. He died in February, 1715.

Godolphin, Charles (1651-1720), esquire, of Godolphin, Cornwall, register general of trading ships; commissioner of customs; and Member of Parliament for Helston Borough, Cornwall County, 1681, 1685-87, and 1689-1701. He was the fifth son of Sir Francis Godolphin, the member of a Cornwall family that could trace its ancestry to the Norman Conquest. Active in political affairs, the family was represented in Parliament almost continuously since the reign of Queen Elizabeth. Its estates were sequestered during the Civil War, but they were released when Sir Francis turned the Scilly Islands over to Parliament. He was elected to the Convention Parliament (1660) and was knighted at the coronation of Charles II. Charles attended Wadham College, Oxford, and the Middle Temple, from which he was called to the Bar in 1677. His interest in education was acute as he founded the Godolphin schools at Salisbury and Hammersmith. Although he was not an outstanding parliamentarian, he provoked fierce debate when he offered a proviso for the succession of William and Mary. He died in July, 1720.

Goodriche, Sir Henry (1642-1705), baronet, of Ribston, Yorkshire, army officer; ambassador to Spain, 1678-82; deputy lieutenant and justice of peace for West Riding; privy councilor for William III; and Member of Parliament for Borobridge, Yorkshire, 1673-1705. The eldest son of Sir John Goodriche, first baronet, who had suffered deeply for his support of Charles I during the Civil War, he succeeded to the baronetcy in 1670. As colonel of his own infantry regiment, he participated in military operations in Flanders during 1678. At the beginning of the War of the League of Augsburg, he was appointed lieutenant general of Ordinance, retaining this post until 1702. He married Mary, the sister of Baron Dartmouth, and died in March, 1705.

Gorges, Edward (1631-1708), esquire, of Wraxall, commissioner to deal with recusants, 1675; a deputy lieutenant of Somerset, 1670-85; and Member of Parliament (Whig) for Somersetshire in 1689. His father was Samuel Gorges, the owner of extensive estates in Somersetshire. These properties had been compounded for £582, during the Civil War. Gorges was removed from his office of deputy lieutenant for his refusal to agree to the repeal of the religious penal laws. He attended Gray's Inn in 1648. He married Grace, the daughter of William Winter of Clapton, and died in 1708.

Goring, Charles (1668-1713), esquire, of Leighthorn, Sussex County, Member of Parliament for Bramber Borough, Sussex, in 1689. The family owned almost 5,000 acres of land in Sussex, and Charles succeeded his grandfather as third baronet in 1702. He married Elizabeth Bridger and died in January, 1713.

Gough, Sir Henry (1649-1724), knight, of Oldfallings, Staffordshire, sheriff of Staffordshire, 1671-72, and Member of Parliament (Tory) for Tamworth Borough, Staffordshire, 1685-87, 1689-1701 and Litchfield City, 1705-08. The son of John Gough, he succeeded his father in 1665 and was knighted at St. James Palace in April, 1678. At this time he purchased the manor of Perry Hall. To secure his education he studied at Christ Church, Oxford, and the Middle Temple. In 1696 Gough was one of the ninety-three Members of Parliament who refused to sign the Association roll. He married Mary, the daughter of Sir Edward Littleton, and died in January, 1724.

Gower, William Leveson (1640-1691), baronet, of Lilleshall, Yorkshire, army officer, and Member of Parliament (Tory) for Merton, Surrey County, 1673, Newcastle-under-Lyme, Staffordshire, 1671-81 and 1689-91, and Shropshire, 1681. The third son of Sir Thomas Gower, baronet, he was the adopted heir of his great-uncle, Sir Richard Leveson, who willed him the vast estate of Trentham in Staffordshire. After 1668 he lived at the estate and took the name Leveson. He succeeded his cousin as fourth baronet in October, 1689. In 1683 he was one of the persons to go on the Duke of Monmouth's bail. Gower married Lady Jane, the daughter of John Granville, the Earl of Bath, and died in December, 1691.

Granville, John (1665-1707), esquire, of London, army officer; lieutenant general of ordinance, 1702-05; privy councilor, 1702; lord warden of the stannaries 1702-05; lord lieutenant of Cornwall, 1702-05; ranger of St. James Park, 1703-07; lord proprietor of Carolina, 1706; and Member of Parliament (Tory) for Launceston, Cornwall County, 1685-87, Plymouth, Devonshire, 1689-

98, Newport, Cornwall County, 1698-1700, Fowey, Cornwall County, 1701, and Cornwall County, 1701-03. He was the second son of John, first Earl of Bath and was created Baron Granville of Partheridge in March, 1703. Granville entered Christ Church College, Oxford, in March, 1680, and was created D.C.L. in 1706. After entering the Earl of Bath's regiment as an ensign, he participated in the Battle of Steinkirk. He was promoted to the rank of captain in 1693, major in 1702, and lieutenant colonel in 1706. He married Rebecca, the widow of the Marquis of Worcester, and died in December, 1707.

Gregory, Sir William (1624-1696), knight, of How Cople, Herefordshire, circuit judge; recorder of Gloucester, 1672; speaker of the House of Commons, 1679; baron of the Exchequer 1679-86; justice of the Common Pleas, 1689-96; and Member of Parliament (Whig) for Weobly Borough, Herefordshire, 1678-79, and Hereford City, Herefordshire, 1689. The second son of Reverend Robert Gregory, vicar of Frownhope and rector of Sutton St. Nicholas, Herefordshire, he was educated at Hereford Cathedral School, All Souls College, Oxford, and Gray's Inn. He was called to the Bar in 1651 and become a bencher in 1673 and a serjeant-at-law in 1677. Although he was chosen speaker of the House in 1679, when Charles refused to approve the selection of Edward Seymour, he served only four months. In the office he was firm, temperate, and impartial. While in office he guided the Habeas Corpus Bill through the House. He was knighted in 1679. Appointed to the court of Exchequer in 1679, he developed a vast legal practice both at Westminster as well as on the Oxford circuit. The treason trial of Sir Miles Stapleton was held before Gregory and Sir William Dolben. Four years later in 1685, he was removed from the bench for a decision unfavorable to dispensing power and the next year was relieved of his recordership by orders from James II. In 1689 he was appointed justice to the Court of Common Pleas. He died in May, 1696.

Grenvill, Bernard (1630-1701), esquire, of Stowe, Cornwall County, groom of the bedchamber, and Member of Parliament for Liskeard Borough, Cornwall, 1661-78; Launceston Borough, Cornwall, 1678-79; Saltash Borough, Cornwall, 1681; Plymouth Borough, Devonshire, 1685-87; Saltash, 1689-90; Launceston,

1690-95; Lastwithiel Borough, Cornwall, 1695-98. He was the son of Sir Bevil Grenvill, a royalist in the Civil War and Member of Parliament from the county or borough of Launceston since 1621, and a younger brother of John, the Earl of Bath. The family had been located at Stowe since the eleventh century and its estates survived the sequestration of the Commonwealth. Grenvill was created M.A. at Oxford in 1663 and died in 1701.

Grey, Anchitell (1624-1702), esquire, of Risley, Derbyshire, the noted compiler of parliamentary debates; deputy lieutenant of Leicestershire, 1681; and Member of Parliament (Whig) for Derby Borough, Derbyshire, 1665-81, 1689-90, and 1690. The second son of Henry, Lord Grey and Earl of Stamford, who had been a Roundhead during the Civil War, he was the younger brother of Thomas, Lord Grey of Groby. In the Civil War, Grey was a commissioner of Dorset County who served as host for Prince Charles at Bridgewater in 1645. After his election to Parliament in 1665, he served as the chairman of numerous committees and at the time of the Popish Plot deciphered the Colemon Letters for the convenience of Parliament. His compilation of debates was based upon notes which he took while in attendance or upon information from members present whom he usually identifies. He died at Risley, Derbyshire, in July, 1702.

Grey, John (1628-1709), esquire, of Enfield Hall, Staffordshire, county judge, and Member of Parliament (Whig) for Leicester Borough, Leicestershire, 1677-80 and 1689. He was the third son of Henry, Lord Grey and Earl of Stamford, a parliamentarian in the Civil War, who was imprisoned in 1659 for complicity in the Booth rising and a brother of Lord Grey of Groby, the Regicide, and Anchitell Grey, the compiler of parliamentary debates. Although his father was in favor with Charles for his support of the Restoration, the family remained Whig. John supported Whig policies in the 1680's but became a Tory toward the end of his career. He died in February, 1709.

Grimston, Sir Samuel (1643-1700), baronet, of Gorhambury, Hertfordshire, Member of Parliament (Whig) for St. Albans Borough, Hertfordshire, 1668-81, and 1689-1700. He was the son of Sir Harbottle Grimston, a moderate parliamentarian during the Civil War, who had been excluded at Pride's Purge, elected to the Council of State upon the return of the excluded members and chosen speaker of the Convention Parliament (1660). Members of the family had long opposed the growth of absolutism. The elder Sir Harbottle had been imprisoned in 1627 for his refusal to pay a forced loan while the younger opposed the attempts to relax the penal laws and the king's interference with the choice of speaker of the House. Grimston was a well-educated, accomplished gentleman. After attending Cambridge University (Clare), he entered Lincoln's Inn and was admitted to the Bar in 1670. He succeeded to his father's baronetcy in 1685. As he was out of favor with the king, he retired to private life during the reign of James II and was excluded from pardon when a manifesto was issued on the eve of the projected invasion of 1692. Grimston married Elizabeth, the daughter of Heneage Finch, and Lady Anne, the daughter of John Trifton, the Earl of Thanet, and died in October, 1700.

Grosvenor, Sir Thomas (1656-1700), baronet, of Eton near Chester, army officer; mayor of Chester, 1685; sheriff of Cheshire, 1688-89; and Member of Parliament (Whig) for the city of Chester, 1679-1700. He was the son of Roger Grosvenor and the grandson of Sir Richard Grosvenor, who had accumulated extensive estates and coal mines at Wrexham. The wealth of the family was considerably increased by the marriage of Thomas to Mary, the eleven-year-old daughter of Alexander Davis, a Middlesex scrivner, who had secured possession of London property during the plague by holding titles to land of persons who fled and did not return. Extensive London property, including the later developed Grosvenor Square, came to Thomas as his wife's dowry. Although the original Grosvenor estates were sequestered and lost during the Civil War because of loyalist support, the property was restored to the family upon the Restoration. At that time the estates and property returned an income of £3,000. Thomas succeeded to the baronetcy in 1664. Rewarded for its support of the royalist cause in the Civil War, the family remained loyal to the crown until late in James II's reign. During the reign of Charles II, Sir Thomas, as jury foreman, had required assertions of loyalty from those in Cheshire who had shown sympathy for the Duke of Monmouth during his swing through the country. At the time of Monmouth's invasion, he mustered a cavalry troop at Chester which was incorporated in the Earl of Shrewsbury's regiment after the battle of Sedgemoor. While stationed at Hounslow Heath with his troops, the king offered him a "regiment and a peerage" if he would support the repeal of the Test Act and the penal laws.[87] Unwilling to support James's policy, Grosvenor resigned his commission, and went to the House where he cast his vote against repeal. During the Revolution, he was sheriff of Cheshire. He died in June, 1700.

Grubbe, Walter (1655-1715), esquire, of Patterne, Wiltshire, Member of Parliament for Devizes Borough, Wiltshire, 1685-87, and 1689-95. The son of Thomas Grubbe, he attended Trinity College, Oxford, and Gray's Inn. He married Rebecca, the daughter of Randolph Brereton, and died without issue in September, 1715.

Guy, Henry (1631-1710), esquire, of Tring, Hertfordshire, mayor of St. Albans; groom of the bedchamber to Charles II, James II and William III; cupbearer to the queen; secretary to the commissioners of the treasury; a commissioner of customs; and Member of Parliament (Whig) for Heydon Borough, Yorkshire, 1670-81, 1685-87, 1689-95, and 1702-08. The son of Henry Guy, he attended Christ Church College, Oxford, from which he received an M.A. degree in 1663 and Gray's Inn as well as the Inner Temple. He was not called to the Bar, however, and soon entered politics. As the cupbearer to the queen he became a close friend of Charles II. Because of this association the path to preferment was cleared for him. A number of positions were held by him in the reigns of three kings, the most important being secretary to the commissioners of the treasury. In this post he controlled the expenditure of public funds. In 1695 he was accused of accepting bribes and was committed to the Tower, but the following year he along with others guaranteed a Dutch loan of £300,000. Guy's political positions brought him great wealth. In 1669 he was granted the estate of Great Tring where he built a magnificent house from a plan prepared by Sir Christopher Wren "and adorned it with gardens of unusual form and beauty." It was here that he entertained William III in June, 1690. Besides this property, sold in

1702, he held a lease on Hemel Hempstead manor and owned some Irish estates granted by the king. Respected for his understanding of court procedures, his associates valued his steadfast friendship. Lord Halifax said: "a fitter man for a friend could not be found in England." [38] Upon his death in February, 1710, he left an estate valued at £100,000.

Guybon, Sir Francis (d. 1704), knight, of Thursford, Norfolk County, Member of Parliament (Tory) for Thetford Borough, Norfolk County, 1689-90. The younger son of Sir Thomas Guybon, knight, who had been sheriff in 1642, he married Isabella Matthews, and died in 1704.

Guyse, Sir John (1654-1695), baronet, of Elmore, Gloucester, army officer; mayor of Gloucester, 1690; and Member of Parliament (Whig) for Gloucester County, 1679-81, and 1689-95. The son of Sir Christopher Guyse, first baronet, he attended Christ Church College, Oxford, and succeeded to the baronetcy in 1670. Upon the approach of the Revolution, he mustered a troop of infantry to augment William's forces when he landed and was commissioned a colonel by the Prince. At the time of William's march toward London, Guyse was placed in command of the garrison left to guard Exeter. The following year he resigned his commission because of a quarrel with his lieutenant colonel, John Foulkes, whom the king supported. He had earlier killed a man in a duel on the college green at Oxford. Guyse married Elizabeth Grubham and died of smallpox in November, 1695.

Gwynn, Francis (1648-1734), esquire, of Llansannon, Glamorganshire, recorder of Totness; steward of Brecknock; groom of the bedchamber of Charles II; clerk of the council, 1679-85; under secretary of state, 1681-83, 1688-89; under secretary of the treasurer; privy councilor of Ireland; commissioner of accounts, 1711-14; commissioner of trade, 1711-13; and Member of Parliament (Tory) for Chippenham Borough, Wiltshire, 1673-78, Cardiff Borough, Glamorganshire, 1685-87; Christ Church Borough, Southamptonshire, 1689-95, 1701-10, 1717-22, Callington Borough, Cornwall County, 1695-98, Totness Borough, Devonshire, 1699-1701, 1701-15, and Wells Borough, Somersetshire, 1722-27. The son of Edward Gwynn, a wealthy Welshman, he was educated at Christ Church College, Oxford, and the Middle Temple. Although he was trained as a lawyer, he chose politics for his career and was initially sponsored by Henry, the Earl of Clarendon. During his political life he served in fifteen Parliaments and held many important posts. Although closely associated with James II, he joined the meeting of the lords at Guildhall in December, 1688, and served as its secretary. He lost his seat in Parliament upon the accession of George I, because he was a Tory, but he returned to Parliament in 1717 and remained until his retirement from politics in 1727. His marriage to Margaret, the daughter of Edward Prideaux, brought him control of considerable property, including Ford Abbey. He died in June, 1734.

Gwynn, Sir Rowland (1658-1726), knight, of Llanelweth, Radnor County, treasurer of the chamber, 1689-93; chairman of the committee of privilege and elections, 1698-1702; and Member of Parliament (Whig) Radnor County, 1678-90, Brecon County, 1690-1702, and Beeralston Borough, Devonshire, 1695-98. He was the son of George Gwynn, Member of Parliament for Radnor and sheriff of Monmouth during the Restoration, and was educated at St. John's College, Oxford, and Gray's Inn. Gwynn was knighted in 1680 and became a Fellow of the Royal Society two years later. He has been described as "an honest country gentleman, and a sturdy Whig" who gave steadfast support to William of Orange.[39] In 1696 he proposed the Association in support of the king and to avenge him if he were assassinated. He married Mary Bassett and died in 1726.

Hales, Edward (d. 1690), esquire, of Paulers Perry, Hampshire, army officer, and Member of Parliament for Hythe, a Cinque Port, 1679-81 and 1689-90. The son of Sir Edward Hales, he attended University College, Oxford, and was commissioned an ensign in his father's regiment of foot in 1686. By the time of the Irish campaign he was a colonel in command of his own regiment and was killed at the Battle of the Boyne in July, 1690.

Halford, Sir Thomas (c. 1664-1689), baronet, of Wistow, Leicestershire, Member of Parliament (Tory) for Leicestershire, 1689-90. The son of Sir Thomas Halford, second baronet, he succeeded to the baronetcy in 1679 and attended Gray's Inn in 1681. He refused to vote for the motion offering William and Mary the throne. He died unmarried in 1689.

Hampden, John (1653-1696), esquire, of Great Hampden, Buckinghamshire, Member of Parliament (Whig) for Buckinghamshire, 1679-80, and Wendover Borough, 1689-90. He was the second son of Richard Hampden and the grandson of John Hampden of ship tax fame in the reign of Charles I. His education was obtained in France where he was deeply influenced by his tutor Francis Tallents, an ejected Presbyterian; Father Richard Simons, author of a *Critical History of the Old Testament* (1678); and the historian, Mezeray. The former two scholars taught him to become a free thinker and the latter confirmed his opposition to the policies of Charles II. After his return from France in 1682 he attached himself to the radical Whig faction and was charged with complicity in the Rye House Plot. In the trial for high misdemeanor at the Court of King's Bench in February, 1684, he was accused of being one of a group of six who met at his home in Bloombury to plan an insurrection. He was declared guilty and imprisoned until he paid a fine of £40,000. For his role in the Duke of Monmouth's Rebellion he was tried for treason. At the trial he pleaded guilty and asked mercy of the court although the Whigs were displeased at his request. Although condemned to death, he was pardoned and freed upon the payment of £6,000 to Lord Jeffreys and Father Petre. His behavior alienated many Whigs, but he was elected to the Convention Parliament, where he became the spokesman for the radical faction of the party. His support for individual rights led to the charge that he supported republicanism, but he denied the accusation. Yet, when he referred in his comment on the resolution to secure England's "Religion, Laws, and Liberties" to the head of the state as the chief governor, he may have revealed his innermost sentiments. In other assertions in the same speech, however, he supported the Whig principles about the action of James, the status of the throne, and the necessity to assert constitutional principles. After observing that the Commons had voted that James had abdicated, he asserted that the task was incomplete, since the throne must be filled and action taken "to declare the constitution and Rule of the government." For guidance in the action he urged an examination of the vote in the Convention Parliament of 1660 that "the Government was in king, lords, and commons." An early decision about fundamentals, he believed, was required "for the safety of the people." [40] His views on religious toleration were large and generous. Although he favored a grant of toleration to dissenters, he objected to clauses of the Toleration Act which limited indulgence to Trinitarians. His opposition to William's policies produced his defeat in the election of 1690 and brought an end to his political life. An attempt was made to return in 1696 when he stood for a vacancy in Buckinghamshire. The opposition of Whig leaders, particularly Lord Wharton, created his defeat. Anguish and despondency over his failure led to his suicide in December, 1696. He married Sarah, the daughter of Thomas Foley, and Anne Cornwallis.

Hampden, Richard (1631-1695), esquire, of Great Hampden, Buckinghamshire, privy councilor; a lord commissioner of the treasury, 1689; chancellor of the Exchequer, 1690-94; and Member of Parliament (Whig) for Buckinghamshire, 1656-57, 1681, and 1690-94, and Wendover Borough, Buckinghamshire, 1660, 1661-79, and 1689-90. The son of John Hampden, "the Patriot," he endeavored to promote parliamentary and nonconformist objectives during the Protectorate and the Restoration. In the Protectorate he was elected as Member of Parliament from Buckinghamshire and was appointed to the other House as Lord Hampden by Oliver Cromwell. As a member of the House of Lords, he voted to offer the English crown to the Lord Protector. While a Member of Parliament in the Restoration he was widely known for his generosity to persecuted dissenters and during the Great Plague, he welcomed the Presbyterian leader, Richard Baxter, to his home at Great Hampden. His liberalism led him later in Charles II's reign to attempt the promotion of parliamentary power through his support of the investigation of the Popish Plot and his promotion of the motion to exclude the Duke of York from the throne. His role in creating the revolutionary settlement was more significant. At the first session of the Convention Parliament he seconded the motion that would make William the caretaker of England until the settlement had been made and served as chairman of the committee of the whole house when the vacancy of the throne was declared as well as a manager of the conference with the lords when the words "abdicated" and "vacancy" were debated. Furthermore, his comments in the debates added to the ideas that justified the Whig action when William of Orange was given control of the government and James II was set aside. Early in the sessions he supported a motion to thank the Prince "for the great action he has done in delivering the nation from Popery and Slavery" and concluded that the House should ask him to "continue the Administration of the Government, till the lords and commoners should make further application to him." William's regal-like powers would be further enhanced by Hampden's suggestion that the Prince upon the house request issue letters authorizing elections to fill vacancies in the commons.[41] Moreover, Hampden argued in the conference with the Lords that the throne was vacant by the action of the king. The acceptance of this view created a condition for awarding the crown to William. By earlier action the Lords had substituted the word "deserted" for "abdicated." Hampden argued that the Commons had chosen the word because of its meaning and applicability to the political situation. Although he admitted the broad application of the word, he did not believe it was "too large to be applied to all the recitals in the beginning of the commons vote, to which they meant it should be applied." Nor would he admit that voluntary action would be required to apply the principle of abdication. The failure of common law to contain the word abdicate he ascribed to its unwillingness to recognize a condition which would require the use of it. In Hampden's opinion James had abandoned the throne.[42] This action he affirmed made the throne vacant. This term which was objectionable to the Lords had been used in earlier incidents in English history. The acceptance of the word did not mean, however, that the English crown would become elective. If the throne were full, the Lords would assert who occupied it, and the people would recognize in whom the royal government resided by some public royal action. The acceptance of the Commons decision would make possible the solution of an important problem.[43] Too, Hampden supported religious limitations for the Crown. In debate he supported Colonel Birch's resolution that it was "inconsistent with a Protestant State to be governed by a Popish Prince." Speaking on the motion, he stated that papal supremacy had been unknown in England until after the Norman Conquest and William I had complained of the great grievance in the power of papal appeals after he had given recognition to papal supremacy by receiving a nuncio. Although legislation had been enacted on the status of papal authority in the fourteenth century, Henry VIII was the first sovereign to eliminate papal power from England, and England had accepted the separation from Rome as well as the laws against nuncios.[44] Hampden's work was so lightly regarded that he was selected to carry the resolution on the popish king as well as the vacancy to the House of Lords. Hampden's political as well as personal inclinations led him to give staunch support to the new government, and he was richly rewarded for his loyalty. Upon resignation from office in 1694 the king offered him a peerage or a pension, but Hampden refused by stating that "he would die a country gentleman of the ancient family as he was, which was honor enough for him."[45] He married Letitia, the daughter of William, Lord Padget, and died in December, 1695.

Hanmer, Sir John (c. 1621-1701), knight and baronet, of Hanmer, Flint County, Wales, army officer; sheriff of Gloucestershire, 1664-65; justice of peace, Flint County, 1680; a commissioner of taxes for Flint County, 1689; and Member of Parliament (Whig) of Evesham Borough, Worcestershire, 1669-79, Flintshire, Wales, 1681, Flint Borough, Flintshire, 1685-87 and 1689-90. He was the eldest son of Sir Thomas Hanmer, second baronet, who had been a Member of Parliament for Flint County and a cup bearer to Charles I. He attended Eton and King's College, Cambridge. The Hanmer family had been established in Wales since the reign of Edward I and in the seventeenth century its estates provided an income of £3,000 a year. Continuing the family's support of the Stuart line, Sir John supported the restoration of Charles II by contributing £600 and by recruiting a troop of cavalry. For his loyal support he was knighted in August, 1660. In 1678 he succeeded his father as third baronet. Besides his political activities he pursued a military career. Entering active service as a captain in the Duke of Buckingham's regiment in 1672, he had risen to the rank of lieutenant colonel by the time of Monmouth's Rebellion and for a time he was on duty in James II's forces at Hounslow Heath. During the Revolution he was the chief figure in a plot to capture the garrison at Hull to secure it for the Prince. When William assumed command of the English army, Hanmer was given a colonelcy and command of the North Devon infantry regiment which he led to Ireland in 1689. After the Irish campaign in which he fought with the king at the Battle of the Boyne, he attained the rank of major general. He married Mary, the daughter of Joseph Alston, and died in 1701.

Harbord, William (1635-1692), esquire, of Gunton, Norfolk, army officer; paymaster general of the forces; vice-treasurer of Ireland; privy councilor; ambassador to Turkey under William III; and Member of Parliament (Whig) for Dartmouth Borough, Devonshire, 1661-79, Thetford Borough, Norfolk, 1679-81, and Launceston Borough, Cornwall, 1681, 1689. The second son of Sir Charles Harbord, a man of great wealth, who had been surveyor of land revenues under Charles I and Charles II and Member of Parliament for Launceston Borough 1661-79, he traveled and engaged in trade in Turkey during the Protectorate. After his return to England, Harbord entered politics as a Member of Parliament and as secretary to the Earl of Essex, lord lieutenant of Ireland, who used him as a political informant and as his representative at court and in Parliament. In Parliament he supported Whig policies although he drew a pension of £500 a year from the king and was on the payroll of the French government. Although he attacked Catholicism and supported the Exclusion Bill, he would not support Monmouth's claim to the throne, but he did propose that a solution of the succession question would be the appointment of William of Orange as protector of the realm. After instructing Henry Sidney to inform the Prince of his friendship and good wishes, Harbord considered taking refuge in Holland and was absent from England during the reign of James II. After serving in the Imperial Army while in Europe, he went to Holland and accompanied William on his invasion of England. Although an enthusiastic proponent of the Revolution and a member of the Convention Parliament, he was not an active participant in the debates. In his comments, however, he defended the authority of Parliament over the Crown and proposed that Parliament retain control of revenues to insure that the king would administer the government according to law. He recognized the necessity for the maintenance of an army by Parliament for protection from dangers at home and abroad. He married Mary Dick from whom he acquired an estate, Grafton Park, Northumberland, and Catherine, the daughter of Edward Russell and sister of the Earl of Oxford. He died enroute to Belgrade in June, 1692.

Harby, Edward (1633-1689), esquire, of Adston, Northampton, sheriff of Northamptonshire, and Member of Parliament from the same county in 1689. The son of Edward Harby, he attended Wadham College, Oxford, in 1652. He died in May, 1689.

Harley, Sir Edward (1624-1700), knight, of Brampton Castle, Parliamentary Army officer; governor of Monmouth, 1644, Canon Frome, 1645, and Dunkirk, 1661; and Member of Parliament (Whig) from Herefordshire, 1646-48, 1656-58, 1660 and from Radnor Borough, Wales, 1661-81, 1689-90, and 1693-98. He was the first son of Robert Harley, a large landowner in Hereford, Salop, and Radnor counties, who had served in Parliament under Charles I. Edward was educated at Shrewsbury School, Gloucester, Magdalen Hall, Oxford, and Lincoln's Inn. Because of his frail constitution he left school and drifted into politics, but his initial effort to enter Parliament failed. At the outbreak of the Civil War he entered the army of Sir William Waller as a captain and rose to the rank of general before the end of the fighting. In an early engagement he was hit by a musket ball which he carried throughout his life, and on several later occasions he displayed unique courage and military prowess. Elected to Parliament in 1646 he staunchly supported the Presbyterian cause and was in conflict on several occasions with Cromwell and his subordinates. At various times he was impeached, excluded from Parliament, and forbidden to live in his native Herefordshire. Harley supported the movement for the Restoration and greeted Charles upon his landing at Dover. For his fidelity the king appointed him governor of Dunkirk. Upon his refusal of a viscountship, Charles made him a knight of Bath in November, 1660. During the reign of Charles II Harley remained a loyal supporter of the crown, although he opposed measures that would restrict religious toleration and promote political disability because of religion. While he supported the cause of nonconformists and attended Baxter's sermons, he retained his membership in the Anglican Church. Upon the accession of James, neither Harley nor any member of his family took the oath of allegiance. And, when James issued his order that his Declaration of Indulgence be read, Harley tried to prevent the Bishop of Hereford from reading it. At the Revolution he and his son, Robert, raised a cavalry troop and took control of Worcester, and he was made governor of the county. He then sent his two sons to offer his family's services to the Prince of Orange. In William's Parliaments he served as a respected member of the Country party. His interest in religion was expressed in two pamphlets: "An Humble Essay toward the Settlement of Peace and Truth in the Church," 1681 and "A Scriptural and Rational Account of the Christian Religion," 1695. Harley married Mary, the daughter of Sir William Button, and Abigail, the daughter of Nathaniell Stephens by whom he had four sons, Robert, Earl of Oxford, Edward, Nathaniel, and Brian. He died in December, 1700.

Harley, Robert (1661-1724), esquire, of Brampton Castle, Herefordshire, militia officer, 1688; sheriff of Herefordshire, 1689; speaker of the House of Commons, 1701-05; privy councilor, 1704; secretary of state, 1704-08; chancellor of the Exchequer, 1710; lord treasurer, 1711-14; and Member of Parliament for Tregory Borough, 1689-90 (Whig) and New Radford, Wales (Tory), 1690-1711. The eldest son of Sir Edward Harley, knight, he was educated at a private school kept by Mr. Birch at Shilton where Simon Harcourt and Thomas Trevor were classmates and the Inner Temple; but he was not called to the Bar. At the time of the Revolution he helped his father form a cavalry troop and seized Worcester in the name of William of Orange. After the accession of the Prince, Harley entered Parliament in a by-election through the influence of the Boscawens and continued to serve until his elevation to a peerage. Although his background was Whig, he became a Tory and a supporter of the Anglican Church. Showing great aptitude for politics, he rose rapidly during Queen Anne's reign. She created him Earl of Oxford and appointed him as lord treasurer. He married Elizabeth, the daughter of Thomas Foley and Sarah, the daughter of Simon Middleton of Edmonton. He died in May, 1724.

Hart, Sir Richard (d. 1701), knight, of Hanham, Somersetshire, sheriff of Bristol, 1680; mayor of Bristol, 1680; and Member of Parliament (Tory) from Bristol City, 1681, 1685-87, and 1689-95. The eldest son of Alderman George Hart, he was active in Bristol politics during the reigns of Charles II and James II until he was removed by royal order in June, 1686. Although he was injured by the policy of James II, he voted against offering the crown to William and Mary. Hart was married three times, the third wife being Elizabeth, the daughter of Sir William James, attorney-general, 1674-79. He died in January, 1701.

Harvey, Michael (c. 1635-1712), esquire, of Clifton, Dorset, justice of peace in Dorset, and Member of Parliament for Weymouth and Melcombe Regis, Dorsetshire, 1679-81, and 1689-1701. He was the son of Michael Harvey, a London merchant, and attended Emmanuel College, Cambridge, as well as Gray's Inn. His death occurred in February, 1712.

Harvey, William (1663-1731), esquire, of Chigwell, Essex, Member of Parliament for Old Sarum, Wiltshire, 1689-1705, 1708-10; Appleby, Westmorland, 1705-07; Weymouth and Melcombe Regis, Dorsetshire, 1711-13, 1714-15; Essex County, 1715-16 and 1722-27. He was the son of Sir Eliah Harvey and, after receiving his preparatory education at St. Paul's School, he attended Trinity College, Cambridge. He died in October, 1731.

Hawles, Sir John (1645-1716), esquire, of Monckton, Dorsetshire, solicitor general 1695-1702, and Member of Parliament (Whig) for Old Sarum, Wiltshire, 1689-1690; Wilton, Wiltshire, 1695, 1702-05; Beeralston, Devonshire, 1698-1700; Cornwall County, 1701; St. Ives, Cornwall County, 1701-02; and Stockbridge, Southamptonshire, 1705-10. The second son of Thomas Hawles, who had supported the parliamentary cause during the Civil War as leader of a band known as "club men" at Salisbury, he was educated at Winchester School, Queen's College, Oxford, and Lincoln's Inn. After being called to the Bar in 1670, he rose to eminence as a lawyer. For seven years he served as solicitor general and was one of the managers in the impeachment of Sacheverell. He was knighted in November, 1695. Hawles' legal interests extended beyond the practice of law. He wrote three treatises on law and politics: "Remarks upon the tryals of E. Fitzharris, S. College, Count Kroningsmark, the Lord Russell," London, 1689; "A Reply to a Sheet of Paper Entitled the Magistrary and Government of England Vindicated," London, 1689; and "The Englishman's Right; A Dialogue between a Barrister-at-Law and a Juryman," London, 1763. A staunch supporter of William of Orange, he did not enter Parliament until after the settlement had been made since his election was held in March, 1689. He died in August, 1716.

Hawtrey, Ralph (b. 1615), esquire, of Rislipp, Middlesex County, Member of Parliament (Tory) for Middlesex County, 1689. The son and heir of Francis Hawtrey, he attended Gray's Inn in 1631.

Hayne, William, a merchant, of Dartmouth, Devonshire, Member of Parliament (Tory) for Hardness Borough, Devonshire, 1689.

Heljar, William (1662-1747), esquire, of East Coker, Somersetshire, served as sheriff of Somersetshire, 1701-01; deputy lieutenant of Somersetshire, 1703; and Member of Parliament (Tory) for Ilchester Borough, Somersetshire, in 1689 and Somerset County, 1715-22. The son of William Heljar, he attended Trinity College, Oxford, and Lincoln's Inn. He married Joanna Hale and Anne Harbin and died in 1747.

Henning, Henry (d. 1699), esquire, of Pakeswell, Dorset County, Member of Parliament for Weymouth and Melcombe Regis Borough, Dorsetshire, 1679-94. He was the son of Edward Henning and married the daughter of Thomas Achim. He died in 1699.

Herbert, Arthur (1647-1716), esquire; naval officer; army colonel; groom of the bedchamber; master of the robes, 1684; privy councilor; first lord of the admiralty, 1689; and Member of Parliament (Whig) for Dover, a Cinque Port, 1685-87, Plymouth Borough, Devonshire, 1689. He was a younger son of Sir Edward Herbert, who had been attorney-general to Charles I and keeper of the great seal to Prince Charles, 1653-54. Choosing the navy as a career, Herbert had risen to the rank of admiral by 1680 and had felt the rigors of sea action. In

1666 on a return voyage from Gibraltar he lost his ship in collision with another. During the Third Dutch War, he was severely wounded, and later he lost an eye in an accidental explosion. After service in the Mediterranean 1680-83, he was appointed master of the robes in 1684. In the following year he was elected to Parliament from Dover. Because he refused on the grounds of conscience to agree to vote for the repeal of the Test Act, the king dismissed him from all employments worth about £4,000 in March, 1687, and had his accounts carefully audited. Herbert's political difficulties made him susceptible to overtures from William of Orange to use his influence in the navy for the support of the Prince's cause. After the lords prepared their invitation for William, Herbert was the courier and arrived in Holland soon after the bishops' trial. Here he offered his services to the Prince, who appointed him admiral of the fleet that brought the invasion forces to Torbay. In March, 1689, Herbert was made first lord of the admiralty and commander-in-chief of the Channel fleet. In the latter capacity, he permitted the French navy to escape from Bantry Bay. Although William, upon a visit to the fleet, after Bantry Bay created Herbert the Earl of Torrington, he was court-martialed on a charge of mismanagement but was acquitted. After this incident, he was removed of all employments although he frequently attended the House of Lords where he spoke on naval affairs. He married Anne Pheasant in 1668 and Anne, the widow of Thomas Carew. He died in April, 1716.

Herbert, Charles (d. 1691), esquire, of Aston, army officer; auditor of Wales, 1689-91; and Member of Parliament (Whig) from Montgomery Borough, Wales, 1689-91. He was the third son of Sir Edward Herbert, who had been a Member of Parliament and attorney-general under Charles I and had preferred charges of treason against the five members in January, 1642. Herbert was commissioned a captain in the Duke of York's regiment in 1678 and had risen to the rank of colonel by the time of the Revolution. His attempt to enter Parliament from Montgomery Borough was unsuccessful but his petition to remove his opponent was granted, and he represented the district from 1689 until 1691. In April, 1689, he was given command of the 23rd infantry which he led in the Irish Campaign. He was described as "very assiduous, but too easy to the officers." [46] At the Battle of Aghrim, Herbert and Colonel Earle were taken prisoners. After the escape of the latter, Herbert was brutally murdered when the Irish troop realized that he would probably be rescued.

Herbert, Francis (1667-1719), esquire, of Oakley Park, Shropshire, Member of Parliament for Ludlow Borough, Shropshire, 1689-90, 1698-1705, and 1715-19. The son of Richard Herbert of Dolegcog, Montgomery County, he attended Christ Church College, Oxford, and Gray's Inn. He died in February, 1719.

Herbert, Henry (1654-1709), esquire, baron, of Ribbesford, Worcestershire, army officer; a lord of trade, 1707-09; and Member of Parliament (Whig) for Bewdley Borough, Worcestershire, 1677-79, 1689-94 and Worcester City, 1681. He was the only son of Sir Henry Herbert, who had been gentleman of the privy chamber, master of the revels, and Member of Parliament. After studying at Trinity College, Oxford, where he was complimented for his diligence, he attended Lincoln's Inn as well as the Inner Temple. Upon his father's death, he stood for election as Member of Parliament in Bewdley. Although he was returned, the election was contested but the committee on elections decided in his favor in 1677. During James II's reign Herbert supported the opponents of the Crown. In 1688 he conferred with William of Orange in Holland, and at the Revolution raised forces in Worcestershire for the Prince and supported his cause in the Convention Parliament. In 1694 he was created Baron Herbert of Cherbury. Although he received a dowry of £8,000 by his marriage to Ann, the daughter of Alderman Ramsey of London, he was generally in financial trouble and sought favors from the Crown to recoup his fortune. He died in January, 1709.

Herbert, James, esquire, of Kingsey, Buckinghamshire, Member of Parliament for Westbury Borough, Wiltshire, 1685-87, and Queensbury Borough, Kent, 1689. He was the second son of James Herbert and the grandson of Philip Herbert, who had been lord chamberlain to Charles I and the constable of Queensborough Castle.

Herle, Edward (d. 1721), esquire, of Landue, Cornwall,

Member of Parliament for Granpound Borough, Cornwall County, 1689.

Herne, Joseph (d. 1699), esquire, merchant, of London, alderman of London; Member of the committee on the East India Company, 1678-86, 1687-93, 1698-99; governor of the East India Company, 1690-92; and Member of Parliament (Tory) for Dartmouth Borough, Devonshire, 1689-90. Educated at the Inner Temple, he pursued mercantile and financial interests in London and married the daughter of Sir John Frederick, knight, alderman, sheriff, and lord mayor of London. He was knighted in September, 1690, and died in 1699.

Hervey, Sir Thomas (1625-1694), knight, of St. Edmundsbury, Suffolk, Member of Parliament for St. Edmundsbury Borough, Suffolk County 1679-81, 1685-87, and 1689-90. The third son of William Hervey he inherited the family estates from his brother John in 1679. In 1641 he matriculated at Pembroke College, Cambridge. After the Restoration he was knighted by Charles II. He married Isabella, the daughter of Sir Humphrey May, vice-chamberlain of the household to Charles I, and died in May, 1694.

Hillersdon, Thomas (1653-1698), esquire, of Elston, Bedfordshire, Member of Parliament for Bedford Borough, Bedfordshire, 1689-98. The son of Thomas Hillersdon, he attended Christ Church College, Oxford and the Inner Temple. He died in February, 1698.

Hobart, Sir Henry (1658-1698), knight and baronet, of Bickling, Norfolk County, army officer and Member of Parliament (Whig) for King's Lynn, 1681, Norfolk County, 1689-90, 1695-98, and Beeralston Borough, Devonshire, 1694-95. The Hobart family had held extensive estates in Norfolk County for one hundred fifty years. Sir John Hobart, the great-uncle of Sir Henry, had served as chief justice of the Court of Common Pleas and had accumulated great wealth before his death in 1625. Since Sir John died without heirs, his estates were inherited by his nephew John, the son-in-law of John Hampden, "the Partiot," who became the third baronet and who was the father of Sir John. The later attended Thetford School and St. John's College, Cambridge. He was knighted in 1671 and succeeded to the baronetcy in 1683. Hobart was among the first to support the revolutionary movement in 1688 and, as a Member of the Convention Parliament, supported the vacancy and the candidacy of William of Orange for the kingship. He was equerry to William III and general of horse at the Battle of the Boyne during the Irish campaign. Hobart married Elizabeth, the granddaughter of Sir John Maynard, and was killed in a duel with Oliver Le Neve at Canston Heath in August, 1698.

Hoby, John, esquire, Member of Parliament for Great Marlow Borough, Buckinghamshire, 1689.

Hoby, Thomas, esquire, of Breamore, Southampton County, Member of Parliament for Great Marlow Borough, Buckinghamshire, 1681, and for Salisbury City, Wiltshire, 1689.

Holles, John (1662-1711), Baron Haughton, of Edwinston, Nottingham County, gentleman of the bedchamber, 1689-91; lord lieutenant of Middlesex, 1689, of Nottinghamshire, 1694, of East Riding, York, 1699, and of North Riding, York, 1705-11; and Member of Parliament (Whig) for Nottinghamshire, 1689. He was the eldest son of Gilbert Holles, third Earl of Clare, who had been an aggressive member of the Whig party during the reigns of Charles II and James II and who had supported a petition that asked the king to summon a Parliament in November, 1688. Like his father, John Holles, Baron Haughton, was a loyal Whig and a staunch Protestant. Although elected to the Convention Parliament, he did not serve in the Commons because he was elevated to the Lords two days after his election upon the death of his father. In the House of Lords he actively promoted the accession of William and Mary. For his work he was appointed gentleman of the bedchamber to the king, was selected as bearer of the queen's sceptre with the cross at the coronation, and was chosen as lord lieutenant of Middlesex County in March, 1689. In the latter capacity he ordered, in June, 1689, a thorough county search for Catholic arms and horses. After he inherited the Cavendish estates from his wife's father, he asked William for a dukedom. When the king refused his request, Holles resigned from his offices. The king's decision, however, was reversed when Holles became one of the richest men in England with the inheritance of the estates of Denzel

Holles. He was now created Marquis of Clare and Duke of Newcastle-on-Tyne, May, 1694. With an income of £40,000 yearly, he lived in an elegant fashion at Waldeck, Nottingham. When William returned from his European campaign in the autumn of 1695, Newcastle entertained the royal party at Waldeck for five days at a cost in excess of £5,000. He married Margaret, the daughter and heiress of Henry Cavendish, Duke of Newcastle, and died in July, 1711, from injuries received when he fell from his horse.

Holmes, Sir Robert (1622-1692), knight, of Mallow, County Cork, captain in the Coldstream Guards; naval officer; governor of Isle of Wight, 1670, and Hurst Castle, 1686; and Member of Parliament (Tory) for Winchester City, Southampton, 1669-79, Newport Borough, Isle of Wight, 1685-87, and Yarmouth Borough, Southampton, 1689. The third son of Henry Holmes of Mallow in Ireland, he saw service with the king's army during the Civil War and with Turenne under the Duke of York in the French forces. When James became lord high admiral, Holmes was given a captain's commission and saw service in African waters. In 1664 he sailed to America and took possession of New Amsterdam for England. Upon being denied a promotion to the rank of rear admiral, he tore up his commission and contemplated leaving the service. Because of his close association with James he was knighted and promoted to rear admiral in 1666. Entering politics in 1670, he was elected as Member of Parliament from Winchester. About the same time, he was appointed governor of the Isle of Wight. During his service there he built a large home where he entertained the king on three occasions. During the Dutch War he was commander of the squadron sent to intercept the Smyrna fleet. When he failed in an impossible task, he was blamed for the misfortune and was dropped from the lists in 1673. After this time he divided his activities between parliamentary duties and the governorship of the Isle of Wight. Although a close friend of the king, he accepted the Revolution without protest and after the Battle of Beachy Head, he secured valuable information about movements of the French fleet. He died unmarried in November, 1692.

Holt, Sir John (1642-1710), knight, of Redgrove, Suffolk

County, recorder of London, 1685-86; king's serjeant, 1686; chief justice of the Court of King's Bench, 1689-1710; and Member of Parliament (Whig) for Beeralston Borough, Devonshire, 1689. The son of Sir Thomas Holt, serjeant-at-law and recorder of Reading and Abingdon, he attended Abingdon grammar school, Winchester College, Oriel College, Oxford, and Gray's Inn. After being called to the Bar in 1663, he developed a lucrative law practice and a wide reputation for his knowledge of law. Following his defense of Danby, he acted as counsel for Lord Powis and Lord Arundell who were accused of involvement in the Popish Plot as well as Lord Russell for his alleged role in the Rye House Plot. Other cases which he handled were those involving Thomas Pilkington, Sir Patience Ward, and the East India Company. Because of his sound legal opinions and his reputation as a lawyer, he was knighted, and appointed recorder of London and king's serjeant in 1686. His tenure as recorder was terminated after he gave a decision contrary to the wishes of the king in the case of a soldier charged with desertion. Although he sympathized with the Whig political views, he would have nothing to do with the extremists of the party. However, he would have served as counsel for the bishops if he had not been a king's counsel. He served the Convention Parliament as legal advisor and as member of the lower House. In the latter capacity he was appointed one of the managers of the conference with the Lords on its amendments to the vacancy resolution. In the debate with the Lords in the Painted Chamber, Holt explained the nature of a magistracy and argued that the word "abdicated" provided a more exact meaning for James's action than the Lord's word "deserted." In regard to the magistracy, he believed that the office "is under a trust, and any acting contrary to that trust is a renouncing of the trust though it be not a renouncing by formal deed, though not in writing, that he who hath the trust, acting contrary, is a disclaimer of the trust . . . if the actings be such as are inconsistent with and subversive of this trust. . . ." Thus, Holt believed that James had abdicated through his actions. The Lords, however, had rejected the word and offered the term "deserted" as a substitute in the resolution, giving as a reason that the word, "abdicated" was unknown in Common Law and when used in Civil Law it meant a "voluntary express act of renunciation." Holt reasoned, however, that the important factor was the recognized meaning of the word. "Abdicated" met the latter requirement because it had been used by the Roman writers, such as Cicero, and was included in Minshew's *Dictionary*. According to this author, the word signified "renounced" which was the meaning that the Commons intended that it have. The fact that the word was not used in Common Law was unimportant to Holt because few words in use were as old as Common Law and new words have been added in "the several successions of time." As for the use of the word "abdicated," which in Civil Law according to the Lords was a "voluntary express act of renunciation," Holt conceded that the Commons had used "abdicated" because it had that meaning. If the Lords had referred to a formal act of renunciation he knew of more that had been made by the king, but he stated that taking action "inconsistent with the being and end of a thing . . . [is] an abdication and formal renunciation of that thing." The conference members accepted Holt's interpretation that by the action of the king on the throne he had renounced his magistracy and had abdicated. Later in the debates on the Bill of Rights and the succession Holt was asked about the status of dispensing power by both Houses of Parliament and replied that it was a part of England's constitutional law.[47] Later in 1689 he was appointed chief justice of the Court of King's Bench and privy councilor. When Somers was dismissed, Holt was offered the position as lord chancellor, but he refused because of ill health. He married Anne Cropley in 1675 and died in March, 1710.

Holt, Richard (b. 1632), esquire, of Portsmouth, Southampton, Member of Parliament for Lymington Borough, Southampton, 1685-87, 1689-90, and Petersfield Borough, Southampton, 1690-98. He was the son of John Holt and attended St. John's College, Oxford, as well as the Middle Temple.

Honeywood, Sir William (1654-1748), baronet, of Evington, Kent, Member of Parliament (Whig) for Canterbury City, Kent, 1685-87 and 1689-98. He was the son and heir of Sir Edward Honeywood, who owned over 5,600 acres of land in Kent

County. Honeywood attended Jesus College, Oxford, and succeeded to the baronetcy upon the death of his father in 1670. He married Anne Harbord and died in 1748 at age ninety-four.

Horner, George (1654-1707), esquire, sheriff; deputy lieutenant and justice of peace for Somerset, 1680; colonel of militia, 1681; visitor of Sexey's School, Burton, 1690; and Member of Parliament (Whig) for Somerset County, 1685-87 and 1689. He was the son and heir of Sir George Horner, knight, who had been sheriff and Member of Parliament for Somersetshire. A staunch supporter of the Crown, he was one of the militia officers whom the Whig leaders sought to remove in 1681. Not long afterwards, however, he was removed as deputy lieutenant by James II and at the Revolution signed the declaration in support of William of Orange. His election in Somerset County was seriously opposed by John Speke, but Horner was returned and was reappointed deputy lieutenant in 1691. By his marriage to Elizabeth Fortescue he had six children and died in 1707.

Hotham, Sir John (1682-1689), baronet, of Scarborough, Yorkshire, Member of Parliament for Beverley Borough, Yorkshire, 1660-81, and 1689. The son of Sir John Hotham, knight, who was executed during the Civil War on the charge of betraying a cavalry regiment in which he was a captain into royalist hands and who owned 20,000 acres of land in Yorkshire, he attended Peterhouse at Cambridge and succeeded his grandfather as second baronet in 1666. He married Elizabeth, the daughter of Sapcote, Viscount Beaumont of Swords, and died in 1689.

Houghton, Sir Charles (1644-1710), baronet, of Houghton Tower, Lancashire, Member of Parliament (Whig) for Lancaster County, 1679-81 and 1689. He was the eldest son of Sir Richard Houghton of an old Lancashire family and a loyal supporter of Parliament during the Civil War as well as member of the Presbyterian party after the Restoration. Sir Charles succeeded his father, a Member of Parliament during Charles II reign, as fourth baronet in 1678 and was called to the House of Lords as Lord Houghton in February, 1689. He married Mary, the daughter of Viscount Massareene of Ireland, and died in 1710.

Howard, Charles (1669-1738), Viscount of Morpeth, Cumberland, governor of Carlisle, 1693-1738; lord lieutenant of Cumberland and Westmorland, 1694-1712, and 1714-38; a gentleman of the bedchamber, 1700-02; deputy earl marshall, 1701-06; privy councilor, 1701; first lord of the treasury, 1701-02 and 1715; one of the justices of the realm, 1714; master of the harriers and foxhounds, 1730; and Member of Parliament (Whig) for Morpeth Borough, Northumberland, 1689-92. The son and heir of Edward Howard, second Earl of Carlisle, who had been a Whig Member of Parliament for Morpeth, Cumberland, and Carlisle during the reign of Charles II, he served as Member of Parliament for Morpeth as Viscount Morpeth until he succeeded to the earldom upon the death of his father in 1692. Morpeth was a powerful political figure in the reigns of Anne and George I. He married Anne Capel, the daughter of Arthur Capel, Earl of Essex, and died in May, 1738.

Howard, Philip (d. 1717), esquire, army officer, and Member of Parliament (Whig) for Westminster City, Middlesex County in 1689. He was the seventh son of Thomas Howard, the Earl of Berkshire, and the brother of Elizabeth Howard, Dryden's wife. Howard was commissioned a captain in the First Foot Guards in 1668 and rose to the rank of lieutenant colonel by 1702. Probably because of his relationship with Dryden, he figures in the latter's "Seasonal Argument" as a gentleman of the Duke of York's bedchamber with a pension of £300 a year. He died in 1717.

Howard, Sir Robert (1626-1698), knight, of Vasherne, Wiltshire, secretary to the commissioners of the treasury and auditor of the Exchequer under Charles II; privy councilor in 1689; commander of militia cavalry, 1690; and Member of Parliament (Whig) for Stockbridge Borough, Southampton, 1660-78 and Castle Rising Borough, Norfolk County, 1679-98. The sixth son of the Earl of Berkshire and the nephew of Sir Robert Howard, he attended Magdalen College, Cambridge, and attained a considerable reputation as a dramatist. He was the author of "The Committee" as well as four other plays, one of which Dryden, his brother-in-law, helped compose. He also wrote some historical works and poems. He fought with the royalist forces in the Civil War and was knighted in 1644 for gallantry in the rescue of Lord Wilmot from parliamentary troops at the Battle of Cropredy Bridge. During the Commonwealth he languished in prison at Windsor Castle. Although a strong Whig during the Restoration, he held several important financial posts and supported Charles II's requests for additional funds. During the Revolution, Howard was one of William's strongest and ablest supporters. Before the Convention met, he spent a whole day hunting and driving with the Prince. In the debates on the state of the nation and on the vacancy of the throne as well as in the conferences with the Lords, Howard made significant contributions to the philosophy as well as the mechanics of the settlement. He introduced the compact idea of government as the basis for the rationalization of the disposition of the king by the Convention. After asserting that James, because of his behavior, was no longer king, he said: "The constitution of the government is actually grounded upon [a] pact and covenant with the people." [48] Because the king had violated the compact, by a series of illegal acts, he believed that "there is an abdication of the government, and it is dissolved into the people." He believed it was now their responsibility to formulate a settlement. Among the features of this arrangement was the religion of the sovereign. Howard opposed the retention of a Catholic king because James had arbitrarily governed the Church, and through his subversion of ecclesiastical power, the sovereign had attempted to control souls as well as bodies. Thus, "The king would not be satisfied with arbitrary government in the laws temporal, but in the laws of the church too." [49] After limitations had been devised for the Crown and the candidacy of William for the kingship advanced, opposition to the Prince developed. It was Howard who reminded the Convention members that if William's wishes were not granted, he would return to Holland. He married Ann Kingswill, Honora, the daughter of the Earl Thormond, and Annabella Dives. Howard died in September, 1698.

Howard, Thomas (b. 1654), esquire, of London, Member of Parliament (Whig) for Bletchingly Borough, Surrey, in 1689. He entered Winchester School in 1667, at age thirteen, upon the recommendation of Bishop Merley.

Howe, John (1657-1722), esquire, of Stowell, Gloucestershire, known as "Jack How," vice chamberlain to Queen Mary, 1689-

92; Keeper of the Mall, 1689-92; privy councilor; vice admiral of Gloucestershire, 1702; paymaster general of guards and garrisons, 1703-14; joint clerk to the privy council of Great Britain under Queen Anne; and Member of Parliament (Whig) for Cirencester Borough, Gloucestershire, 1689-95, and for Gloucester County, 1698-1705. The son of John Grubham Howe, a Member of the Cavalier Parliament, he led a gay social life at the court until he was excluded for making unsubstantiated allegations about the behavior of the Duchess of Richmond. During his ostracism he composed poems and drafted barbed lampoons. Becoming interested in politics at the Revolution, he was returned to Parliament from Cirencester as a Whig. In the Convention Parliament he supported William of Orange and denounced the condition of "Popery and Slavery" created by James II.[50] Later, he fought against measures and policies which he believed were unconstitutional. Early in William's reign he urged severe action against Danby and Halifax, who had helped fashion the policies of James II. Following judicial proceedings against him for injury to a servant, Howe joined the Tories and leveled his assaults against the king's policies After he referred to the Partition Treaty as "felonious," William remarked that if it were not for the inequality of rank, he would challenge Howe to a duel. Because of his support of generous treatment for Prince George, he enjoyed preferential treatment by Queen Anne and held most of his powerful offices during her reign. He married Mary, the daughter and co-heir of Humphrey Baskeville, and died in June, 1722.

Howe, Sir Scroope (1648-1712), knight, of Langar, Nottinghamshire, groom of the bedchamber, 1689-1702; surveyor general of roads for William III; comptroller of excise for Anne; and Member of Parliament (Whig) for Nottingham County, 1673-81, 1689-98, and 1710-12. He was the eldest son of John Grubham Howe, who represented Gloucestershire from 1661 to 1678, and a brother of John Howe, who was a Member of the Convention Parliament from Cirencester. After being knighted, he attended Christ College, Oxford, receiving an M.A. degree in 1665. As a staunch and uncompromising Whig, he represented Nottinghamshire during the reigns of Charles II, William III, and Anne. In 1678 he was entrusted to carry the impeachment articles to the House of Lords. He was among the persons who in 1680 agreed to deliver a presentment to the Middlesex grand jury against the Duke of York for not attending the Anglican Church, but the judges dismissed the jury before the presentment could be made. In 1685 he was indicted for his remarks about the Duke of York although the indictment was withdrawn when Howe made his submission. Howe played an important role in the revolutionary movement. With the Earl of Devonshire, he devised plans for inviting the Prince of Orange to England and pronounced his support of William in November, 1688. Upon the Prince's landing he assisted the Earl of Nottingham in the formulation of a declaration which explained their revolutionary action. It read as follows: "We owe it rebellion to resist a King that governs by law; but he was always accounted a tyrant that made his will the law; and to resist such a one, we justly deem no rebellion, but a necessary and just defense." [51] When the Convention Parliament met, Howe supported the vacancy resolution and the selection of William and Mary as the joint sovereigns of England. In 1701 he was created Baron Clenawley and Viscount Howe in Ireland, but he did not take his seat in the House of Lords. He married Anne, the daughter of the Earl of Rutland, and Juliana, the daughter of Lord Arlington. He died in January, 1712.

Hungerford, Sir Edward (1632-1711), knight, of Farleigh Castle, Wiltshire, lord lieutenant of Wiltshire, 1681, and Member of Parliament for Clippenham Borough, Wiltshire, 1660-81, New Shoreham Borough, Sussex County, 1685-87, 1689-90, 1690-95 and for Steyning, Sussex County, 1695-1702. The member of an old Wiltshire family that had represented the county since the fourteenth century, he was the son of Anthony Hungerford, who sat for Malmesbury in the Long Parliament and who was disabled and imprisoned in the Tower for his support of the royalist cause. With the addition of the Farleigh estates, in 1653, Sir Edward's possessions consisted of thirty manors in Wiltshire and the neighboring counties. Noted for his extravagance, he was called "the spendthrift of Farleigh Castle" while attending Queen's College at Oxford. By 1679, when he had disposed of almost all of his land, he obtained royal sanction to establish a market at Charing Cross. This was sold in 1685 as well as the manor and castle of Farleigh the following year. By his death he had become impoverished. His petition for calling a Parliament in 1680 and his staunch opposition to the court brought him royal disfavor and his removal as lord lieutenant of Wiltshire in 1681. He was thrice married and died in 1711.

Hunt, John (1639-1721), esquire, of Compton Pauncefote, Somerset County, justice of peace, 1683; deputy lieutenant, 1691; and Member of Parliament (Tory) for Milbourne Port Borough, Somerset 1677-81, 1685-87, 1689-90, 1702-05; for Ilchester, Somerset, 1690-95, 1695-98; and for Somershire, 1702. He was among those who refused during the reign of James II to sanction the repeal of the religious penal laws and was the leader of the opposition to the action of Sheriff Strode at the Bruton sessions in 1687. He died in 1721.

Hussey, Sir Edward (1662-1725), baronet, of Caythorpe, Lincolnshire, Member of Parliament (Whig) for Lincoln City, 1689-95, 1698-1700, and 1701-08. He was the third son of Sir Charles Hussey and the cousin of Sir Thomas Hussey, who was a Member of Parliament from Lincoln County in the Convention Parliament. Hussey succeeded his brother as third baronet in 1680 and inherited the Honington baronetcy from his cousin, Sir Thomas, in 1706. He attended Trinity College, Cambridge. He married Charlotte, the daughter of the Dean of Lincoln, and Elizabeth, the daughter of Sir Henry Divine, and died in 1725.

Hussey, Sir Thomas (1639-1706), baronet, of Honington, Lincolnshire, army officer, sheriff and deputy lieutenant of Lincolnshire, and Member of Parliament for Lincoln City, 1681, and for Lincolnshire, 1685-87 and 1689-98. The son of Thomas Hussey, who had been a Member of Parliament for Grantham, he attended Lincoln School under Mr. Lovelace and Christ's College, Cambridge. After entering the army as an ensign in the Earl of Peterboro's regiment, he became an adjutant in the Duke of York's regiment and was transferred to a Tangier unit. Following his service in Africa, he commanded a cavalry troop at the Battle of Sedgemoor. By the time of the Revolution he had received a lieutenant colonelcy. He married Sarah Langham and died in December, 1706.

Hyde, Edward (1661-1723), viscount, army officer, 1685-89; master of horse to Prince George, 1685-90; page of honor to James II at his coronation; governor of New York and New Jersey, 1701-08; and Member of Parliament (Tory) for Wiltshire, 1685-87, 1689-95, and for Christchurch Borough, Southampton County, 1695-1701. He was the son and heir of Henry Hyde, second Earl of Clarendon, and after attending Christ Church College, Oxford, he was commissioned as a lieutenant colonel in the King's Own Regiment of Dragoons. This unit was attached to the Scotch regiments which were returned from Holland to help suppress Monmouth's Rebellion, but the troops were not involved in the action of Sedgemoor. After 1685 he was colonel of his own regiment of dragoons and master of the horse to Prince George. Although he had received many favors from the royal family, he was among the first officers to desert James II, and many of his troops followed him to William's headquarters. He continued as master of the horse to Prince George after the Revolution and was appointed captain general and governor of New York and New Jersey in 1701. The year following the conclusion of his New York governorship he succeeded his father as the third Earl of Clarendon and became a privy councilor in 1711. He married Catherine Oliver secretly and died in March, 1723.

Hyde, Robert (1651-1722), esquire, of West Hatch, Wiltshire, Member of Parliament (Tory) Hindon, Wiltshire, 1677-78, 1685-87, 1689-98 and for Wiltshire, 1702-22. The son of Alexander Hyde, the Bishop of Salisbury, he attended Magdalen Hall, Oxford, and the Middle Temple. He was called to the Bar in 1673. He died in April, 1722.

Hyde, William (1635-1694), esquire, of Langtoft, Lincolnshire, army officer and Member of Parliament for Stamford Borough, Lincolnshire, 1679-81, 1688-94. He was the son of Humphrey Hyde and was educated at Oundle and Queen's College Cambridge. In 1680 he was captain of a Lincolnshire militia company. He died in November, 1694.

Isham, Sir Justinian (1658-1730), baronet, of Lamport, Northamptonshire, army officer and Member of Parliament (Tory) for Northampton Borough, Northamptonshire, 1685-87, 1689-90, and 1695 and Northamptonshire for eleven Parliaments, 1698-

1730. He was the third son of Sir Justinian Isham, second baronet, who had suffered severe fines and sequestrations during the Protectorate and who served as Member of Parliament for Northampton County, 1661-75. He succeeded his brother, Sir Thomas, as fourth baronet and inherited the Isham estates of almost 5,000 acres of land. Sir Justinian, the fourth baronet, attended Christ Church College, Oxford, and Lincoln's Inn. Although the Isham family had supported the royalist cause during the Interregnum, Sir Justinian became involved in the political intrigue of the Revolution. Upon the landing of William, he appeared under arms at Nottingham to help form a troop of guards to protect Princess Anne in her escape from the court. Although he was offered command of the troop, he refused the honor and served in the operation as a coronet. He married Elizabeth, the daughter of Sir Edmund Turner, and died in May, 1730.

James, Sir Roger (c. 1622-1697), knight, of Reigate, Surrey, Member of Parliament for Reigate Borough, Surrey County, 1661-81, and 1689-90. The son of Sir Roger James, he was educated at Clare College, Cambridge, and the Inner Temple. He married the daughter of Sir Anthony Ancher.

Jenkinson, Sir Robert (1655-1710), baronet, of Walcot and Hawkesbury, Oxfordshire, deputy lieutenant of Oxfordshire in 1689 and Member of Parliament (Tory) for Oxfordshire in four parliaments, 1689-1710. He was the son of Sir Robert Jenkinson, a friend of Sir Matthew Hale and Robert Boyle, and a descendant of Anthony Jenkinson, the ambassador to Constantinople and Moscow. Sir Robert, the first baronet, had invested a large sum of money in estates in Oxford and Gloucester counties and had served as a Member of Parliament in the Protectorate and Restoration. His son inherited the title and estates in 1677. He was educated at Brasenose College, Oxford, and the Inner Temple. He married Sarah, the daughter of Thomas Tomlins, and died in January, 1710.

Jennens, William, esquire, member of Parliament for Saltash Borough, Cornwall County, 1679, and for Wallingford Borough, Berkshire, 1689.

Jennings, Sir Jonathan (1633-1707), knight, of Ripon, justice of peace for West Riding; high sheriff of Yorkshire in 1690;

and Member of Parliament (Tory) for Ripon Borough, York-shire, 1659-60 and 1689-95. The son of Jonathan Jennings, bar-rister-at-law, and the brother of Sir Edward Jennings, sheriff of Yorkshire in 1675, he was educated at Ripon School under Mr. Palmes, Christ's College, Cambridge, and Gray's Inn. He was knighted in March, 1678. After he fought a famous duel with George Aisley of York, he was convincted of manslaughter but escaped punishment by a royal pardon. He died in January, 1707.

Jephson, William, esquire, Member of Parliament (Whig) for East Grinstead Borough, Sussex County, 1679, and for Chipping Wycombe Borough, Buckinghamshire, 1689.

Jervoyse, Thomas, esquire, Member of Parliament from South-ampton County, 1689.

Johnson, Sir Henry (1659-1719), knight, of Friston Hall, Suf-folk, and Blackwall, Middlesex, Member of Parliament (Tory) for Aldborough Borough, Suffolk County, 1689-1719. An eminent shipbuilder, he was knighted in March, 1685, and married Martha, the daughter of John Lovelace, the third Baron of Lovelace. Although she was disinherited by her father's will, the House of Lords resolved that she was entitled to the baronetcy of Wentworth; their decision was approved by the queen. She accordingly walked as a peeress at Anne's coronation. He died in September, 1719.

Johnson, Sir William (b. 1671), esquire, of London, Member of Parliament (Tory) for Aldborough Borough, Suffolk County, 1689. Educated at Eton, he received a commission as ensign in the Scots Foot Guards and became a wealthy East India merchant.

Jones, Edward (d. 1696), esquire, of Buckland, Brecon County, alderman, 1687, and mayor of Brecon, 1686; justice of peace, 1685; sheriff of Brecon County, 1694; and Member of Parliament (Tory) for Brecon County, Wales, 1685-87, 1689-90, and 1695-96. The son and heir of Edmund Jones, a barrister and a commissioner of array for Charles I, he was apparently a loyal follower of James II since he served as justice of peace in 1685 and mayor of Brecon under the new charter issued by the king. He died in 1696.

Jones, Richard (1641-1712), Earl of Ranelagh (Ireland),

Chancellor of Irish Exchequer, 1668-74; farmer of Irish revenues, 1674-81; gentleman of the bedchamber, 1679; paymaster general of the army, 1685-1702; and Member of Parliament (Tory) for Plymouth Borough, Devonshire, 1685-87; Newtown Borough, Southampton, 1685-95; Chichester, Sussex County, 1695-98; Marlborough Borough, Wiltshire, 1698-1700; and West Looe, Cornwall County, 1701-03. The only son and heir of Arthur Jones, Viscount of Ranelagh, he succeeded his father as third Viscount in 1669 and was created Earl of Ranelagh in 1677. After receiving his early education under John Milton, he studied at Oxford University but did not matriculate. His education was completed under a tutor on a three-year tour of Europe. He was one of the original Fellows of the Royal Society. As the result of conviction on the charge of misappropriation of £72,000 as paymaster general of the army, he was expelled from the House of Commons. Ranelagh married Elizabeth, the daughter of Baron Willoughby, and Margaret, the daughter of the Earl of Salisbury, and died in 1712.

Kaye, Sir John (1640-1706), baronet, of Woodsome, York, justice of peace for West Riding; privy councilor to James II; militia officer, 1688; and Member of Parliament for Yorkshire in four Parliaments, 1685-98, and 1701-06. He was the son of Sir John Kaye, a royalist cavalry colonel during the Civil War, whose estates suffered severely in the Protectorate. Kaye succeeded to the baronetcy in 1662. In politics he was a moderate member of the court party but was sympathetic toward the dissenters and did not pursue a rigid enforcement policy in local administration. When James asked his questions of prospective candidates about the repeal of religious disabilities, Kaye refused to answer them and assembled a militia force of 7,000 men when rumors were afloat that Irish soldiers were marching to attack York. He married Ann Lister and died in 1706.

Kendall, James (1648-1708), esquire, of Killigarth, Cornwall County, captain in the Coldstream Guards; a commissioner of Irish revenue; a commissioner of the admiralty, 1696-99; governor of the Barbados, 1690-94; and Member of Parliament for West Looe, Cornwall County, 1685, 1689-90 and 1690-94. A member of one of the three great families of Cornwall, he was the brother of Thomas Kendall. After attending Westminster

School, he studied at Lincoln's Inn. Following his service as Member of Parliament from West Looe in two Parliaments, he was appointed governor of the Barbados and became very wealthy.

Kendall, Walter (1626-1693), esquire, of Pelynt, Cornwall County, member of Parliament for Lostwithiel Borough, Cornwall County, 1679-81, and 1689-90. He married Jane, the daughter of Sir John Carew, and, when he died without issue in September, 1693, he was succeeded by his brother, Charles Kendall.

Kirkby, Roger (d. 1709), of Kirkby, Lancashire, army officer; governor of Chester, 1693; and Member of Parliament for Lancaster Borough, 1685-1702. The grandson of Roger Kirkby, who occupied Lancaster Castle when it was stormed by Colonel Birch, and the son of Richard Kirkby, who represented the borough, 1661-81, he served as Member of Parliament for the constituency in seven Parliaments and, when he died in February, 1709, he was the last of the Kirkbys of Kirkby.

Kirke, Percy (1646-1691), esquire, major general, of Westminster City, Middlesex, army officer; governor of Tangier, 1682-84; and Member of Parliament for West Looe, Cornwall County, in 1689. The second son of George Kirke of Charing Cross, who had been gentleman of the robes to Charles I and groom of the bedchamber as well as keeper of Whitehall Palace to Charles II, he chose the army as a career and was commissioned an ensign by the Duke of York in the Lord Admiral's Regiment (Marines). Because of his excellent combat record with the Duke of Monmouth's regiment in French service on the continent, Kirke was promoted rapidly, attaining the rank of lieutenant colonel and the command of the Queen's Second Regiment, known as the Old Tangier Regiment, or "Kirke's Lambs," with its badge, a Paschal lamb. Upon the termination of English control over Tangier in 1684, Kirke returned to England and became a brigadier general. He was present at the Battle of Sedgemoor on July 6, 1685, in command of his regiment when Monmouth's Rebellion was ended. Since Kirke was responsible for the restoration of order, much of the odium of Jeffrey's "Bloody Assizes" has fallen on him. After the Battle of Sedgemoor, he executed nineteen prisoners and marched from Taunton to Bridgeport, escorting a large body of prisoners and two wagon loads of wounded. Within a week of the battle, he had executed a hundred prisoners without trial. Although he was not a barbaric officer, he was a tough and brutal soldier. Kirke was recalled to London with his troop in August, 1685, and he remained near London until 1688. At odds with the king over his refusal to reject Anglicanism, he was sent to the Tower for his refusal to advance upon Devises. Yet, he was believed to be involved in a plot to seize James II at Warminster. Three days after his landing at Torbay, William promoted him to major general. After service at the relief of Derry and at the Battle of the Boyne, Kirke was promoted to lieutenant general and given command over all forces. In the summer of 1691 he fought in the Flanders Campaign and died of wounds at Brussels in October, 1691. Kirke had married Mary, the daughter of George Howard, the fourth Earl of Suffolk.

Knatchhull, Sir John (1636-1696), baronet of Mersham, Kent, Member of Parliament (Whig) for New Romney, Kent, 1660, and for Kent County, 1685-95. He was the son of Sir Norton Knatchhull, first baronet, who had been a Member of Parliament for New Romney and Kent County during the reign of Charles I and inherited the baronetcy as well as 4,600 acres of land in Kent in 1685. Sir John attended Trinity College, Cambridge, and the Inner Temple although he was not called to the Bar. His education, however, most likely motivated him to keep a diary of the events of 1688-89 from which the account of the arrest of James II at Feversham was printed. He succeeded to the baronetcy in 1684. He married Jane Monins and died in December, 1696.

Knight, Sir John (d. 1718), knight, of Bristol, sheriff, 1681 and mayor, 1690, Member of Parliament (Tory) for Bristol City, Gloucestershire, 1689-95. Called "the younger," he was probably a relative of Sir John Knight, "the elder," who had earlier been mayor and Member of Parliament from Bristol. The younger Knight was a wealthy merchant and participated actively in city affairs. As sheriff of the city, he developed a reputation as a zealous foe of nonconformity, and for his policy he was knighted in 1682. His policy toward Catholics was equally severe. In 1686 he apprehended eight or ten Catholics, together with their priests, who planned to celebrate Mass and sent them to Newgate. For his anti-papal zeal he was imprisoned in 1686 although the charge was terrifying citizens. In the sessions of the Convention Parliament, Knight made several remarks in the debate on the state of the nation and voted against the crown being offered to William and Mary. His Jacobite sympathies led him to become involved in the attempt to restore James II in 1696, and he was imprisoned after the discovery of the assassination plot, but, since no charge was filed, he was freed in September, 1696. During his later life, he lost his fortune and lived in obscurity on a small estate in Somerset until his death in 1718. He was married and had a daughter, Anne.

Knyvett, Thomas (1656-1693), esquire, of Ashwellthorpe, Suffolk, Member of Parliament (Tory) for Dunwick Borough, Suffolk, 1685-87, and for Eye Borough, Suffolk, 1689-90. He was the son and heir of Sir John Knyvett and died unmarried in September, 1693.

Kynaston, Edward, of Hordley, Shropshire, sheriff (1682) and Member of Parliament (Tory) for Shropshire in 1689. The son of Roger Kynaston, he married Amy, the daughter of Thomas Barker.

Lambton, William (1646-1724), esquire, of Lambton Hall, Durham, Member of Parliament (Whig) for Durham County, 1685-87, 1689-98, and 1700-02. He was the son of Henry Lambton and the grandson of Sir William Lambton, who was killed at the Battle of Marston Moor fighting for Charles I. Lambton attended Queen's College, Oxford, and died in 1724.

Langham, Sir William (1631-1701), baronet, of Cottesbrooke, Northampton, sheriff of Northampton, 1671-72, and Member of Parliament (Whig) for Northampton Borough, Northampton County, 1679-81, and 1689-95. He was the fourth son of Sir John Langham, a Levant merchant, who had been sheriff of London and Member of Parliament. Sir William attended Emmanuel College, Cambridge, the University of Leyden, and the University of Padua from which school he received an M.D. in 1648. He was incorporated at Cambridge University in 1652, made an honorary Fellow of the Royal College of Physicians in 1664, and knighted in 1671. He succeeded to the baronetcy in 1699. Langham married Elizabeth Haslewood, Alice Rolle, and Martha Palhill. He died in September, 1701.

Lascelles, Thomas (d. 1697), Member of Parliament for Northallerton Borough, Yorkshire, 1660, and 1689-97. He was the brother of Francis, a justice of peace, a committeeman for Yorkshire, and colonel in the Parliamentary Army during the Civil War as well as one of the judges at the trial of Charles I, although he did not sign the death warrant. Thomas was named in the ordinances of Parliament for raising forces and money under Lord Fairfax and signed the Solemn League and Covenant. He died in 1697.

Lawton, John (1656-1736), of Lawton, steward of the manor of Newcastle, 1700-02, 1707-10, 1716-17, and Member of Parliament (Whig) for Newcastle-under-Lyme Borough, Staffordshire, 1689-90, 1695-98, and 1706-08. The son of John Lawton, mayor of Newcastle, 1692-93, he married Anne, the daughter of Henry Montagu, first Earl of Manchester and sister of the Earl of Halifax, and died in 1736, leaving an estate of £1,800.

Lee, Henry (1657-1734), esquire, of Southfleet, Kent, army officer; commissioner of the victualling office, 1711; and Member of Parliament (Whig) for Hindon Borough, Wiltshire, 1685-87, 1689-95, and 1698-1715. The son of John Lee, he attended Balliol College, Oxford, and the Inner Temple. He married Dorothy Howe and died September, 1734.

Lee, Richard (d. 1724), esquire, of Winslade, Devonshire, army officer and Member of Parliament for Barnstaple Borough, Devonshire, 1679-81 and 1689. He died in September, 1724.

Lee, Thomas (1661-1702), esquire, of Hartwell, Buckinghamshire, Member of Parliament for Aylesbury Borough, Buckinghamshire, 1689-99, and 1701-02. He was the son and heir of Sir Thomas Lee, first baronet, and inherited the baronetcy in February, 1691. Lee married Alice, the daughter of Thomas Hopkins, a London merchant, and died in 1702.

Lee, Sir Thomas (1635-1691), baronet, of Hartwell, Buckinghamshire, commissioner of the admiralty, 1689-91, and Member of Parliament (Whig) for Aylesbury Borough, Buckinghamshire 1661-81 and 1690-91 and Buckingham County, 1689-90. He was the son and heir of Thomas Lee and was created baronet in 1660 for his role in the Restoration. Among other accomplishments he and his stepfather, Sir Richard Ingoldsby, encouraged Sir Bulstrode Whitelock to take the great seal to the king in Europe. From the Restoration until his death he served almost continuously in Parliament. In the House he was an active debater and was greatly admired for his elegant speeches. At the Convention Parliament he was one of the principal speakers on constitutional questions. Lee had welcomed the arrival of William of Orange and labored to solve constitutional problems in a manner which would establish the Prince as king and secure English laws and liberties. As a member of the House committee which met with the Lords in conferences in the Painted Chamber, he argued that England was without a government because of the abdication of James II and proposed that the original contract provided for a procedure to solve problems in "extraordinary cases and necessities," yet, he argued that the government was hereditary and, when the question of the vacancy had been settled, the House would "declare their minds" about the occupant of the throne at the time the question would "arise in the proper way." [52] He married Anne Davis and died in February 1691.

Lewes, Thomas, esquire, Member of Parliament (Whig) for Chipping Wycombe Borough, Buckinghamshire, 1679-81 and 1689.

Lewis, John, esquire, of Coedmore, Cardigan County, Wales, sheriff of Brecon County, 1684, and Member of Parliament for Cardigan County, 1685-87, 1689-90, 1698-1700, and for Cardigan Borough, Cardigan County, 1693-98, and 1701. The son of James Lewis of Coedmore, he married the daughter of Ludovick Lewis in Brecon County. By this marriage he inherited estates in that county.

Lewis, Richard, esquire, army officer; wagon master general, 1694; and Member of Parliament (Tory) for Westbury Borough, Wiltshire, in 1689.

Lewkenor, John (1658-1706), esquire, of West Dean, Sussex County, Member of Parliament (Whig) for Sussex County, 1678-79, and for Midhurst Borough, Sussex, 1679-81, 1685-87, 1689-1705.

Liddell, Henry (c. 1650-1723), baronet, of Ravensworth Castle, Durham County, sheriff of Durham County, 1721-23, and Member of Parliament for Durham City, 1689-98, Newcastle Borough, Durham County, 1700-03, and 1705-10. The son of Sir Thomas Liddell and Anna, the daughter of Sir Henry Vane, he married Catherine, the daughter of Sir John Bright, and succeeded his father as third baronet in 1687. He died in September, 1723.

Littleton, Sir Thomas (1647-1710), baronet, of North Ockendon and Stoke Milburgh, Shropshire, lord of the treasury, 1696-99; a privy councilor; speaker of the House of Commons, 1698-1700; treasurer of the navy, 1700-10; and Member of Parliament (Whig) for New Woodstock Borough, Oxfordshire, 1689-1702; Castle Rising Borough, Norfolk County, 1702-05; Chichester Borough, Sussex County, 1705-08; and Portsmouth Borough, Southampton County, 1708-10. His father was Thomas Littleton, a poor baronet, who had sat in the Long Parliament, fought for Charles I in the Civil War, and was a member of the Cavalier and Exclusion Parliaments. As the son, Sir Thomas, was the younger, he was early apprenticed to a trade and became highly trained in business methods and habits. After the death of his brother he was educated at St. Edmund Hall, Oxford, and at the Inner Temple from which Inn he was called to the Bar in 1671. Upon the death of his father in 1681, he succeeded to the baronetcy. Elected to the Convention Parliament from Woodstock, he took a leading role in the discussion of the constitutional issues. When the dispute arose over the choice of words to be used in declaring the throne vacant, Littleton was chosen as one of the managers of the Commons conferees. He has been highly praised for the effectiveness of his work. His work attracted the attention of the Duke of Shrewsbury, who recommended him to William III. Littleton occupied several responsible financial posts and was elected speaker of the House of Commons before the end of William's reign. He married Ann Baun and died in January, 1710. Macaulay described him as "one of the ablest and most consistent Whigs in the house of commons." [53]

Love, William (1600-1689), esquire, of London, councilor of state, 1660; a member of the committee of the East India Company, 1657-62; deputy governor of the Levant Company,

1661-62; London alderman; and Member of Parliament (Whig) for London, 1661-81 and 1689. An independent in religion and a draper in business, he was an alderman in London before the Restoration. Because of his strict enforcement of the Clarendon Code, he was removed from office in 1662. During Charles II's reign, he, along with Sir Robert Clayton, Sir Thomas Player, and Thomas Pilkington, represented London in the House of Commons as members of the Country party. Besides his drapery business, he had interests in the Levant and East India Companies. He died in 1689.

Lowther, Sir John (1655-1700), baronet, of Lowther, Westmorland, privy councilor, 1689; vice chamberlain of the household, 1689-94; lord lieutenant of Cumberland and Westmorland, 1689-94; first lord of the treasury, 1690-92; lord privy seal, 1699; a lord justice of the realm, 1700; and Member of Parliament (Whig) for Westmorland County, 1677-79, 1681, 1685-87, and 1689-96. The eldest son of Colonel John Lowther of Lowther, who owned numerous manors in Cumberland and Westmorland counties and who was Member of Parliament for Appleby Borough, Westmorland County, he was the thirty-first knight in the family. Since his grandfather outlived his father, Sir John was reared by the former. After attending public schools at Kendal and Sedbergh, Yorkshire, he was sent to Queen's College Oxford, and, thence, on the Grand Tour of Europe. He was called to the Bar from the Inner Temple in 1677, two years after he had succeeded his grandfather as second baronet. Upon his election to Parliament, he became affiliated with the Country party although his family had been moderate Cavaliers by tradition. As a devoted Anglican, he supported the Test and Corporation Acts, but he was certain that the repeal of these measures would create civil disorders and opposed the manipulations of the Duke of York. When the Duke became a Catholic, Lowther and his colleagues viewed his future accession to the throne with apprehension. Plans were devised as early as 1668 for the exclusion of James. However, no measure was introduced until 1679. While Sir John was a strong supporter of the Bill, he opposed the efforts to unseat the king in 1685. The policies of James II soon alarmed him, and he not only supported the opposition efforts of Sir Edward Seymour but he also inquired of the House what safeguards were being taken against the growing threat of France. Yet, his efforts were received without sympathy. He also supported the Duke of Somerset who had refused in August, 1687, to introduce D'Adda, the Papal nuncio at Windsor Castle. In 1688 he became a zealous promoter of the Revolution when he was convinced that James was determined to establish Catholicism and absolutism. He cooperated with those leaders who were encouraging William to invade England. With the aid of his tenants he seized a shipload of munitions destined to reinforce the Catholic garrison at Carlisle, secured control of the garrison, and influenced Westmorland and Cumberland to declare for the Prince. With the laws and religion of England secured by the action of the Convention, Lowther became a moderate Tory and was held in high regard by William III who rewarded him with offices and created him Baron of Lowther and Viscount Lonsdale in 1696. He married Katherine, the daughter of Sir Henry Thynne, first Baronet of Kempsford, and died in July, 1700.

Lowther, Sir John (1643-1706), baronet, of Whitehaven, Cumberland County, commissioner of the admiralty and Member of Parliament (Whig) for Cumberland County, 1665-81, 1685-87, 1689-1700. He was the son of Sir Christopher Lowther, who had been sheriff of Cumberland County and who had inherited the possessions of the dissolved monastery of St. Bees. Although Sir Christopher had established coal colleries at Whitehaven, little progress was made until Sir John devised a plan for large-scale mining operations. Additional grants from the king provided a site for the construction of a harbor to which the coal was transported on the backs of ponies. Before his death, he had become very wealthy from his mining operations. Sir John inherited the baronetcy as an infant in 1644 and attended Balliol College, Oxford, in 1657. He married June, the daughter of Wooley Leigh of Surrey, and died in January, 1706.

Lowther, Richard (c. 1640-1713), esquire, of Maulds Meaburn, Westmorland County, Member of Parliament (Tory) for Appleby Borough, Westmorland County, 1688-90. The son of Sir John Lowther of Lowther, he attended Queen's College, Oxford, and the Inner Temple and was a Levant merchant.

He married Barbara, the daughter of Robert Pricket of Yorkshire, and died of smallpox in December, 1713.

Luttrell, Francis (1659-1690), esquire, of Dunston Castle, Somersetshire, army officer and Member of Parliament (Tory) for Minehead Borough, Somersetshire, 1679-90. He was the son of Thomas Luttrell and the grandson of George Luttrell, who had unsuccessfully defended Dunston Castle for over a year against the siege of Colonel Blake's army and who later acted as sheriff of Somerset. Francis inherited the 15,000 acre estate from his brother, Thomas. He was educated at Christ Church College, Oxford. Luttrell was commissioned as a captain by William of Orange in November, 1688, to raise a regiment of infantry which is now the 19th Infantry Regiment. Later he received a commission to be colonel of his own regiment of foot, now the Prince of Wales' Own. He married Mary Tregonwell of Dorsetshire and died in December, 1690.

Machell, John (d. 1704), esquire, of Hills, Sussex, Member of Parliament (Whig) for Horsham Borough, Sussex, 1681-1701. A member of a Cumberland family, he purchased the Hills estate producing a yearly income of £1,000 and resided there until his death in 1704. At the restoration he was a royalist and was chosen to be initiated in the Order of the Royal Oak. As a Member of James II's Parliament, he was asked to reply to the questions about the repeal of the Test and penal laws. He said: "As to ye first and second questions he is very willing to consent unto them provided his religion and property may be secured. As to the third question he wholly consents." Machell, however, supported the Revolution and its settlement. His daughter, Isabella, married Viscount, Lord Irwin, and his grandson, Richard Ingram, inherited the Hills estate.

Mackworth, Sir Thomas (d. 1694), baronet, of Normanton, Rutland County, sheriff of Rutland County, 1666-67, and Member of Parliament (Tory) for Rutland, 1679-94. He was the son of Sir Henry Mackworth, thrice sheriff of Rutland, who rebuilt the Manor house at Normanton and succeeded his father as third baronet in 1640. Mackworth married twice and died in 1694.

Mainwaring, George (1642-1695), of Chester, alderman and mayor of Chester, 1681-82, and Member of Parliament for Chester City, 1689-95. He was the son of Randle Mainwaring, who had been a colonel in the royal army during the Civil War. He married Elizabeth Bradshaw of Chester and died in August, 1695.

Mainwaring, Sir John (1656-1702), baronet, of Over Peover, Chester County, army officer; deputy lieutenant, 1689; and Member of Parliament (Whig) for Chester County, 1689-1702. He was the son of Thomas Mainwaring, formerly sheriff of Cheshire and the owner of over 5,000 acres of land in the counties of Salop, Chester, Flint, and Denbigh. He attended Brasenose College, Oxford, and succeeded to the baronetcy in 1689. As deputy lieutenant and cavalry captain he assisted Lord Delamere and other noblemen in support of William of Orange at the time of the Revolution. Mainwarng married Elizabeth, the daughter of Roger Whitley, who had attended Prince Charles in exile and had received a commission as colonel of a regiment at the Restoration. He died in 1702.

Mallock, Rawlyn (1650-1691), esquire, of Cockington, Devonshire, Member of Parliament (Tory) for Ashburton Borough, Devonshire, 1677-78 and for Totness Borough, Devonshire, 1689-90. The son of Roger Mallock of Exeter City, he attended Wadham College, Oxford, and died in August, 1691.

Manaton, Amborse (1648-1696), esquire, of Kilworthy, Devonshire, Member of Parliament for Newport Borough, Cornwall County, 1670-81; Camelford Borough, Cornwall County, 1689-96; and Tavistock Borough, Devonshire, 1696. The son of Ambrose Manaton of Trecarry, Cornwall, he attended Exeter College, Oxford, and Gray's Inn. He died in June, 1696.

Manaton, Henry (b. 1655), esquire, of Trecorell, Cornwall County, Member of Parliament for Camelford Borough, Cornwall County, in 1689. The second son of Ambrose Manaton, he lived at Harewood in Colstock. His family owned two-thirds of the town and dominated the elections after 1688.

Manley, John, esquire, of Manley Hall, Litchfield, Stafford County, mayor in Cromwell's army; postmaster general under William III; and Member of Parliament for Bridport Borough, Dorsetshire in 1689. He married Margaret, the daughter of Isaac Dorislaus, who was murdered at the Hague when he was the Commonwealth's ambassador in Holland.

Mansell, Bussy (1623-1699), esquire, of Brinton Ferry, Glamorganshire, Wales, justice of peace, 1651; and sheriff, 1645, 1677, of Glamorganshire as well as an army officer and civilian official during the Civil War and Commonwealth; and Member of Parliament (Whig) for Cardiff, Glamorganshire, 1660 and 1681, Glamorganshire, 1679-81 and 1689-99. The youngest but surviving son of Arthur Mansell, he married Catherine, the daughter of Sir Hugh Perry, knight and alderman of London, who brought him an estate of £1,100. Besides his interests as patron of three livings, Mansell was concerned with Welsh coal mining operations. As a zealous parliamentarian he was closely associated with Lord Fairfax and Cromwell in military and political affairs. After the death of his first wife, Catherine, he married again and died in May, 1699.

Mansell, Thomas (1668-1723), esquire, of Morgam, Glamorganshire, Wales, vice-admiral and sheriff of Glamorganshire, 1701; controller of the household to Queen Anne, 1704-08 and 1711-12; a privy councilor, 1704; a commissioner of the treasury, 1710-11; a teller of the Exchequer, 1712-14; and Member of Parliament (Tory) for Cardiff Borough, Glamorganshire, 1689-98 and for Glamorganshire, 1699-1712. He was the second but surviving son of Sir Edward Mansell, baronet, a vice-admiral, who, because of his importance in South Wales, was visited by the Duke of Beaufort during his "Progress" as Lord President of Wales. Educated at Oxford University where he received B.A. and M.A. degrees, he extended the influence of his father and became influential not only in his county but in London as well. After succeeding to the baronetcy in 1706, he was created Baron Mansell of Morgam. While in London he was friendly with Robert Harley and Swift, who refers to him in the *Journal to Stella*. He married Martha, the daughter and heir of Francis Millington, a London merchant and a commissioner of customs during the reign of Charles II. He died in December, 1723.

Master, Thomas (1644-1710), esquire, of Cirencester, Gloucestershire, Member of Parliament (Tory) for Cirencester Borough, Gloucestershire, 1685-87, and 1689-90. He was the eldest son of Thomas Master, a Member of the Convention Parliament of 1660, whose family owned considerable land at Aston, Warwickshire. Thomas attended Christ Church College, Oxford, and married Elizabeth Driver. He died in September, 1710.

Mathewes, Sir John, knight, of Evesham, Worcestershire, army officer; alderman, 1684; mayor of Evesham, 1685; and Member of Parliament (Tory) for Evesham Borough, Worcestershire, 1685-87, and 1689-90. The son of William Mathewes, mayor of Evesham in 1662, he was a London merchant who was knighted April, 1677. Since he was appointed alderman of Evesham following the issuance of a new city charter, he was, without a doubt, a staunch Tory.

May, Sir Algernoone (d. 1704), knight, of Old Windsor, Member of Parliament for New Windsor Borough, Berkshire, 1689. He died in May, 1704.

May, Thomas, esquire, Member of Parliament for Chichester Borough, Sussex County, 1689.

Maynard, Sir John (1602-1690), knight, of Devon and London, legal council for Exeter, 1638, Plymouth, 1641; a member of the Westminster Assembly; a member of the council of state, 1659; solicitor general under Richard Cromwell; recorder of Plymouth; king's serjeant; a commissioner of the great seal, 1689; and Member of Parliament (Whig) for Chippenham Borough, Wiltshire, 1624-25; Totness Borough, Devonshire, 1640-48 until excluded; Plymouth Borough, Devonshire, 1656-58, 1678-81, 1689-90; Newton Borough, Southamptonshire, 1659; Exeter Borough, Devonshire, 1660; and Beeralston Borough, Devonshire, 1661-78, 1685-87. The son of Alexander Maynard of Tavistock, Devonshire, who was a barrister from the Middle Temple and a justice of peace, he was educated at Exeter College from which he received an A.B. degree and the Middle Temple. After he was called to the Bar in 1626, he soon developed a large practice on the western circuit and in Westminster, and by 1640 he was a wealthy man. Maynard was a well-known parliamentary leader in the Long Parliament and the Commonwealth. In his long political career, the ardent Presbyterian barrister fought against arbitrary power and for individual rights. He had an important part in the impeachment of William Laud and the Earl of Strafford while he defended parliamentary privilege after the king's attempt to arrest the five members. When a measure was adopted to depose King

Charles, Maynard withdrew from the House because he believed it was not a lawful assembly. Yet, he performed legal
work for the Commonwealth and served in its later Parliaments.
At the time of the Restoration, he was a member of the council
of state and a Member of the Convention Parliament. Upon
his accession Charles II made Maynard a king's serjeant and
knighted him. During Charles's reign he represented the Crown
in most of the state trials and in most of the Popish plot
prosecutions. While he supported a strong monarchy, he rose
to defend parilamentary rights and powers when these were
threatened. At the Revolution he was invited to the meeting
of the Lords and Commons to consider the constitutional crisis
created by the flight of James II. After the arrival of William in
London, Maynard was summoned to an audience as the dean
of the barristers. William congratulated him on having outlined
his rivals and Maynard replied: "And I had like to have outlined the law itself had not your highness come over." [54] In the
debates of the Convention Parliament, he interpreted the crisis
in a strict constructionist view of the constitution and believed
an alteration of the succession and the establishment of guarantees to secure religion, laws, and liberties were the only requirements for a suitable settlement. The basis of government, he
believed, was the contract and its form was mixed, not monar-
chical, with its beginnings in the people with laws and rules to
protect their interests and liberties. The king might transgress
the constitution to the extent that the people would no longer
have him but the constitution would be the same since the laws
and rules were still applied. Yet, the breach of the constitution
created an abdication and a vacancy. To solve the problem the
Commons intended to supply the defect by altering the succession and filling the vacancy. This action would not, however,
make the throne elective. Since the foundation of government
was in the people, they had justification for the action in the law
of nature "to provide ourselves and the public weal in . . . an
exigency." Some guarantees were required to provide security
in the future. The first of these, Maynard thought, should be
a provision to bar Catholics from the throne. He felt that any
Catholic prince of Europe would destroy all Protestants in his
country if he could. James, by accepting Catholicism, had made

himself incapable of ruling. The second feature of the guarantees would be conditions for the acceptance of the Crown to prevent future transgressions. Several suggestions were made by previous speakers including a proposal that a new Magna Carta be drafted. Maynard rejected the proposal and offered this counsel: "Take care of overloading your horse, not to undertake too many things. I would go only to things obvious and apparent, and not into particulars too much." His ideas prevailed and the guarantees took the form of the clauses composed by the Somers Committee.[55] Soon after the settlement had been completed, Maynard opposed a bill that would make Mary queen while William was out of England and he fell out of favor with the court. During his long lifetime he married four times and outlived all of his children but his youngest daughter. He died in October, 1690.

Medlicott, Thomas (1627-1716), esquire, of Abingdon, Berkshire, justice of peace; deputy lieutenant; and Member of Parliament (Whig) for Abingdon Borough, Berkshire, 1689. The son of James Medlicott, a dyer in Abingdon, he was educated at Merchant Taylors' School, Christ's College, Oxford, and the Middle Temple. He was called to the Bar from this Inn in 1653. At the coronation of William III, he was awarded the parliamentary medal. He died in December, 1716.

Michell, Robert, esquire, of Petersfield, Southampton, Member of Parliament for Petersfield Borough, Southamptonshire, 1689.

Middleton, Sir Richard (1655-1716), baronet, of Chirk, Denbigh County, Wales, justice of peace, 1680; sheriff; custos rotulorum of Denbigh County; and Member of Parliament for Denbigh County, 1685-87 and 1689-1716. The son of Thomas Middleton of Cefu Parish, Denbigh County, he was educated at Brasenose College, Oxford, and in Europe since he was originally destined for the clergy. Upon the death of his eldest brother, he succeeded to the baronetcy in 1684 and purchased the lordship of Ruthin in Denbigh County. He married Francis, the daughter of Sir Francis Whitmore, knight, and died in April, 1716.

Middleton, Sir Thomas (1654-1702), knight, sheriff of Sussex County, 1670, and Member of Parliament (Whig) for Harwick

Borough, Essex County, 1679-81, 1688-90, 1690-95, and 1698. The son of Thomas Middleton, a Member of Parliament excluded at Pride's Purge, he received an M.A. degree from Cambridge and was knighted in 1675. He married Mary Langham and died in June, 1702.

Mildmay, Henry (b. 1640), esquire, of Wanstead, Essex County, Member of Parliament (Whig) for Essex County, 1679-81 and 1689-95. He was the second son of Sir Henry, who had been a Member of Parliament, master of the king's jewel house and member of the council of state during the Commonwealth but who had his titles and estates forfeited and was deported to Tangier at the Restoration. Henry attended Gray's Inn and sat in the Exclusion Parliaments as well as the first two under William III. No close relative of Sir Henry, however, could enjoy influence or favors during the reigns of Stuart rulers.

Miller, Sir Thomas (1635-1705), knight, of Chichester Borough, Sussex County, alderman and mayor of Chichester, army officer, and Member of Parliament for the town, 1688-90 and 1690-95. The son of Mark Miller, alderman of Chichester, he inherited a large fortune and was knighted in December, 1689. In 1705 he was created first baronet. He was married in 1665 and died in December, 1705.

Milner, John, esquire, Member of Parliament for Hindon Borough, Wiltshire, 1689. He was clerk of the Merchant Taylors' Company who took the oath of allegiance and supremacy when the new company charter was issued in 1684.

Mompesson, Sir Thomas, knight, of Corston, Somersetshire, Member of Parliament (Whig) for Salisbury City, Wiltshire, 1679-80; Old Sarum, Wiltshire, 1681-87; and Wilts County, 1689. He was knighted in 1661.

Monke, John (b. 1659), esquire, of Storrington, Sussex County, Member of Parliament for New Shoreham Borough, Sussex County, 1689-90. The son of John Monke, gentleman of Storrington, he attended Oriel College, Oxford.

Monson, Sir Henry (1653-1718), baronet, of Burton, Lincolnshire, Member of Parliament (Tory) for Lincoln City in five Parliaments, 1675-89. He was the son of Sir John Monson, a Member of Parliament in the Cavalier Parliament, and grandson of Sir John Monson, second baronet, Doctor of Civil Laws, who had been a Member of Parliament for Lincoln County during the reign of Charles I. The family held considerable estates in Lincoln and Surrey counties. Sir John succeeded to the estates and baronetcy in 1683. Although elected to the Convention Parliament, he gave up his seat when he refused to take the oaths to William and Mary. He married Elizabeth, the daughter of Viscount Newhaven, and died in April, 1718.

Montagu, Charles (1661-1715), esquire, of Horton, Northamptonshire, clerk of the privy council, 1689-92; a lord of the treasury, 1692-94; privy councilor, 1694-1702; chancellor of the Exchequer, 1694-99; first lord of the treasury, 1697-99, 1714-15; auditor of the Exchequer, 1699-1714; a lord justice of England, 1698; and a Member of Parliament (Whig) for Maldon Borough, Essex County, 1689-95, and for Westminster City, Middlesex County, 1695-1700.

He was the fourth son of George Montagu, a Puritan Member of the Rump and Cavalier Parliaments, and a grandson of Henry, first Earl of Manchester. After education in a private school in Northampton, he studied at Westminster School and Trinity College, Cambridge, where he developed friendships with Isaac Newton and Matthew Prior. From Cambridge he received M.A. and LL.D. degrees and was made a Fellow in 1683. Although he was trained for the clergy, he developed an interest in politics which he made his career. His poetic skill opened an avenue of unusual attainment in politics. At the death of Charles II, he composed laudatory verses for his deceased king which attracted the attention of Lord Dorset. The latter invited him to London and introduced him to the fashionable circle of the metropolis. In 1687, he and Prior wrote "The Town and Country Mouse," a burlesque on Dryden's "The Hind and the Panther." Dorset's reference to the poem when Montagu was introduced to William amused and impressed the phlegmatic Dutchman, who immediately gave Montagu a pension of £500. He had, however, earlier attracted the attention of William. Montagu had signed the letter of invitation to the Prince and joined the revolutionary forces in Northampton. Entering the Convention Parliament as a younger Whig, he rose to prominence in William's reign. His most significant achievements were in the fields of finance, banking, and currency. For his accomplishments he was created Baron Halifax (1700) and Earl of Halifax (1714). He married Anne, the widow of Robert, the third Earl of Manchester, and died in May, 1715.

Montagu, Robert (1668-1693), esquire, Member of Parliament for Huntingdon County, 1689-93. The second son of Robert, third Earl of Manchester, he was an elder brother of Charles Montagu, Earl of Halifax. He was educated at St. Paul's School, Trinity College, Cambridge, and the Middle Temple but was not called to the Bar. Although he served in Parliament several years, he performed no notable services. He died in December, 1693.

More, Richard (1637-1698), esquire, of Lindley, Shropshire, officer in the Parliamentary Army; a commissioner for compounding estates, 1646-58; and Member of Parliament for Bishop's Castle, 1681-98. He was the son of Samuel More, a zealous parliamentarian during the Civil War and the grandson of Richard More, a Puritan Member of the Long and Short Parliament. The family had owned extensive estates in Shropshire and was outstanding among the dissenters in a county that was largely royalist. It continued to support the old Whig tradition into the eighteenth century. Richard was educated at Gray's Inn and became a serjeant. He was twice married. His first wife was Anne, the daughter of Isaac Pennington, lord mayor of London, who was a leader of parliamentarian affairs at the outbreak of the Civil War. More died in 1698.

Morgan, James, esquire, Member of Parliament for Weobley Borough, Hereford, 1689.

Morgan, Sir John (1650-1693), baronet, of Kinnersley Castle, Hereford County, army officer; governor of Chester; and Member of Parliament for New Radnor Borough, Wales, 1681, Herefordshire, 1685-87, and 1689-92. He was the eldest son of Sir Thomas Morgan, Member of Parliament, general of horse under General Monck, governor of Jersey for Charles, and a nephew of the notorious Sir Henry Morgan, governor of Jamaica. Sir John was educated at Lincoln College, Oxford, and succeeded his father as second baronet in 1679. He chose a military career and became colonel of a regiment of Royal Welsh Fusiliers.

He married Hester, the daughter of James Price of Radnor County, and died in February, 1693.

Morgan, Thomas (1664-1700), esquire, of Tredegar, Monmouth County, member of the common council of Brecon, 1698; justice of peace and sheriff of Monmouth County, 1689; and Member of Parliament for Brecon Borough, 1689-90, and Monmouth County, 1685-87, and 1690-1700. The eldest son of William Morgan, a Member of Parliament for Monmouth County during the Commonwealth and Restoration, he married Martha, the daughter of Sir Edward Mansel, baronet, and died in 1700 with an estate worth £7,000.

Morice, Sir William (1628-1690), baronet of Werrington, Devonshire, army officer and Member of Parliament for Newport Borough, Cornwall, 1685-87, and 1689-90. He was the son of Sir William Morice, a recruiter from Devonshire who had served as sheriff of Devonshire and governor of Plymouth during the Commonwealth as well as Secretary of State for Charles II. Educated at Exeter College, Oxford, he was created first baronet in 1661 "in consideration of his father's well-known services." Sir William married Gertrude, the daughter of Sir John Bampfylde, and the daughter of Richard Reynell. He died in February, 1690.

Morland, George (1643-1712), esquire, of Durham City, mayor of Durham, 1690, and Member of Parliament (Tory) for Durham City, 1689-90 and 1690-95. The son of John Morland, alderman of Durham, he was educated at Durham School and Magdalen College, Cambridge. He died in March, 1712.

Morley, Francis, esquire, Member of Parliament (Tory) for Winchester City, Southampton County, 1689-90. He was probably the son of the widely known Calvinistic Bishop of Winchester, George Morley. Francis was created M.A. at Christ Church College, Oxford, in 1663.

Morley, William (1662-1693), esquire, of Halnaker, Sussex County, Member of Parliament (Tory) for Arundel Borough, Sussex County, 1689-93. The second son of William Morley, he was educated at St. John's College, Oxford. He died in 1693.

Morley, Sir William (c. 1640-1701), knight, of Halnaker, Sussex County, Member of Parliament (Tory) for Midhurst Borough, Sussex County, 1678-79, 1685-87, 1689-1700. The son of Sir William Morley by his first wife, he was educated at St. John's College, Oxford, and the Inner Temple. He was knighted April, 1661, and died in 1701.

Morton, Sir James (b. 1652), knight, of Kidlington, Oxford County, Member of Parliament for Steyning Borough, Sussex County, 1681, 1685-87, and 1689-90. He was the youngest son of Sir William Morton, justice on the Court of King's Bench, who had fought in the royalist army during the Civil War. Sir James was educated at Trinity College, Oxford, and the Inner Temple although he was not called to the Bar.

Morton, John (1627-1699), baronet, of Milborne, Dorset County, gentleman of the privy chamber, 1660, and Member of Parliament (Whig) for Poole Borough, Dorsetshire, 1661-79, and Weymouth and Melcombe Regis Borough, Dorsetshire, 1679-90. The son of George Morton, a Member of Parliament in Charles I's reign and a staunch loyalist, he succeeded to second baronet in 1661 and married twice, the second time to Elizabeth, the daughter of Reverend Benjamin Culme. He died in January, 1699.

Mountagu, Edward, esquire, Member of Parliament for Northampton County, 1689.

Mountagu, William, of Evesham, esquire, Member of Parliament for Stockbridge Borough, Southampton, 1689.

Moyle, Sir Walter (1627-1701), knight, of Beke in St. Germains, Cornwall County, sheriff of Cornwall County, 1671, and Member of Parliament for Cornwall County, 1654-55, 1655-58; Lostwithiel Borough, Cornwall County, 1659, 1660; and St. Germains Borough, Cornwall County, 1689-90. The son of John Moyle of St. Germains, a friend of Sir John Eliot, he was knighted at Whitehall in 1663. He received his education at Exeter College, Oxford, and the Inner Temple while he was admitted to the Bar in 1661. Sir Walter, a writer of some reputation, married Thomasine, the daughter of Sir William Morice, and died in September, 1701.

Munn, Thomas (1645-1692), esquire, of Iklesham and Hastings, Sussex, Member of Parliament for Hastings, Sussex, a Cinque Port, 1681 and 1689. He was the son of John Munn of Otteridge, Kent, and attended Peterhouse College, Cambridge. He died in February, 1692.

Musgrave, Sir Christopher (1632-1704), knight and baronet, of Eden Hall, Cumberland County, army officer; lieutenant general of ordnance, 1681-87; governor and mayor of Carlisle, 1677; justice of peace and deputy lieutenant of Cumberland; clerk of the robes to Queen Catherine; a teller of the Exchequer and privy councilor under Queen Anne; and Member of Parliament (Tory) for Carlisle City, Cumberland County, 1661-90; Westmorland County, 1690-95; Appleby, Westmorland County, 1695-98, 1700-01, 1702-04; Oxford University, 1698-1700; and Totness Borough, Devonshire, 1701-02. The third son of Sir Phillip Musgrave, baronet, who had fought under the royal banner at Marston Moor, at Worcester, and with the Countess of Derby on the Isle of Man, he was knighted in 1671 and succeeded his brother, Richard, as fourth baronet in 1687. The family owned almost 12,000 acres of land in Cumberland, Westmorland, and Durham counties. Although educated at Queen's College, Oxford, and Gray's Inn, Musgrave was soon commissioned as a captain of foot guards and chose politics as a career. His early political interest began in the Commonwealth when he conspired to effect the restoration in the Booth rising and was committed to the Tower for his efforts. A staunch Tory in the Restoration he was rewarded with offices and a pension of £200. He fought vigorously against the Exclusion Bills and supported the policy of surrendering charters. Under James II, however, he was removed as lieutenant general of ordnance because he refused to agree to the repeal of the Test and Corporation Acts. As the leader of the Jacobites and Tories in the Convention Parliament he fought for retaining James in some status. When the question about the seat of authority after the king had fled was discussed, Musgrave raised doubts about the authority of the Convention to settle the question. He said: "I would be clear whether the interest is to depose the king; if he has forfeited his Inheritance to the Crown, I would know from the Long Robe whether you can depose the King or no." [56] He, moreover, opposed the proposition that James by his action had broken the contract, destroyed the constitution, and forfeited the crown. Adhering to the ideal of the hereditary monarchy as an element in the compact, he believed the king could violate the contract and not destroy the constitution. To avoid disturbing the constitution, he would distinguish between the right to, and the exercise of the right to, the crown.[57] Still, he believed the exercise of the executive powers should be in hands other than James's. He remarked: "I believe we are in great danger, should the king return again." After the status of James had been determined, however, Musgrave supported the motion to secure the laws and liberties of the nation and urged that a vote be taken on it. The house then proceeded to vote favorably and to appoint the Somers Committee.[58] Musgrave continued as leader of the Tories and country gentleman during William's reign. In this capacity he caused some embarrassment to the king. After the accession of Anne, he became a teller of the Exchequer. He was married twice and died in July, 1704.

Musgrave, Philip (1661-1689), esquire, of Eden Hall, Cumberland County, clerk of the privy council and of the deliveries in the ordnance under James II and Member of Parliament for Appleby Borough, Westmorland County, 1679-87 and 1689. He was the eldest son of Sir Christopher Musgrave, baronet and Member of Parliament from Carlisle, and married Mary, the daughter of the first Baron Dartmouth. He was educated at Queen's College, Oxford. He died in June, 1689.

Napier, Gerard (1661-1689), baronet, of Crichel, Dorsetshire, Member of Parliament for Dorcester Borough, Dorsetshire, 1689. The son of Nathaniel Napier, his family was Scottish, probably descended from the Earls of Lennox who settled in Dorsetshire. Gerard was educated at Wareham College, Oxford, and Lincoln's Inn. He died in December, 1689.

Napier, Sir Nathaniel (1636-1709), baronet, of Edmundsham, Dorsetshire, sheriff of Dorsetshire and Member of Parliament for Dorsetshire, 1677, Corfe Castle Borough, Dorsetshire, 1679-81, 1685-87; Poole Borough, Dorsetshire, 1689-98; and Dorchester Borough, Dorsetshire, 1702-05. He was the third son of Sir Gerard Napier, a royalist soldier in the Civil War, who entertained Charles II and Queen Catherine at his estate during the plague of 1665. He attended Oriel College, Oxford, but soon withdrew because of ill health. Almost immediately he married Blanch, the daughter of Sir Hugh Wyndham, a justice of the

Court of Common Pleas, and lived the life of a country gentle-man at Edmundsham. Sir Nathaniel was knighted in 1661 and succeeded his father as second baronet in 1673. He kept a journal of his extensive travels and was well versed in languages, in architecture, and in painting. He died in January, 1709.

Napier, Sir Robert (1642-1700), knight and baronet, of Pucknoll, Dorsetshire, sheriff of Dorsetshire, 1680, and Member of Parliament (Tory) for Weymouth and Melcombe Regis Borough, Dorsetshire, 1689-90, Dorchester Borough, 1690, 1698-1700. He was the son and heir of Robert Napier a Royalist during the Civil War, who was the brother of Sir Gerard Napier. He was educated at Trinity College, Oxford, and the Middle Temple, from which Inn he was called to the Bar in 1660. Sir Robert was knighted in 1681 and created a baronet the following year. He married Sophia Evelyn, of Surrey, a spinster, and died in October, 1700.

Neale, Thomas, esquire, army officer and Member of Parliament for Lugersdall Borough, Wiltshire, 1678-80, and for Stockbridge Borough, Southampton County, 1689. He was elected at Stockbridge in December, 1689, to replace William Montagu, who was expelled from the House.

Nevile, Sir Christopher (c. 1635-1692), knight, of Amber, Lincoln County, Member of Parliament for Lincoln County, 1689-90. He was the eldest son of Sir Gervase Nevile, knight, who was probably related to Henry Nevile, the republican. Sir Christopher was educated at Sidney College, Cambridge, and Gray's Inn. He was knighted in 1674. He married Katharine, the daughter of Thomas Estoft, and died in November, 1692.

Newdigate, Sir Richard (1644-1710), baronet, of Arbury and Harefield, Warwickshire, Member of Parliament for Warwick County, 1681, 1685-87, 1689-90. He was the son of Sir Richard Newdigate, baronet, serjeant-at-law, and one of the three lord chief justices appointed by Cromwell in 1654. He succeeded his father as second baronet in 1678. He was educated at Christ Church College, Oxford, and Gray's Inn. Sir Richard was married twice and died in 1710.

Newland, Sir Benjamin (1633-1699), knight, of London, London alderman and Member of Parliament (Tory) for South-ampton Borough, Southampton County, 1678-81, 1685-87, and 1689-99. He was the son of William Newland, a mercer, from Newport, Isle of Wight, and pursued a business career as a grocer. He was educated at Pembroke College, Cambridge, and was knighted in 1679. He married the daughter of Robert Rich-bell, a London alderman, in 1661. He died in 1699.

Newport, Andrew (1623-1699), esquire, of High Ercall, Shropshire, army officer; a commissioner of customs in the Res-toration; and Member of Parliament (Tory) for Montgomery County, 1661-78; Preston Borough, Lancashire, 1685-87; and Shrewsbury Borough, Shropshire, 1689-98. He was the second son of Richard Newport, first Baron of Newport, a Member of Parliament and a loyal follower of the king during the Civil War. Andrew attended Christ Church College, Oxford. Under the Protectorate he joined the younger, more devoted royalists led by John Mordaunt and took an active part in the abortive rising of July, 1659. After the Restoration he became a com-missioner of customs and an army captain. He died unmarried in September, 1699.

Newport, Richard (1641-1723), of Shropshire, custos rotu-lorum, 1708-12; lord lieutenant of Shropshire, 1704-12, 1714; and Member of Parliament for Shropshire County, 1661-81, 1689-98. He was the son of Francis, Earl of Bradford, a Shropshire landowner, who was imprisoned twice during the Common-wealth for his support of the royalist cause and who was rewarded by William III for his adherence to the seven bishops. Richard was awarded an M.A. degree from Christ Church College, Oxford, and succeeded his father as Earl of Bradford in 1708. He married Mary, the daughter of Sir Thomas Wil-braham, and died in 1723.

Newton, Sir Isaac (1642-1727), professor, of Cambridge, Cambridge County, warden of the mint, 1696; master of the mint, 1699; and Member of Parliament (Whig) for Cambridge University, 1689-90 and 1701-02. He was the son of Isaac New-ton of Woolsthrope, Lincoln County, a small freehold farmer, who died before his son was born. He was educated at a grammar school and at Trinity College, Cambridge, where he received an A.B. degree in 1665 and an M.A. in 1668. After serving a short time as Fellow, he was appointed to the Lucasian chair of natural philosophy in 1669 and was elected Fellow of the Royal Society in 1672. In 1703 he became president of the society and was elected to that office annually for the next quarter century. Well grounded in the new mathematics before he entered Trinity College, his contributions to scientific knowledge were formulated before he completed his academic studies there. In the years 1665-66 he had formulated the binomial theorem, differential and integral calculus, and the idea of universal gravity. His *Principia* was published in 1687 through the financial and editorial assistance of Halley. During the same year Newton was involved in university affairs that led to participation in politics as a defender of freedom. When the king's request that Alban Francis, a Benedictine monk, be awarded an M.A. degree was refused by the University, Newton, along with the vice-chancellor and seven others, argued the case before the Ecclesiastical Commission. The presentation was unsuccessful and the vice-chancellor was removed and the others sent home. Probably because of Newton's opposition to the king's attack on academic freedom, he was chosen as a Whig member of the Convention Parliament from Cambridge University. His work in the Convention's sessions, however, was not auspicious. He delivered no speeches in the debates and he served on only three committees. Two of these, however, were concerned with religious freedom and might well reveal Newton's interest in religious affairs. His letters show that he was active in convincing the university faculty that the elements of the revolutionary settlement should be accepted. In Parliament his political perception was developed by his association with John Locke, John Somers, and Charles Montagu. When the latter became chancellor of the Exchequer, Newton was appointed master of the mint and was largely responsible for the reformation of coinage. He was knighted by Queen Anne in 1705 and died unmarried in 1727.

Nicholas, Edward (1663-1726), esquire, of Gillingham Parish, Dorsetshire, Member of Parliament (Tory) for Shaftesbury, 1689-1726. He was the first son of John Nicholas, of London, and the cousin of the Earl of Northampton. He attended New College, Oxford, in 1679 and received a D.C.L. degree in 1702. He died in April, 1726.

Nicoll, Humphrey, esquire, Member of Parliament for Bossiney Borough, Cornwall County, 1689.

Norris, Sir Edward (1636-1713), knight, of Weston, Oxford County, deputy lieutenant of Oxford County, 1689, and Member of Parliament for Oxfordshire, 1675-79, 1700-08, and Oxford City, 1689-1700. He was the second son of Sir Francis Norris, knight, the natural son of Francis, Earl of Berkshire, and a cousin of the Earl of Abingdon. He was educated at Queen's College, Oxford, and Lincoln's Inn. He was knighted in 1662. Norris married Jane, the daughter of Sir John Clerke, baronet, and died in October, 1713.

Norris, Thomas (1653-1700), esquire, of Speke Hall, Lancashire, sheriff of Lancashire, 1696, and Member of Parliament (Whig) for Liverpool Borough, Lancashire, 1689-95. He was the eldest son of Thomas Norris, who had supported the royalist cause in the Civil War. Norris married Magdalene, the daughter of Sir Willoughby Aston, and died in June, 1700.

Northleigh, Henry (1643-1694), esquire, of Woolborough, Devonshire, Member of Parliament (Tory) for Okehampton Borough, Devonshire, 1677-79, 1689-94. He was the second son of Henry Northleigh and attended King's College, Cambridge. He died in January, 1694.

Norton, Richard (1615-1691), esquire, of Southwick, Hampshire, army officer; governor of Portsmouth; and Member of Parliament for Southampton County, 1645 (until excluded), 1653, 1654-55, 1656-58, 1659, 1660, 1678-79, 1690, and Portsmouth Borough, Southampton County, 1661-78, 1679-81, 1689-90. A noted republican during the Civil War, he was the son of Daniel Norton and the grandson of Sir Daniel Norton of Southwick, Hampshire. He was educated at Brasenose College, Oxford, and Gray's Inn. Known as Colonel "Dick" Norton, he was a "very fierce commander in the First Rebellion." [59] Although a republican during the Civil War, he was said to have entertained four kings at his home in Southwark. He married Elizabeth Fiennes and died in November, 1691.

Okeden, William (1662-1694), esquire, of Crichill, Dorsetshire, Member of Parliament (Tory) for Corfe Castle Borough, Dorsetshire, 1689-90, and Wareham Borough, Dorsetshire, 1690-94. The son of William Okeden, he attended Trinity College, Oxford. He married Mary, the daughter of John Wyndham of Orchard Wyndham, and died in 1694.

Onslow, Denzell (d. 1721), esquire, of Purford, Surrey County, commissioner for victualling the navy, 1706-21, and Member of Parliament (Whig) for Haslemere Borough, Surrey County, 1679-81, and 1689-90, and the County of Surrey, 1695-98. During the reigns of Anne and George I he represented Guildford Borough in Surrey. He was the third son of Sir Richard Onslow, Member of Parliament during the reigns of Charles I and Charles II as well as during the Commonwealth, and a close friend of Shaftesbury. Onslow married Sarah, the widow of Sir John Lewis and the daughter of Sir Thomas Foote, and died in 1721.

Onslow, Foot (1655-1710), of London, commissioner of excise, 1694-99; first commissioner of excise, 1699-1710; and Member of Parliament (Whig) for Guildford Borough, Surrey County, 1689-1700. He was the second son of Sir Arthur Onslow, the brother of Denzell, and the brother of Arthur and Richard. After attending St. Edmund Hall, Oxford, he entered business and became a London merchant. He married Susanna, the widow of Arnold Calwell and the daughter and heiress of Thomas Anlaby, East Riding, York, and died in May, 1710.

Onslow, Sir Richard (1654-1717), baronet, of West Clandon, Surrey County, army officer, lord lieutenant and custos rotulorum of Surrey County, 1716; a lord of the admiralty, 1690-93; speaker of the House of Commons, 1708-10; a privy councilor, 1710, 1714; chancellor of the Exchequer and lord treasurer, 1714-15; a teller of the Exchequer for life after 1715; and Member of Parliament (Whig) for Guildford Borough, Surrey County, 1679-81, 1685-87, Surrey County, 1689-1710, 1713-16 and St. Mawes Borough, Cornwall County, 1710-13. He was the eldest son of Sir Arthur Onslow, first baronet of West Clandon, Surrey, and Mary, the daughter of Sir Thomas Foote, lord mayor of London in 1649. He was educated at St. Edmund Hall, Oxford, and the Inner Temple, but he received no degree from Oxford and was not called to the Bar. He succeeded to the baronetcy in 1688 and was raised to the peerage as Baron Onslow in 1716. At one time he was governor of the Levant Company. He also owned extensive estates in Surrey and Sussex counties. In his politics he defended the rights and liberties of the subjects and supported the Protestant religion. Onslow married in 1676 Elizabeth, the daughter of Sir Henry Tulse, lord mayor of London, and died in December, 1717.

Osborne, Peregrine (1658-1729), Viscount of Kiveton, Yorkshire, naval officer and Member of Parliament (Tory) for Berwick-on-Tweed Borough, Northumberland County, 1677-79, for Corfe Castle Borough, Dorsetshire, 1679, and for York City, Yorkshire, 1689-90. He was the third although only surviving son of Thomas Osborne, the Duke of Leeds. In 1674 he had been created Viscount Osborne (Dumblain) in a Scottish peerage and was summoned to the House of Lords in 1690 as Baron Osborne of Kiveton. Known as the Earl of Danby, 1689-94, and the Marquis of Carmarthen, 1694-1712, he became the second Duke of Leeds upon his father's death in 1712. Osborne saw considerable naval action during the reign of William III. As the captain of the *Windsor Castle*, he saw action at Barfleur in 1692 and commanded the covering squadron at the attempted landing at Camaret Bay in 1694. He became rear admiral of the Red in 1697 and vice-admiral of the Blue in 1702. With his father and brother he was in arms in support of William of Orange in 1688, although he later expressed regret for having deposed James II. He married Briget Hyde in 1682 and died in June, 1729.

Owen, Arthur (d. 1753), esquire, of Orielton, Pembrokeshire, Wales, lord lieutenant, 1707; sheriff of Pembrokeshire, 1707; and Member of Parliament for Pembroke Borough, Pembroke County, 1679-1727. He was the surviving son of Sir Hugh Owen, second baronet, who served as sheriff and Member of Parliament for Pembroke County. According to legend he, by a rapid ride from Wales, arrived at Westminster to cast his vote for the Act of Settlement in 1701 which was approved by a majority of one vote. He succeeded his father as third baronet in 1699. He married Emma, the daughter of Sir William Williams, speaker of the House of Commons, and died in June, 1753.

Owen, Sir Hugh (1645-1699), baronet, of Orielton, Pembroke County, Wales, sheriff of Anglesby County, 1688, and Member of Parliament for Pembroke Borough, Pembrokeshire, 1676-79, Pembrokeshire, 1679-81, and 1689-95. The son of Sir Hugh Owen, first baronet, sheriff and Member of Parliament who supported the parliamentary cause, he was educated at Christ Church College, Oxford, and the Inner Temple. He succeeded to the baronetcy in 1670. Owen married Anne, the daughter of his uncle, Henry Owen, thereby uniting the Pembroke and Anglesby estates of the family. He also married Catherine Arnwell. He died in January, 1699.

Owen, Sir Robert (1658-1698), knight, of Clenennon, Carnarvonshire, Wales, sheriff of Merioneth, 1688, and Member of Parliament (Tory) for Merioneth County, 1681, and for Carnarvon Borough, Carnarvon County, Wales, 1689-97. He was the son of William Owen of Porkington, Shropshire, and the grandson of Sir John Owen, the Welsh royalist commander during the Civil War. He was educated at Oriel College, Oxford, and the Inner Temple and was knighted in 1678. Owen was a dedicated Tory, upholding the status of the Crown and the Anglican religion in political disputes. His loyalty to the Duke of York created considerable opposition to his candidacy for a seat in Parliament in 1681. Yet, after the accession of James, he remained loyal and offered to raise forces to oppose William as late as November, 1688. His marriage with Margaret Wynn of Glyn added considerable land to the family holdings. He died in March, 1698.

Oxenden, Sir James (1643-1708), baronet, of Deane, Kent County, Member of Parliament (Whig) for Sandwich, a Cinque Port, Kent, 1679-81, 1689-90, 1701-02, and for Kent County, 1698-1700. He was the son and heir of Sir Henry Oxenden, first baronet, and the brother-in-law of the first Earl of Rockingham. His family owned over 5,000 acres of land in Kent County. He was knighted in 1672 and succeeded his father as second baronet in 1686. He was educated at Trinity College, Cambridge, and Gray's Inn. At the Convention Parliament Oxenden made one speech in the debates. During the state of the nation discussion he expressed the opinion that the king had made a "voluntary departure" in order to enlist the help of foreign powers to retain his position.[60] He married Elizabeth Chute and Arbella, the sister of the first Earl of Rockingham. He died in September, 1708.

Palmer, Nathaniel (c. 1656-1717), esquire, of Fairfield in Stogursey, deputy lieutenant of Somersetshire, 1689, and Member of Parliament (Tory) for Minehead Borough, Somersetshire, 1685-87, 1689-90, for Bridgewater Borough, Somersetshire, 1695-98, 1710-13, 1713-14, and for Somerset County, 1699-1708. He was the son of Colonel Peregrine Palmer, a veteran officer of European armies and a royalist colonel in the battles of Edgehill, Marston Moor, and Naseby, who owned estates in Somerset County. Nathaniel was one of the deputy lieutenants removed by James II for refusing to agree to the repeal of the penal laws. He signed the declaration in favor of the Prince of Orange and was reappointed deputy lieutenant in 1691. He married Frances, the daughter of Sir William Wyndham, and died in 1717.

Palmes, William (b. 1640), esquire, of Lundley, Yorkshire, Member of Parliament (Whig) for Malton Borough, Yorkshire, 1668-81, 1689-1713. He was the younger son of Sir Brian Palmes, knight, and the grandson of Sir Guy Palmes, knight, sheriff (1622), and justice of peace of Yorkshire. He attended Wadham College, Oxford.

Papillon, Thomas (1623-1702), esquire, of Papillon Hall, Lubenham and of Acrise Place, Kent, member of the council of trade and foreign plantations, 1660; sheriff of London, 1682; first commissioner for victualling the navy, 1689-99; and Member of Parliament (Whig) for Dover, a Cinque Port, Kent County, 1673-81, and for London, 1685-89. He was the third son of David Papillon of Putney. After attending school at Drayton, Northamptonshire, he was articled to a London merchant and in 1638 he began as apprenticeship in the Mercers' Company, which he completed in 1646. Following his participation in civil disorders in London, he fled to France but returned to England and established himself as a general merchant. For many years he was a director of the East India Company. Although his political activity was limited before 1660, he became an active participant in government during and after the Restoration. He was appointed to the newly created Council of Trade and Foreign Plantations and served as Member of Parliament for Dover, 1672-81. As a member of the Council of Trade, he sponsored free trade within the United Kingdom and opposed measures that restricted commerce. As a Member of Parliament, he fought for increased parliamentary power, individual rights, and the interests of the dissenting sects. In a dispute over his candidacy for sheriff of London in 1682, Papillon was fined £10,000 and fled to Holland to avoid payment. Upon his return at the Revolution, he was elected Member of Parliament and served this constituency until 1700. He was a vigorous proponent of the Revolution and of freer trade. His pamphlet, "A Treatise Concerning the East India Trade," first printed in 1680, was reprinted in 1696. He married Jane, the daughter of Thomas Broadnax of Kent, and died in May, 1702.

Parker, Anthony (1658-1693), esquire, of Kirkham, Lancashire, justice of the Court of King's Bench under James II and Member of Parliament for Clitheroe Borough, Lancashire, 1689-93. He was the son of Christopher Parker and the son-in-law of Thomas Stringer, a barrister of Gray's Inn, who had represented Clitheroe, 1675-81. He was educated at Trinity College, Oxford, and at Gray's Inn being called to the Bar in 1681. He married the daughter of Sir Thomas Stringer and died in November, 1693.

Parker, Henry (1640-1713), esquire, of Honington, Warwickshire, justice of peace, 1682; recorder of Evesham, Worcestershire, 1684-88; and Member of Parliament (Tory) for Evesham Borough, Worcestershire, 1679-1700, and for Aylesbury Borough, Buckinghamshire, 1704-05. He was the only son of Henry Parker of London and the nephew of Sir Hugh Parker, baronet. He attended the Middle Temple and acted as recorder of Evesham until removed by James II in 1688. He succeeded his uncle, Hugh, as second baronet in 1697. Parker married Margaret, the daughter of Alexander Hyde, Bishop of Salisbury, and died in 1713.

Parkhurst, John (1644-1731), esquire, of Catesby, Northamptonshire, Member of Parliament for Durham City, 1661-78, Northamptonshire, 1678-81, 1690-95, 1698-1701, and for Brackley Borough, Northamptonshire, 1689-90. The third son of

Robert Parkhurst of Burford, Surrey, he attended Lincoln College, Oxford. He died in May, 1731.

Parsons, Sir John (d. 1717), knight, of London, London alderman; a commissioner for victualling the navy, 1683-88; a regimental colonel, 1710-14; and a Member of Parliament for Reigate Borough, Surrey County, 1685-87, 1689-98, and 1701-17. A London businessman, he was a master of the Brewer's Company, 1689-90, as well as a warden of the Fishmongers' Company, 1706-08. He was knighted in August, 1687, and died in January, 1717.

Patten, Thomas (1662-1726), esquire, of Preston and Thornley, Lancaster County, Member of Parliament for Preston Borough, Lancaster County, 1689-90. He was the eldest surviving son of William Patten, alderman and mayor of Preston, 1655-56. He was a barrister-at-law. Patten married Margaret Blackburne of Oxford and died in 1726.

Pelham, Sir John (1624-1703), of Holland, Sussex County, Member of Parliament (Whig) for Hastings Borough, Sussex County, 1645, until excluded at Pride's Purge, Sussex County, 1654-55, 1656-58, 1660-98. He was the eldest son of Sir Thomas Pelham, second baronet, and succeeded his father as third baronet in August, 1654. Although he served in two of the Commonwealth Parliaments, he supported the restoration of Charles II. He was noted for his moderation and deep public spirit. Pelham married Lady Lucy, the second daughter of the Earl of Leicester, and died in 1703.

Pelham, Sir Nicholas (1651-1739), knight, of Catfield, Sussex County, Member of Parliament for Seaford, a Cinque Port, Sussex County, 1671-81, and Lewes Borough, Sussex County, 1702-05, and 1726-27. He was the eldest son of Sir Thomas Pelham by his third wife, Margaret, the daughter of Sir Henry Fane, who had served as Member of Parliament during the early Stuart reigns and during the Civil War, and the brother of Sir John. He was knighted as a boy by Charles II in 1661. He was educated at Christ Church College, Oxford, receiving an M.A. degree in 1665. Pelham married Jane, the daughter of James Huxley, and died in 1739.

Pelham, Thomas (1653-1712), esquire, of Holland, Sussex County, commissioner of customs, 1689-91; lord commissioner of the treasury, 1689-91, 1698-99, 1701-02; vice-admiral of Sussex, 1705; and Member of Parliament (Whig) for East Grimstead Borough, Sussex County, 1678-79, for Lewes Borough, Sussex County, 1679-1702, and for Sussex County, 1702-05. The eldest son of Sir John Pelham, he succeeded his father as fourth baronet in 1703 and was created Baron Pelham of Laughton in 1706. As a loyal member of the Whig party, he promoted the Revolution of 1688. In the Convention Parliament he argued for the vacancy of the throne for the succession of William and Mary and for their election as joint sovereigns. Pelham married Elizabeth, the daughter of Sir William Jones, the attorney-general to Charles II, and Lady Grace, the daughter of Gilbert Holles, Earl of Clare, and the sister of John, Duke of Newcastle. He died in February, 1712.

Pendarves, Alexander (1665-1725), esquire, of Roscrowe, Cornwall County, Member of Parliament (Tory) for Penryn Borough, Cornwall County, 1689-98, 1699-1700, 1700-05, 1710-14, Helston Borough, Cornwall County, 1714, Launceston, 1721-25. Pendarves was the son of John Pendarves of Penryn, Cornwall County; he attended Exeter College, Oxford, and Gray's Inn. Pendarves married Mary Granville, the charitable and accomplished Mrs. Delany, the friend of Jonathan Swift and John Wesley. He died in March, 1725.

Penruddocke, Thomas (b. 1647), esquire, of Compton Chamberlaine, Wiltshire, Member of Parliament for Wilton Borough, Wiltshire, 1678-79, and 1689-90. He was the son of Colonel John Penruddocke, who was beheaded at Exeter in 1655 for participation in a royalist uprising against Cromwell. He was educated at Winchester School and Magdalen College, Oxford. In 1687 he partially accepted the king's proposals on the Test and penal laws. Penruddocke married Frances, the daughter of John Hanham of Dean's Court, Dorsetshire.

Philipps, Hector, (c. 1635-1693), esquire, of Treyghi, Cardigan, Wales, commissioner for securing the peace of Cardigan, Carnarvon, and Pembroke counties; justice of peace, 1680; sheriff of Cardigan County; mayor of Cardigan, 1657, 1666, and 1678; and Member of Parliament (Whig) for Cardigan Borough, Cardigan County, 1679-81, 1685-87, and 1689-93. He was the younger son of George Philipps, sheriff of Cardigan County in 1606, and the brother of Colonel James Philipps, a Parliamentary Army officer who created an unsavory reputation through his vigorous sequestration of royalist estates during the Commonwealth. Hector, who had attended the Middle Temple, held political views similar to those of his brother and helped with the sequestering of the estates and with the preservation of peace. He inherited his brother's estates. He married Mary, the daughter of Colonel Philip Skippon, distinguished soldier of European wars and the Civil War and governor of London, and Mary Owen. He died in March, 1693.

Pierrepont, Evelyn (1665-1726), esquire, of Thoresby, Nottinghamshire, commissioner for the union of Scotland, 1706; privy councilor, 1708; lord lieutenant of Wiltshire, 1711-26; chief justice in Eyre North-of-the-Trent, 1714-16; and Member of Parliament (Whig) for East Retford Borough, Nottingham County, 1689-90. He was the third son of Robert Pierrepont, first Earl of Kingston, and the brother and heir of William Pierrepont, fifth Earl of Kingston-upon-Hull, who had been a member of the Long Parliament and one of the leaders of the Independent party during the Commowealth. After attending Winchester School, Evelyn studied at Christ's College, Cambridge, and was granted an LL.D. in 1705. In 1690 he succeeded his brother as fifth Earl of Kingston and was created Marquess of Dorchester in 1706. He became the Duke of Kingston in 1715. One of the leaders of the fashionable world in his age, he was a staunch Whig and a member of the Kit Cat Club. Pierrepont married in 1687 Mary, the daughter of the Earl of Denbigh, and later Isabella, the daughter of the Earl of Portland. He died in March, 1726.

Pierrepont, Francis, esquire, Member of Parliament for Nottingham Borough, Nottinghamshire, 1689.

Pilkington, Thomas (c. 1620-1691), esquire, of London, alderman, 1680; sheriff, 1681; lord mayor of London, 1689; and Member of Parliament (Whig) for London City, Middlesex County, 1679-81 and 1689. The son of Thomas Pilkington, he came to London as a boy and apprenticed himself as a skinner. Not long after he established himself as a skinner, he became a successful businessman and served as master of the Skinners' Company on three occasions. Although he attracted public notice late in life, he was popular with London citizens for his opposition to court policies. Engaging in controversy in his first Parliament, he, by supporting the Whig cause, had a stormy political career. He attacked the Duke of York in parliamentary debate and as sheriff of London entertained at his home on Thomas Street, Monmouth, Shaftesbury, Essex, and other leading Whigs. Because he manipulated the grand jury in the case of Shaftesbury's suspected treason, Pilkington was scolded by the judges and fined £800 for libel in March, 1682. When he and Shute defeated court candidates for sheriff in the election of sheriff, the lord mayor charged them with riotous behavior and they were fined £4,100 of which Pilkington's share was £500. The alleged rioting of the candidates for sheriff was the basis for suspending the city charter by the writ of *quo warranto* in 1683. After his term as sheriff expired, he was charged by the Duke of York of *scandalum magnatum* on the ground that Pilkington had failed to welcome the Duke upon his return from Scotland and had made the comment that James had burned London and was now coming to cut its citizens' throats. The jury fined Pilkington £100,000 and he spent the next four years in prison. His fortune changed with the Revolution. After his release from prison, he was elected alderman and lord mayor of London and a Member of the Convention Parliament. He was knighted by William III in April, 1689. He married Hannah Bromwich of London and died in December, 1691.

Pincent, Sir William (1640-1719), baronet, of Erthfont, Wiltshire, sheriff of Wiltshire, 1694, and Member of Parliament (Whig) for Devizes Borough, Wiltshire, 1685-90. He was the son of William Pincent and attended Oriel College, Oxford. In 1687 he was created first baronet. He died in 1719.

Pitt, Thomas (1653-1726), esquire, of Stratford, Dorsetshire, East India Merchant; governor of Fort St. George, 1697-1709; commissioner to build new churches, 1716; governor of Jamaica, 1716; and Member of Parliament for Old Sarum, 1689-90, 1690-95, 1695-98, 1710-26. He was the second son of John Pitt, the rector of Blanford St. Mary, Dorsetshire. Getting his training at sea as a boy, he entered the East India trade as an interloper before he was of age. After establishing himself at Balasore in

1674, he became involved in a prolonged legal struggle with the company that did not end until 1694. After Pitt had served for a time as agent of the company, he became governor of Fort St. George, a post which he held from 1697-1709. During this period he acquired the large diamond which he sold to the Regent of France for £135,000 at a gigantic profit. After his return to England he purchased considerable tracts of land in Berkshire, Cornwall, Dorset, Hampshire and Wiltshire counties. He married Jane Innes in 1678, and died in 1726.

Pole, John (1649-1708), esquire, of Shute, Devonshire, Member of Parliament (Tory) for Lyme Regis, Dorsetshire, 1685-87, 1689-90, Bossiney, Cornwall County, 1698-1700, Devonshire, 1701-02, East Looe, Cornwall County, 1702-05 and Newport, Cornwall County, 1705-08. He was the son of Sir Courtney Pole, second baronet, who had been Member of Parliament and sheriff, and succeeded to the baronetcy in 1695. Pole married Anne, the daughter of Sir William Morice, one of the secretaries of state during the reign of Charles II, and died in 1708.

Poley, Sir John (1637-1705), knight, of Boxton Hall, Suffolk, Member of Parliament (Tory) from Sudbury Borough, Suffolk County, 1689. He was the son of Sir William Poley who had been a Member of Parliament for Sudbury in 1623 and 1628 and died in 1705.

Pollen, John (b. 1642), esquire, of Andover, Southamptonshire, Member of Parliament (Whig) for Andover Borough, Southamptonshire, 1689-90. The son of John Pollen of Lincolnshire, who became a London merchant, he followed his father's career in business after he studied at Gray's Inn. Pollen married Anne, the widow of Nicholas Venables, and the daughter of William Bernard.

Pollexfen, Sir Henry (1632-1691), knight, of Sherford, Devonshire, attorney general, 1689; chief justice of the Court of Common Pleas, 1689-91; and Member of Parliament (Whig) for Exeter City, Devonshire, 1689. The eldest son of Andrew Pollexfen he attended the Inner Temple and was called to the Bar in 1658. Before long he had developed an extensive practice as the attorney for the defense in state trials. As a prominent Whig he developed popular support through his aid to those caught in the web of absolutism under Charles II and James II.

Although his reputation was diminished by his role as crown prosecutor of those who participated in Monmouth's Rebellion, his status was enhanced when he along with John Somers defended the seven bishops. A strong supporter of William of Orange, Pollexfen played an active role in the Convention. Not only was he adviser to the peers on the legality of the crisis, but he also served as Member of Parliament from Exeter. In his comments in the debates of the Convention he clarified the legal status of James II and the nature of the settlement. In the debates much concern was expressed about whether the Crown was demised or vacant. Pollexfen expressed himself on this question as follows: "It is an unnecessary question to carry at first sight; and if the crown be vacant, trouble yourselves no further in the matter. If the crown be demised, you must think of the succession of it." [61] In the conference in the Painted Chamber, the question of the right to and the exercise of the kingship arose. Pollexfen urged the Lords to consider these features of the kingship as one and the same thing. In this manner James could be set aside. ". . . We do insist . . . that if the right of kingship be still . . . due to him, we cannot in justice agree to keep him from it. And if it be not his due right, but by these acts, his subversion of the constitution, his breaking the Original Contract, and violation of the fundamental laws, he hath abdicated it . . . and this abdication hath put him by his right, and so his right is gone from him . . . , then, I think we may lawfully go on to settle the peace and welfare of the nation." When this aspect was under discussion, Pollexfen proposed drafting conditions which would guarantee the ascendancy of Parliament in drafting the limitations. Before offering the crown to the successor to James, he urged that the legislative role and authority of Parliament should first be fixed.[62] He stated: "First make a Settlement of the Laws, that they may be asserted, and those must all be consulted by lords and commons and then settle the crown." [63] Soon after the settlement was completed Pollexfen was knighted, appointed as attorney-general, and, then, elevated to a judgeship. He died in June, 1691.

Pollexfen, John (1638-1697), merchant, of London, member of the Council of Trade and Foreign Plantations, 1675, and the board of trade, 1696-97; and Member of Parliament for Plympton Borough, Devonshire, 1679-81, and 1689. He was the younger son of Andrew Pollexfen of Andover, Southampton and the brother of Henry Pollexfen, judge on the Court of Common Pleas. John moved to London and became a merchant and a writer on economic policy. He was influential on public policy through his membership on commercial commissions and on public opinion through his tracts on economic subjects. Characteristic of the free-traders of the seventeenth century, he agitated for an elimination of monopoly and privilege and permitting "trade to take its own course." [64] He did, nevertheless, favor some state regulation of industry and commerce. His ideas were counterpoised against those of Charles Davenant. Pollexfen married Mary, the daughter of Sir John Lawrence, and died in 1697.

Pooley, Henry (1653-1707), esquire, of Bradley, Suffolk, Member of Country Parliament (Tory) for Eye Borough, Suffolk, 1685-95, West Looe Borough, Cornwall County, 1703-05, and for Ipswich Borough, Suffolk, 1705-07. The son and heir of Sir Edmund Pooley, knight, he was educated at Bury School, Jesus College, Cambridge, Gray's Inn, and the Middle Temple. He was granted a B.A. degree by Cambridge in 1673. and was a Fellow from 1673-75. He was called to the Bar from the Middle Temple in 1678, and he became a bencher in 1701. Pooley died unmarried in 1707.

Portman, Sir William (1641-1690), baronet, of Orchard Portman, Somerset, justice of peace for Somerset, 1661; deputy lieutenant for Somersetshire and Dorsetshire in the Restoration; colonel of militia; and Member of Parliament (Tory) for Taunton Borough, Somersetshire, 1661-79, Somerset County, 1679-81, and Taunton Borough, Somersetshire, 1685-87, 1689-90. He was the only son of Sir William Portman, fifth baronet, who sat for Taunton in both the Short and Long Parliaments but was excluded as a royalist in 1644. His family had held estates in Somersetshire since medieval times and his grandfather had been one of James I's first baronets. At his death the estate of Orchard Portman was worth £8,000. Upon his father's death in 1645 he became sixth baronet and was made a Knight of the Bath at the coronation of Charles II. After attending All

Souls College, Oxford, he was elected Fellow of the Royal Society in 1664. Along with Sir Edmund Seymour, Portman was characterized as "one of the most influential Tories in the West," and was a strong supporter of the monarchy and the church. He was a staunch abhorrer during the critical years of Charles II's reign; as late as 1681, he stated that he would not support any party that would not drink to the Duke of York's health. Having received a warning of the Duke of Monmouth's insurrection while attending Parliament in May, 1685, he with Lord Lumley devised security measures which led to Monmouth's capture by them near Ringwood in the New Forest. When Sir William refused to approve the removal of the penal acts, he was removed from his post as deputy lieutenant. This rebuff and his loyalty to the church and state prompted him to abandon James and to join William at Exeter with a large following. The Prince planned to reward Portman with an appointment to high office but he died in March, 1690. Although married three times, he left no issue, and his estates were inherited by a nephew, Henry Seymour.

Powle, Henry (1630-1692), esquire, of Quenington, Gloucestershire, privy councilor 1679, 1689; speaker of the House of Commons, 1689-90; master of the rolls, 1689-92; and Member of Parliament (Whig) for Cirencester Borough, Gloucester, 1660, 1671-81, New Windsor Borough, Berkshire, 1689-90. He was the second son of Henry Powle of Shottesbrook, Berkshire, sheriff of the county, and the brother of Sir Richard Powle, Member of Parliament for Berkshire, 1660-61. He was educated at Christ Church College, Oxford, and at Lincoln's Inn. He was called to the Bar in 1654 and became a bencher in 1659. During the reign of Charles II, his opposition to the exercise of royal prerogative and his support of parliamentary power and rights identified him with the Country party. After the fall of Danby, however, Powle accepted an appointment to the new privy council although he withdrew on Shaftesbury's advice in 1680. While he was not as vigorous in his promotion of the Exclusion Bill as other leading Whigs, he was active in the action taken against Lord Stafford. In the interval between the Oxford Parliament and the Revolution he devoted his energy to his law practice and travel abroad. He became in the period a Fellow of the Royal Society. In 1688 Powle intensified his political activity. On December 16, he and Sir Robert Howard conferred privately with the Prince of Orange. When the Members of Parliament of Charles II's reign were summoned to meet with William and the common councilmen at St. James Palace, Powle headed the delegation of former Members of Parliament and was chosen chairman of the body when it returned to Westminster to consider how to implement the Prince's Declaration. In the session he said that the desire of William was sufficient authority to summon a Parliament. On the following day he read the message that requested the Prince to act as caretaker of the government and to call the Convention Parliament. When the Convention met, Powle was chosen speaker rather than Sir Edward Seymour and in this capacity he exercised great influence on the decisions of the members. He congratulated William and Mary upon their coronation and presented the Bill of Rights to the king on December, 1689. He was rewarded for his work by an appointment to the privy council and to the Bench as master of the rolls. He married Elizabeth, the daughter of Lord Newport, and Francis, the daughter of the first Earl of Middlesex. He died in November, 1692.

Powlett, Charles (1661-1722), earl, of Amport, Hampshire, vice-admiral of Hampshire; lord lieutenant and custos rotulorum of Hampshire and Dorsetshire, 1699; army officer; privy councillor, 1690; a lord justice of Ireland, 1697-1700; governor of the Isle of Wight, 1707-10; a lord justice of the realm, 1714; and Member of Parliament (Whig) for Southampton County, 1681, 1685-87, 1689-98. The son and heir of the first Duke of Bolton, he was styled the Earl of Wiltshire, 1675-89, and the Marquis of Winchester, 1689-99. He succeeded his father as the second Duke of Bolton in 1699. After receiving his education at Winchester and Gray's Inn, he entered politics as a Member of Parliament from Southampton County, in 1681. Before the Revolution, he went to Holland and returned with William's expedition. At Exeter he was appointed commissioner of revenue in November, 1688, and after the Revolution, he held a number of local and national offices under William and Anne. As an infantry colonel, he was one of the few nobles to serve in William's Flanders campaign. Powlett was married three times. His first wife was Margaret, the daughter of Lord Coventry; the third was Henrietta, the daughter of James, Duke of Monmouth. He died in February, 1722.

Powlett, Francis, esquire, of Amport, Southampton, Member of Parliament for Andover Borough, Southampton County, 1679-80 and 1689.

Powlett, William (1666-1729), lord, teller of the Exchequer, 1715, and Member of Parliament for Winchester City, Southampton County, 1689-1729, except that he was elected to represent Lymington Borough, Southampton County in 1710 and 1713. He was the youngest son of Charles, the first Duke of Bolton, and the Earl of Wiltshire's brother. At the burial of the Duke of Gloucester in 1700 he was the supporter of the pall. Powlett married Lady Louisa, the daughter of the Marquis of Monponillon, in Holland and Anne Egerton of Strafford. He died in September, 1729.

Praed, James (1656-1708), esquire, of Trevethoe, Cornwall County, Member of Parliament (Tory) for St. Ives Borough, Cornwall County, 1681, and 1689-1705. He was the son of James Praed, who had been a Member of Parliament in 1661 as a Cavalier. Praed was educated at Exeter College, Oxford, and the Middle Temple. He died before 1708.

Preston, Thomas (1646-1696), esquire, of Holker, Lancashire, army officer and Member of Parliament (Whig) for Lancaster Borough, 1689-97. He was the son of Thomas Preston, deputy lieutenant and sheriff of Lancashire and Member of Parliament for the county, 1664-78, whose estates had been severely damaged by parliamentary forces during the Civil War. He succeeded his father in 1679. Preston was educated at Wharton in Kirkham and St. John's College, Cambridge. He married Mary Dodding and Elizabeth Bradshaigh. He died in January, 1696.

Prideaux, Jonathan, esquire, Member of Parliament (Whig) for Callington Borough, Cornwall County, 1689. He was probably the son of Sir Edmund Prideaux, a London barrister, who became recorder of Exeter and of Bristol, a commissioner of the great seal and postmaster. The family had long been established in southwestern England and owned extensive estates in Devon and Cornwall counties. As a young man Jonathan was tutored by Tillotson. During James II's reign he was involved in the Duke of Monmouth's Rebellion. In order to save his life, he gave Judge Jeffreys a huge bribe to set aside the charges against him.

Puleston, Sir Roger (1663-1697), knight of Emral, Flint County, Wales, commissioner of taxes for Flint County, 1689, and Member of Parliament for Flintshire, 1689-90, and for Flint Borough, Flintshire, 1695-97. The son of Roger Puleston, who had been sheriff of Flint County in 1664, he was knighted in 1680. He married Catherine Chirk and Martha Ryder and died in March, 1697.

Pultney, Sir William (c. 1624-1691), knight, of Misterton, Leicestershire, Member of Parliament (Whig) for Westminster City, Middlesex County, 1678-81, and 1689-90. The son of Sir John Pultney, he attended King's College, Cambridge, and the Inner Temple being called to the Bar in 1654. He was knighted in 1660. At the Convention Parliament he supported the Whig position in regard to the status of James and the role of William. In the state of nation debates he proposed that the terms "abdicated" and "the throne void" should be included in the resolution. These should be incorporated, he believed, because James had broken the contract "without making any provision for the administration of the government." Because of the void in government, the Convention had been called "to supply what he [James] had taken from us." William was appointed caretaker of the nation because the Convention assumed that a "demise" existed.[65] He died in 1691.

Raleigh, Sir Charles (1653-1698), knight, of Downton, Wiltshire, Member of Parliament (Whig) for Downton Borough, Wiltshire, 1685-87, and 1689-98. The son of Gilbert Raleigh, he was educated at Magdalen College, Oxford, and was knighted in 1681. He died in 1698.

Ramsden, John (1657-1718), esquire, of Hull, Yorkshire, justice of peace; alderman and deputy lieutenant for Hull; and Member of Parliament for Hull Borough, Yorkshire, 1685-87, 1689-95. He was the son of William Ramsden, a merchant of Hull. After his training at Chesterfield and Ferriby schools in York, he entered Trinity College, Cambridge, and received a B.A. degree in 1677. He was created a baronet in November, 1689. Late in life he purchased the Norton estate and built a palatial residence. Ramsden married Catherine, the daughter of John, Viscount Downe, and died in 1718.

Rashleigh, Jonathan (1642-1703), esquire, of Menabilly, Cornwall, sheriff of Cornwall County, 1686, and Member of Parliament (Tory) for Fowley Borough, Cornwall County, 1675-81, 1689-95. He was the second son of Jonathan Rashleigh, who had been a Member of the Long Parliament until expelled by Pride's Purge. His family had long been engaged in shipbuilding and trading in the southwest but it had gradually transmuted itself into a landowning family. Rashleigh was educated at Balliol College, Oxford, and the Inner Temple. He married Mary, the daughter of Sir William Clayton, merchant and lord mayor of London, and died in September, 1703.

Rawlinson, Curwen (1642-1689), esquire, of Corke-in-Cartmel, Lancashire, vice-chancellor of Chester and Member of Parliament for Lancaster Borough, Lancashire, 1689. He was the son of Robert Rawlinson, esquire, justice of peace for Lancashire and Cheshire, who had suffered during the Civil War for his loyalty to the Crown. He was educated at Queen's College, Oxford, and Gray's Inn, being called to the Bar from this school. Rawlinson married Elizabeth Monck, the daughter of Nicholas Monck, Bishop of Hereford and a brother of General Monck. He died in August, 1689.

Rebow, Sir Isaac (1658-1727), knight, steward, recorder and mayor of Colchester and Member of Parliament (Whig) for Colchester Borough, Essex County, 1689-90, and 1692-1722. The son of a wealthy merchant, whose wife was the daughter of Francis Tayspill, the wealthiest man in Colchester, he continued to conduct his father's cloth trade, expanding his operations into London. After living at Head Gate for many years, he purchased Colchester Castle from John Wheeley, an ironmonger in 1704. He married Mary, the daughter of James Lemyng, a staunch Anglican and royalist, and died in 1727.

Reynell, Thomas (1630-1698), esquire, of West Ogwell, Devonshire, justice of peace and sheriff of Devonshire, 1677, and Member of Parliament (Whig) for Devonshire, 1654-55, 1656-58, and for Ashburton Borough, Devonshire, 1657, 1678-81, and 1689-90. He was the son of Sir Richard Reynell, who was knighted at his uncle's home by Charles I on one of his visits there. He attended Exeter College, Oxford, and was called to the Bar from the Middle Temple in 1649. Reynell married Mary Bennett and Elizabeth Could and died in March, 1698.

Reynolds, Samuel (b. 1666), esquire, of Colchester, Essex, served as Member of Parliament for Colchester Borough, Essex County, 1681, 1689-94. The son and heir of Samuel Reynolds, he was educated at Colchester School, Jesus College, Cambridge, and Gray's Inn. He married Frances, the daughter of Charles Pelham.

Rich, Sir Peter (d. 1692), knight, of London, London alderman, city chamberlain, 1684-87, 1688-89, 1691; sheriff of Surrey County, 1681-82; regimental colonel, 1690-92; and Member of Parliament (Whig) for Southwark Borough, Surrey County, 1679-81, 1689-90, and for London, 1685-87. A saddler by trade, he was a master of the Saddler's Company, 1678 and 1681. During Charles II's reign, he enjoyed royal favor through his appointment as London alderman after the surrender of the city charter and his receipt of a knighthood in 1685. Although he was removed from his aldermanic post by James II in 1687, he was restored to office in October, 1688. He died in August, 1692.

Rich, Sir Robert (1648-1699), baronet, of Roos Hall, Suffolk, Member of Parliament (Whig) from Dunwich, 1689-99. The second son of Colonel Nathaniel Rich, Member of Parliament, and grandson of Robert Rich of Essex, he was knighted in 1676 and succeeded to the baronetcy in 1677. His father was seventh in descent from Richard Rich, alderman and sheriff of London. By the seventeenth century the family belonged to the landed class. He married Mary, the daughter of Sir Charles Rich of London, whom he succeeded as second baronet and died in October, 1699.

Rich, Sir William (1654-1711), baronet, of Sonning, Berkshire, Member of Parliament (Whig) for Reading Borough, Berkshire, 1689-98, and Gloucester Borough, Gloucestershire, 1698-1700. The son and heir of Sir Thomas Rich, baronet, a vintner and a Levant merchant, Member of Parliament in 1660, he succeeded his father as second baronet in 1667. During the Revolution he gave consistent support to the Whig program.

He married Anne, the daughter of Robert, the first Earl of Ailesbury, and died in 1711.

Robartes, Francis (1650-1718), esquire, of Cornwall, teller of the Exchequer, 1705, and Member of Parliament (Tory) for Bossiney Borough, Cornwall County, 1673-79, Cornwall County, 1679-81, and Lostwithiel Borough, Cornwall County, and other boroughs, 1689-1718. He was the fourth son of Sir John Robartes, first Earl of Radnor, an anti-royalist in the Civil War who fought with Essex at Edgehill and served as lord lieutenant of Devonshire and governor of Plymouth as well as privy councilor and lord lieutenant of Ireland under Charles II. After his education at Christ's College, Cambridge, Francis distinguished himself in literary and musical accomplishments. In 1672 he published a treatise "Discourse concerning the Musical Notes of a Trumpet." For a time he was vice-president of the Royal Society. Francis married Anne, the widow of Hugh Boscawen and daughter of Wentworth Fitzgerald, the Earl of Kildare, and died in February, 1718.

Robinson, Sir William (1656-1736), baronet of Newby, Yorkshire, sheriff of Yorkshire, 1689; lord mayor of York, 1700; and Member of Parliament for Northallerton Borough, Yorkshire, 1689-95, and for York City, 1698-1722. He was the eldest son of Thomas Robinson, esquire, a Levant merchant, who served as Member of Parliament for York during the reigns of Charles II and James II. He inherited the estate of Newby upon the death of his uncle, Metcalf Robinson, in February, 1689, and was thereupon created a baronet. He had been educated at York School under Mr. Langley, St. John's College, Cambridge, and Gray's Inn. Robinson married Mary, the daughter of George Arslabie of Studley Royal, Yorkshire, and died in December, 1736.

Rolle, Samuel, esquire, of Heanton, Devonshire, a relative of Sir John Rolle of Truo, a Levant merchant, and one of the richest commoners of his generation, Member of Parliament for Callington Borough, Cornwall County, 1665-79, and Devon County, 1679-1706.

Rous, Sir John (1656-1730), baronet, of Henham Hall, Suffolk, sheriff of Suffolk County, 1675-79, and Member of Parliament (Tory) for Eye Borough, Suffolk County, 1685-87, and for Suffolk County, 1689-90. He was the son and heir of Sir John Rous, who had been a Member of Parliament during the Restoration. He succeeded his father as second baronet in 1670. After attending St. Catherine's College, Cambridge, he was granted an M.A. degree in 1673. Rous married Philippa Bedingfield and Anne Wood and died in April, 1730.

Rowe, Anthony, esquire, of Middlesex County, Member of Parliament (Whig) for Penryn Borough, Cornwall County, 1689.

Rudd, Sir Rice (1643-1701), baronet, of Aberglasney, Carnmarthen County, Wales, Member of Parliament for Higham Ferrers, Borough, Northamptonshire, 1678-81, and Carnmarthen County, Wales, 1689-1701. He was the only son of Anthony Rudd and the great-grandson of Anthony Rudd, Dean of Gloucester and Bishop of St. David's. In 1664 he succeeded his grandfather as second baronet and from the estates came an income of £1,200. Rudd married Dorothy, the sister of Sir Francis Cornwallis, knight, and died in July, 1701.

Rushout, Sir James (1644-1698), baronet, of Marylands, Essex County, Member of Parliament (Whig) for Evesham Borough, Worcestershire, 1670-81, Worcester County, 1689-90, and Evesham Borough, 1690-98. He was the son of John Rushout, a London merchant, who had immigrated from Flanders to England and was naturalized in 1635. He was created first baronet by Charles II in 1661 and purchased the estate of Northwick Park in Blackley, Worcestershire, from the Childe family in 1665. After studying at Christ Church College, Oxford, he was granted an M.A. degree in 1661. He married Alice Palmer, who brought him immense wealth, and died in February, 1698.

Russell, Edward (1653-1727), esquire, of Chiswick, Middlesex County, naval officer; groom of the bedchamber to the Duke of York; and Member of Parliament (Whig) for Launceston Borough, Cornwall County, 1689-90, Portsmouth Borough, Southampton County, 1690-95, and Cambridgeshire, 1695-97. He was the second son of Edward Russell and grandson of Francis, the fourth Earl of Bedford, as well as the nephew of William Russell, the first Duke of Bedford. The family owned considerable property in southwestern England, acquired at the

time of the confiscation of the monasteries, and in London that
came from lands of the attainted Duke of Somerset. After
receiving his education at Tottenham School and St. John's
College, Cambridge, he was commissioned a lieutenant in the
navy in 1671. In 1683 he resigned from the navy as a captain
and left the court following the execution of Lord Russell, his
cousin. Because of his dissatisfaction with the government, he
actively engaged in the intrigue that led to the invasion of
England by William of Orange. He met often with Shrewsbury
and others in 1687 and was employed to exchange correspond-
ence between the English malcontents and the Prince. After
signing the invitation, along with seven other English leaders,
he carried it to Holland disguised as an ordinary seaman.
He returned with William's expedition in a private capacity,
although he supervised the pilots in the landing at Torbay. For
his role in the Revolution, Russell was well rewarded. He was
appointed privy councilor, treasurer of the navy, admiral of the
Blue, commander-in-chief of the channel fleet, vice-admiral of
England, captain general of the narrow seas, and admiral of
the fleet. He was created Earl of Orford in 1697. Russell married his first cousin, Margaret, the third daughter of William,
the first Duke of Bedford, and died in November, 1727.

Russell, Sir Francis (1638-1706), baronet, of Strensham, Worcester County, army officer and as Member of Parliament
(Tory) for Tewkesbury Borough, Gloucestershire, 1673-90. The
eldest son of Sir William Russell, he succeeded his father as
second baronet in 1669. He had attended the Inner Temple.
Russell had been commissioned a captain of infantry in 1680
and was in command of a troop attached to the Scotch regiments transferred from Holland to suppress Monmouth's Rebellion, but his unit was not engaged at the Battle of Sedgemoor.
When the Revolution occurred, he was among the first army
officers to join William of Orange. He became a cavalry colonel
after the Revolution. He married Anne, the daughter of Sir
Rowland Lytton, knight, and died in January, 1706.

Russell, James (1646-1712), esquire, of Loverstock, Southampton County, Member of Parliament (Whig) for Whitechurch Borough, Southampton County, 1685-87, 1689-95, and
Travistock Borough, Devonshire, 1701-03. He was the son of

William, Earl of Bedford, and the brother of George Russell. After attending Magdalen College, Oxford, and receiving an M.A. degree, he was incorporated at Cambridge University in 1668. Russell married Elizabeth, the daughter of Sir Edmund Wright, lord mayor of London, and Elizabeth Lloyd. He died in June, 1712.

Russell, Robert, esquire, the son of the Earl of Bedford, Member of Parliament (Whig) for Tavistock Borough, Devonshire, in 1689.

Ryves, George (b. 1637), esquire, of Tarrant Grinville, Dorset County, Member of Parliament for Wareham Borough, Dorsetshire, 1685-87, and 1689. He was the son of George Ryves and attended Winchester School.

Sacheverell, William (1638-1691), esquire, of Morley, Derbyshire, lord of the admiralty, 1689, and Member of Parliament (Whig) for Derbyshire, 1670-81, Heytesbury Borough, Wiltshire, 1689-90, and Nottingham, 1691. Soon after attending Gray's Inn, he entered politics as Member of Parliament for Derbyshire. An accomplished orator with great parliamentary skill, he used his talents to oppose court policy. He secured the passage of a resolution in 1673 that removed Catholics from military office and served on the committee that prepared the Test Bill. Not only did he take an active part in the parliamentary investigation of the Popish Plot, but he also sponsored the motion to force James, Duke of York, from the court and king's councils as well as the Exclusion Bill. In the Convention Parliament he spoke with effectiveness on the vacancy resolution as well as on the guarantees that would preserve the laws and religion of England. He was appointed to the Somers Committee and was manager for the Commons in the Conference with the Lords on the vacancy question. He married Mary Stanton and June Newton and died in 1691.

Sackvile, Thomas (1622-1693), esquire, of Selscombe, Sussex County, army officer and Member of Parliament for East Grinstead Borough, Sussex County, 1689-90, and 1690-93. The second son of Thomas Sackvile and the brother of John, he was educated at Christ Church College, Oxford. He died in January, 1693.

St. Aubyn, Sir John (1645-1714), baronet, of Clowance, Cornwall County, sheriff of Cornwall, 1704-05, and Member of Parliament (Tory) for Helston Borough, 1689-95. The member of a landowning family in Cornwall, he was the first son and heir of Sir John St. Aubyn, who had been sheriff of Cornwall and Member of Parliament, and attended Exeter College, Oxford. He succeeded his father as second baronet in 1687. St. Aubyn married Mary, the daughter of Peter Delahay of Westminster, and died in 1714.

St. John, Henry (1652-1742), esquire, of Battersea, Surrey County, deputy lieutenant of Wiltshire, 1683; secretary of war, 1704; and Member of Parliament (Whig) for Wootton Bassett Borough, Wiltshire, 1679-81, 1685-87, 1689-95, 1698-1700 and Wiltshire, 1698-1700. He was the eldest son of Sir Walter St. John, third baronet of Wiltshire and the father of Henry, Lord Bollingbroke. The family owned over 3,000 acres of land in Wiltshire. His education was received at Eton and at Caius and St. John's colleges, Cambridge. After receiving an M.A. degree from Cambridge, he was incorporated at Oxford and was granted a D.C.L. degree from this school in 1702. St. John succeeded his father as fourth baronet in 1708 and was created Viscount St. John in 1716. He married Mary, the daughter of the Earl of Warwick, and Angelica Magdelina, the daughter of George Pelissary, treasurer of the Navy to Louis XIV. He died in April, 1742.

St. John, Oliver (c. 1642-1689), esquire, of Farley, army officer and Member of Parliament for Stockbridge Borough, Southampton County, 1678-81 and 1689. His father was Henry St. John who sent him to Exeter College, Oxford, for his education. He died in 1689.

Samwell, Sir Thomas (1645-1694), baronet, of Upton, Northamptonshire, Member of Parliament (Whig) for Northampton County, June, 1689-1690, and for Northampton 1690-94. The son and heir of Richard Samwell, he succeeded his father in 1662 and was created a baronet in 1675. He married Elizabeth Gooday and Anne Godschalk and died in 1694.

Sanderson, Nicholas, esquire, Member of Parliament from Thirsk Borough, Yorkshire, 1679-81, and from Newark-on-Trent, Nottinghamshire, 1689.

Sandys, Samuel (1638-1701), esquire, of Omersley, Worcestershire, Member of Parliament from Worcester County, 1661-79, Worcester City, 1679, Droitwich Borough, Worcestershire, 1681, 1689-90. He was the son of Samuel Sandys, a Cavalier officer and governor of Evesham, who had his estates sequestered and was imprisoned. The Sandys estates were worth £1,000 a year. The son married Elizabeth, the daughter of Sir John Pettus, knight, and died in August, 1701.

Sanford, John, esquire, Member of Parliament (Tory) from Taunton Borough, Somerset County, 1689.

Saunders, Thomas, esquire, of Milborne Wyke, Somerset County, infantry officer and Member of Parliament (Tory) for Milborne Port, Somerset County, in 1689. He was elected warden of the Company of Grocers.

Saunderson, George (1631-1714), viscount in the Irish peerage, cavalry officer, vice admiral of Lincoln County, 1660, and Member of Parliament for Lincoln County, 1660-81, 1685-87, and 1689-98. The son of Nicholas Saunderson, second Viscount Castleton, and brother of Peregrine Saunderson, fourth viscount, he became the fifth Viscount Castleton in Ireland and raised a regiment in Yorkshire to support William of Orange in 1689. Although an Irish peer, he did not attend the Irish Parliament of James II. Saunderson married Grace Belasyse and Sarah Fanshawe and died in May, 1714.

Savage, Richard (1654-1712), Viscount Colchester, cavalry officer and Member of Parliament (Whig) for Wigan Borough, Lancashire, 1681, and for Liverpool, 1689-94. The second but surviving son of Richard Savage, the third Earl of Rivers, colonel in the royalist army and governor of Donnington, he succeeded his father as the fourth Earl in 1694. He was styled Viscount Colchester from his brother's death in 1680 until 1694. In 1686 he was commissioned an officer in the Fourth Troop of Horse under the command of John Churchill. A handsome, unscrupulous rake known as "Tyburn Dick," in his younger years, he was one of the first to assess the political drift in the fall of 1688. Accompanied by Thomas Wharton and about sixty-five men, he rode into William's camp at Exeter and became the first nobleman to join forces with the Prince. As a Member of the Convention Parliament, he was among the several persons who urged a vote on the vacancy resolution on January

28, 1689. After the settlement he continued his military career with distinguished service in Ireland, Flanders, and the Iberian Peninsula and held many political offices. He served as custos rotulorum of Cheshire, lord lieutenant of Cheshire, Lancashire, and Essex, as well as vice-admiral of the last named counties, constable of Liverpool Castle and the Tower, privy councilor and master general of ordinance. He married Penelope Downes and Margaret Tryon and died in August, 1712.

Savile, William (1665-1700), Lord Eland, Member of Parliament (Tory) for Newark-on-Trent Borough, Nottinghamshire, 1689-95. Educated at Geneva and Christ Church College, Oxford, he was the son of George Savile, first Marquis of Halifax, and succeeded his father as fifth baronet and second marquis in 1695. He married Elizabeth, the daughter of Sir Samuel Grimston, and Mary, the daughter of Daniel Finch, Earl of Nottingham, and died in September, 1700.

Sawyer, Sir Robert (1633-1692), knight, of Heywood, Berkshire, speaker of the House of Commons, 1678; attorney-general, 1681-89; counsel for the seven bishops, 1687; and Member of Parliament (Tory) for Chipping Wycombe Borough, Buckinghamshire, 1673-79, and Cambridge University, 1689-92. The sixth son of Sir Edmund Sawyer, an auditor of the Exchequer, he was educated at Westminster School, Magdalen College, Cambridge, and the Inner Temple. An excellent scholar, he received the A.B. and M.A. degrees from Cambridge and was called to the Bar from the Inner Temple in 1661. As a barrister, he practiced in the Court and on the Oxford circuit. After serving as the prosecutor of persons implicated in the Popish Plot, he was appointed attorney-general. In this capacity he handled some of the most famous cases of his generation and generally sustained the position of the Crown. The breach between Sawyer and James widened after he reluctantly approved the patent of dispensation for Sir Edward Hales and refused to approve the confirmation of Obediah Walker as master of University College, Oxford, on the ground that it was "against all laws since the days of Elizabeth." Although he requested dismissal from his post, he was retained until December, 1687. When the seven bishops were brought to trial, Sawyer was the senior counsel. His stout defense on their behalf ingratiated him with the Tories. Elected to represent Cambridge University to the Convention Parliament, largely because of his repudiation of dispensing power in the case of Obediah Walker and his defense of the seven bishops, he resumed his earlier opposition to James when he had supported the Exclusion Bill. As a member of several committees, among them those working on the Declaration of Rights, the Toleration Act, and the Muting Act, and a frequent speaker he took an active part in the proceedings of the Convention. When issues involving the fundamentals of the constitution and law were under discussion, his legal perception gave his comments great weight. Although he supported the principles involved in the words "abdicated" and "vacancy," he refused to accept the assumption that a vacancy of the throne dissolved the government. He moved that the resolution to bar a Catholic from the throne be passed, but he was uncertain about the legality of William's accession and of the power of the Convention to grant money.[66] When William and Mary had been installed, however, he supported the new regime and served on eighteen committees, including those dealing with privilege, repeal of the Corporation Act, the relief of French Protestant ministers, and new oaths. His political fortune was reversed, however, when he was expelled from the House because of his conduct as attorney-general. Although he was re-elected in 1690, he soon left the Commons to become lord chief justice. He married Margaret, the daughter of Ralph Suckley, Canonbury, Middlesex, and died in July, 1692.

Seymour, Sir Edward (1633-1708), baronet, of Berry Pomeroy, Devonshire, clerk of the hanaper, 1667-1708; speaker of the House of Commons, 1672-78; privy councilor, 1673; treasurer of the navy, 1673-81; commissioner of the treasury, 1691-94; and Member of Parliament (Tory) for Hindon Borough, Wiltshire, 1661-78; Devonshire, 1678-79; Totness Borough, Devonshire, 1679-81, 1695-98; and Exeter Borough, Devonshire, 1685-95, 1698-1708. He was the eldest son of Sir Edmond Seymour, third baronet, who had served as vice-admiral and sheriff of Devon, as well as Member of Parliament during the reigns of Charles I and Charles II. The Seymour family could date its pedigree from the Norman Conquest, and Sir Edward was the descendant of the Lord Protector of Edward VI. Although his extensive estates were plundered and compounded during the Civil War, the family recovered its influence during the Restoration. Entering Parliament from Hindon, Sir Edward soon became a powerful leader of a group from the western counties. As a Protestant Tory he fought against Catholicism and the growth of arbitrary power. Although he played a leading role in the attack upon Clarendon, he subsequently was appointed treasurer of the navy and a privy councilor and was elected speaker of the House of Commons. In the Exclusion Bill debates, he cooperated with Halifax in opposing its enactment while at the same time he was urging the Duke of York to change his religion. Seymour favored permitting James to inherit the crown, but he would have William administer the government as regent. He had eagerly supported the enactment of the Habeas Corpus Act. At the beginning of James's reign Seymour expressed fears of the threat to the Test and Habeas Corpus Acts. In parliamentary debates he spoke against the abrogation of charters, the interference in recent elections, and the increase in the standing army. Because of his opposition to James, his policies won slight support among the Members of Parliament. He was an early sympathizer with the revolutionary movement, and he was one of the first of the gentry to join William at Exeter. Through his initiative, an association in support of the Prince was formed. When William led his forces out of Exeter, Seymour was left in charge of the city. In the Convention Parliament he served as a member from Exeter. Although he was well qualified to serve as a speaker, Henry Powle was chosen because rumors were spread that Seymour was opposed to declaring the throne vacant and selecting William as king. When the Convention began the debate on the state of the nation, he urged the formation of a committee of the whole House and supported the proposal that guarantees for liberties be drafted as conditions for awarding the crown. After the Revolution he was appointed lord of the treasury, privy councilor, and comptroller of the household. After the Whig victory of 1705, he was without office or influence. Seymour married Margaret, the daughter of Sir William Wale, alderman of London, and Letita Popham, both wealthy women, and died in 1708.

Seymour, Henry (d. 1728), esquire, of Orchard Portman, Somersetshire, infantry officer and Member of Parliament (Tory) for St. Mawes Borough, Cornwall County, 1679-81, 1685-87, and 1689. The fifth son of Sir Edward Seymour, he inherited the large estate of Orchard Portman from his uncle, Sir William Portman, baronet, and changed his name to Portman in compliance with the terms of the will. Entering the army as an ensign in 1678 he rose to the rank of captain in the First Regiment of Foot Guards. Seymour married Penelope Haslewood and Meliora Finch and died in February, 1728.

Sherard, Bennett (1621-1700), baron, of Stapleford, Leicestershire, commissioner for assessments, Rutland, 1652; commissioner of militia, Leicester County; custos rotulorum of Rutland, 1660; and Member of Parliament for Leicestershire (Whig), 1679-81, 1685-87, and 1689-95. The son and heir of Sir William Sherard, the first Irish baron to receive a knighthood from James I, he attended St. John's College, Oxford, and supported the parliamentary party during the Civil War. After the Revolution he was attainted by James II for his absence from the Jacobite session of the Irish Parliament. He was an enthusiastic sponsor of the arts. Sherard married Elizabeth Christopher and died in January, 1700.

Sherard, Bennett (1650-1701), esquire, of Whissendine, Rutland County, Member of Parliament for Rutland County, 1689-95. He was the son of Philip Sherard, who received his estate as a gift from his father Sir William Sherard, a Member of Parliament under Charles II. Bennett was educated at Queen's College, Oxford, and the Middle Temple. Sherard married Dorothy, the daughter of Henry, Lord Fairfax, and died in 1701.

Sidney, Henry (1641-1704), esquire, of Long Itchington, Warwickshire, army officer; groom of the bedchamber to the Duke of York; master of the house to the Duchess of York, 1665; envoy to France, 1672, and the Hague, 1679-81; master of the robes, 1675-78; privy councilor, 1689; and Member of Parliament (Whig) for Bramber Borough, Sussex County, 1679-81, and Tamworth Borough, Staffordshire, 1689. He was the fourth son of Robert Sidney, the second Earl of Leicester and a brother of Philip, the third Earl of Leicester, as well as the favorite son of his mother, the daughter of the Earl of

Northumberland, who gave him a small estate in 1659. In 1677 his security was enhanced by the inheritance from his father of the estate of Long Itchington in Warwickshire and £25,000. He was educated through travel abroad with a nonconformist minister, Dr. Thomas Pierce, his nephew, and Harry Savile, the younger brother of Lord Halifax. Sidney held a number of important posts in the household as well as a captaincy in the Bluffs before his election as member of Parliament from Bramber to the Exclusion Parliament. In its sessions he gained the confidence of Sunderland who sent Sidney to Holland to encourage William to visit England. Although the conversations were futile, Sidney became a close friend of the Prince and was appointed general of the English troops in Dutch service at William's request in 1681. While he was out of favor in James's reign, he traveled in Europe, but he returned to England in 1688 and undertook conversations that led to the plans for William's invasion of England. After arrangements had been completed among the English leaders, Sidney left England with royal permission and, in spite of his promise not to do so, went to Holland with a copy of the invitation and assurance of the support of Churchill. He accompanied the expedition to England along with Burnet and Herbert, but he did not play an active part in the settlement activities. His support of the Revolution brought him position and wealth. In 1689 he was created Viscount Sidney and, in 1694, the Earl of Romney. In 1690 after participating in the Irish campaign he was awarded 50,000 acres of confiscated estates with a return of £17,000. Moreover, he held many offices including those of privy councilor, secretary of state for the Northern Department, lord lieutenant of Ireland, master general of Ordnance, lord justice of the realm, and lord warden of the Cinque Ports. At the accession of Queen Anne he was removed from all his posts. Sidney died (unmarried) of smallpox in April, 1704.

Skinner, Thomas, esquire, of Dewlish, Member of Parliament for Wareham, Dorsetshire, 1689. The son of Nicholas Skinner, a London merchant, who had purchased the estate of Michael's Farm from John Bassett in 1663, he inherited his father's estate and business and built a large stone house on his land in 1702.

Skippon, Sir Philip (1674-1692), knight, of Wrentham, Suffolk

County, Member of Parliament (Whig) for Dunwick Borough, Suffolk, 1679-81, and 1689. He was the son of Major General Philip Skippon of the Parliamentary Army, a member of the Long Parliament. The younger Skippon was educated at Cambridge University and at Gray's Inn, and was knighted in April, 1674. He married Anne, the daughter of Thomas Brewster and Anne, the daughter of Sir Thomas Barnardiston. He died in 1692.

Slingsby, Henry (c. 1640-1691), baronet, of Yorkshire, army officer; gentleman of the bedchamber; lieutenant governor of Portsmouth; justice of peace for West Riding, Yorkshire; and Member of Parliament for Portsmouth Borough, Southampton County, 1685-87 and 1689. The son of Sir Henry Slingsby, a royalist member of the Long Parliament, who was beheaded in 1658 for attempting to restore Charles II, he succeeded his father as third baronet in 1687. Entering the army as a coronet in a cavalry regiment in 1661, he rose to the rank of colonel by 1688. In 1683 he was urged by Lord Feversham to ask for a troop of dragoons then being formed, but Slingsby declined to do so because "Lord Churchill is to command them." He died in 1691.

Smith, John (1655-1723), esquire, of Tedworth, Hampshire, Member of Parliament (Whig) for Ludgershall Borough, Wiltshire, 1679, 1681, 1689-90; Beeralston, Cornwall County, 1691-95; Andover Borough, Hampshire, 1695-1713; and East Looe, Cornwall County, 1715-23. The son of John Smith, a member of a respectable Hampshire family with a good estate, he was a close friend of Sidney Godolphin. He was educated at St. John's College, Oxford, and the Middle Temple. After the Revolution he became not only party whip and speaker of the House of Commons but also a lord of the treasury and chancellor and teller of the Exchequer. He died in October, 1723.

Somers, John (1650-1716), esquire, of Clifton in Severn Stroke, Worcester County, junior counsel for the seven bishops and Member of Parliament (Whig) for Worcester City, Worcestershire, 1689-93. He was the son of John Somers, a landowner and attorney, who had fought with the Parliamentary Army during the Civil War and who had become wealthy from his legal practice after 1660. His education was obtained at Col-

lege School, Worcester, Trinity College, Oxford, and the Middle
Temple from which he was called to the Bar in 1676. In this
early legal career he was associated with Sir Francis Winnington, the solicitor general, as well as the Duke of Shrewsbury,
Lord Russell, and Algernon Sidney. His legal interests ranged
the whole field of English law and equity although he was well
versed in constitutional law. This legal knowledge was invalu-
able when Somers played a decisive role as junior counsel at
the bishops' trial. He cited pertinent precedents to prove that
a law could not be suspended without the consent of Parliament. His strong evidence and his appeal to the jury virtually
assured a favorable verdict for the clergymen. After participating in the negotiations with William in the fall of 1688, he
was returned to the Convention Parliament by Worcester and
played a dominant role in the debates dealing with the settlement of the monarchy. Somers expressed his opinion that James
had broken the contract and by fleeing he had, in fact, abdicated the throne. He, indeed, in one of his speeches, voiced the
Commons concensus in his statement that the king by sub-
verting the constitution, breaking the contract, and violating
fundamental laws "hath thereby renounced to be King according to the constitution, by avowing to govern by a despotick
power, unknown to the constitution, and inconsistent with it;
he hath renounced to be King according to the law, such King
as he swore to be at his coronation, such a King to whom the
allegiance of an English subject is due." [67] While the Commons
accepted the "vacancy" resolution, strong opposition developed
in the Lords and only through the cogency of the arguments by
Somers as well as Treby in the conference was the Lords convinced that it should approve the resolution. In the conference
debate on the word "vacancy," Somers referred to its many
uses, and cited a case parallel to the Revolution in the interval
between the reigns of Richard II and Henry IV. At that time
a resignation of the Crown and government by Richard II
occurred. Observing that the throne was void, Parliament
drafted articles against the king and deposed him. Before the
accession of the next sovereign, public offices ceased, and the
throne was declared vacant.[68] Somers also had an important
role in the preparation of conditions upon which the crown

would be awarded. After a lengthy discussion about the motive of the limitations to be drafted, the Convention approved a motion that general conditions should be drafted as a prerequisite for filling the throne, and Somers was appointed to head a committee to prepare the document. As chairman of the committee, he presided over its meetings and probably had the major role in the composition of its report which with little change became the Bill of Rights.[69] After the settlement he became solicitor general, attorney-general, lord keeper of the great seal, speaker of the House of Lords, a lord justice of the realm, and lord chancellor. He was knighted in October, 1689, and was created Baron Somers of Evesham in December, 1697. As additional rewards, the king granted him two royal manors and a pension of £2,100. Before the end of William's reign Somers was dismissed from office and impeached, but the charges were later dismissed. He was lord president of the council under Anne and a privy councilor under George I. Somers was a Fellow and president of the Royal Society and probably the author of "Vindication of Proceedings of the Late Parliament of England," 1689. He died (unmarried) of paralysis in April, 1716.

Somerset, Charles (1660-1698), marquis, of Raglan, Monmouth County, member of the committee of the East India Company, 1683-91; army officer; and Member of Parliament (Tory) for Monmouth Borough, Monmouth County, 1677-78; Monmouth County, 1678-79; Monmouth Borough, 1679-80; Gloucester Borough, Gloucester County, 1681; Gloucester County, 1685-87; and Monmouth County, 1689-95. The son and heir of Henry Somerset, the first Duke of Beaufort, he was styled Lord Herbert in 1667 and created Marquis of Worcester in 1682. He attended Christ Church College, Oxford, receiving an M.A. degree in 1681. The family was closely associated with the Stuart family. Charles II was the godfather at Somerset's birth. He was the steward of a royal manor in Radnor County. After helping with the suppression of Monmouth's Rebellion, he served as a colonel of an infantry regiment, 1685-87. So strong was his loyalty to the Crown, he attempted to hold Bristol for James II after the invasion of William of Orange. Somerset married Rebecca, the daughter of Sir Josiah Child, the wealthy merchant and sometime governor of the East India Company, and died in July, 1698.

Speccott, John (b. 1665), esquire, of Penheal, Cornwall, Member of Parliament (Tory) for Newport Borough, Cornwall County, 1685-87, 1689-95, and for Cornwall County, 1695-1701. He was the son of John Speccott and was educated at Exeter College, Oxford.

Staines, Richard (b. 1650), esquire, of Thirsk, Yorkshire, Member of Parliament from Thirsk Borough, Yorkshire, in 1689. The son of Richard Staines, he was educated at Thirsk School, York, Caius College, Cambridge, and Gray's Inn.

Stanley, James (1664-1736), esquire, of Lancashire, Member of Parliament (Whig) from Clitheroe Borough, Lancashire, 1685-87, from Preston Borough, Lancashire, 1689-90, and from Lancashire, 1690-1702. He was the second son of the eighth Earl of Derby, who had attempted with several gentlemen to support Sir George Booth's Rising but was defeated and captured. His family owned almost 6,000 acres of land in Lancaster and Somerset counties. After the Revolution he served with William III in Ireland and Flanders as a regimental commander, becoming a major general in 1704. After his elevation to the peerage upon his brother's death in 1702, he resigned from his military employments but served as lord lieutenant and vice-admiral of Lancashire as well as privy councilor. He married Mary, the daughter of Sir William Morley of Sussex, and died in February, 1736.

Stephens, Sir William (c. 1642-1697), knight, of Barton, Isle of Wight, army officer and Member of Parliament for Newport Borough, Southampton County, 1685-87, and 1689-95. The son of Dr. William Stephens, he was educated at New College, Oxford University, and the Middle Temple. He was knighted in 1684 and served as lieutenant governor of the Isle of Wight. Stephens died in September, 1697.

Stockdale, William, esquire, of Bolton Yorkshire, Member of Parliament (Whig) from Knaresborough Borough, Yorkshire, 1660, 1661-79, 1679-81, 1685-87, and 1689.

Stonehouse, Sir John (1637-1700), baronet, of Radley, Berkshire, Member of Parliament for Abingdon Borough, Berkshire, 1675-81, 1685-87, and 1689-90. The second son of Sir George

Stonehouse, a Member of Parliament during the Protectorate and Restoration, he was educated at Queen's College, Oxford, and Gray's Inn. He succeeded his father as second baronet in 1675. Stonehouse married Martha, the widow of Richard Spencer, a wealthy London merchant, and died in 1700.

Strangeways, Thomas (1643-1713), esquire, of Melbury Sampford, Dorsetshire, army officer and Member of Parliament (Tory) for Dorsetshire, 1678-81, 1685-87, and 1689-1713. The Strangeways family with marriage connections with influential houses in the southwest had furnished Members of Parliament of royalist inclinations since the reign of James I. Although Sir John Strangeways had opposed the forced loans under Charles I, he supported Strafford in the Long Parliament. Thomas Strangeways, the son of Dr. Strangeways, was educated at Wadham College, Oxford, and in 1685 he was commissioned to raise an infantry regiment in Dorset County, but the unit was not activated. He died in December, 1713.

Stratford, John, esquire, of Coventry, Member of Parliament from Coventry, Warwickshire, 1679-81, and 1689.

Strickland, Sir William (1665-1724), baronet, of Boynton, Yorkshire, Member of Parliament (Whig) for Malton Borough, Yorkshire, 1689-98, 1700-08, 1722-24, Yorkshire, 1708-10, and Old Sarum, Wiltshire, 1716-22, The son of Sir Thomas Strickland, second baronet, he was educated at Exeter College, Oxford, and entered politics as a representative from Malton in the Convention Parliament. In Parliament he was a staunch Whig and a strong party man. He was appointed commissary general of musters by George I. Strickland married Elizabeth Palmes of Lindly and died in May, 1724.

Tancred, Christopher (d. 1705), esquire, of Whixley, Yorkshire, army officer; sheriff of Yorkshire, 1685-86; and Member of Parliament for Aldborough, Yorkshire, 1689. He was the son of Sir Richard Tancred, a Cavalier, who was knighted by Charles II for his loyalty and services during the Civil War. During the reign of William III, he was appointed as master of the buckhounds. Tancred married Catherine Kirklees and died in 1705.

Tanner, John, esquire, Member of Parliament (Tory) for Grampound Borough, Cornwall County, 1661-81, and 1689.

Taylor, Sir Thomas (1657-1696), baronet, of Maidstone, Kent, army officer and Member of Parliament (Whig) for Maidstone Borough, Kent, 1689-96. The son and heir of Sir Thomas Taylor, first baronet, he was educated at St. John's College, Oxford, and succeeded to the baronetcy in 1665. He was appointed as the commander of Upnor Castle in 1695. Taylor married Alice, the widow of Herbert Stapley, and died in February, 1696.

Temple, Sir Richard (1634-1697), knight and baronet, of Stowe, Leicestershire, lord lieutenant by Buckinghamshire; army colonel; commissioner of customs, 1672-94; member of the Council of Foreign Plantations, 1671; and Member of Parliament (Whig) for Warwickshire, 1654-55, Buckingham Borough, Buckinghamshire, 1659, and 1660-97. He was the son and heir of Sir Peter Temple, baronet, the sheriff of Buckinghamshire who processed the ship tax writ that John Hampden refused to obey and who served in the last two Parliaments of Charles I as an ardent Puritan. He was the nephew of Sir William Temple who had assumed that William of Orange would in time ascend the English throne. Temple succeeded to the baronetcy in 1653 and was knighted in 1661. His education was obtained at Emmanuel College, Cambridge, and Gray's Inn. Entering Parliament as a minor in 1654, he became a supporter of the royalist cause prior to the Restoration. After the accession of Charles II, he became a leading member of the Country party in the Cavalier Parliament. Although he was appointed to important crown offices by the king, notwithstanding his prosecution of the Popish Plot, he worked so vigorously to secure the enactment of the Exclusion Bill that James's followers referred to him as the "Stoe monster." Temple was an active proponent of William of Orange and the revolutionary settlement in the Convention, speaking in the debates on ten different occasions. In the state of the nation debate he supported the proposition that the king had broken the original contract. After stating that James had endeavored to destroy the government by attempting to influence elections and revoking charters, he said: "When a king attempts to destroy the roots of government, he differs nothing from a tyrant." [70] After the Convention decided that the king had broken the contract, the discussion turned to the status of the throne. Following the proposal of the terms "demise," "deposition," and "desertion," the members more nearly agreed on the word "renunciation" that was proposed by Temple, who suggested that the king, by his attempt to destroy the government and to eliminate all who would not comply with Catholicism, had acted in a manner inconsistent with the nature of government and relinquished the crown, thereby effecting a renunciation of the crown. This renunciation did not require a formal statement but could be accomplished by the fact as well as by solemn instrument. This renunciation of the crown by the king had created a vacancy of the throne.[71] The Convention subsequently declared that by his actions the king had abdicated and the throne was vacant. After making this decision the members began to consider limitations within which future sovereigns would rule. A factor to come under consideration was the religion of the ruler. The Catholicism of James had caused grave consternation during his reign, and Temple believed that the king's loyalty to the Catholic Church obligated him to "invade" the laws discriminatory to Catholicism. Consequently, he threatened to destroy the Anglican Church by his suspension of ecclesiastical laws. His policy involved the destruction of all who would not comply with Catholicism.[72] A resolution was later enacted which limited the crown to Protestant sovereigns. In further discussion of limitations Temple advanced most of the principles that would provide for parliamentary control of the state. Under the heading "encroachments on parliament," he discussed several points which, if included in a declaration, would ensure the sanctity of parliamentary authority. He recommended that freely elected Members of Parliament should meet in certain and frequent sessions. Should any executive official attempt to interfere with the action of Parliament, he should be called to account. He further suggested that the regular military force should be under the control of the legislature.[73] After the Revolution, Temple continued his active parliamentary role and was restored to his office as commissioner of customs. He married Mary Knap of Oxfordshire and died in May, 1697.

Thomas, Sir William (1641-1706), baronet, of Folkington,

Sussex, Member of Parliament for Seaford, Sussex County, 1661-81, 1685-87, 1701, 1702-06, and Sussex County, 1681, 1689-1700, 1701-02. The son and heir of William Thomas, he was educated at Oriel College, Oxford, and was created baronet in 1660. Thomas married Barbara Springett and died in 1706.

Thompson, Edward, merchant, of York, alderman and lord mayor of York and Member of Parliament (Whig) for York City, 1689-98, and 1700. He was the son of Richard Thompson and the brother of Sir Henry Thompson, a Member of Parliament. In 1685 Thompson, along with four other aldermen, was charged with disloyalty and arrested by an order in council. They were imprisoned at Hull after Monmouth's defeat in July.

Thompson, Francis (1656-1693), esquire, of Humbleton, Yorkshire, Member of Parliament for Scarborough Borough, Yorkshire, 1679-81, 1689-93. The eldest son of William Thompson, he was educated at Brentwood School and St. John's College, Cambridge. He married Arbella, the daughter of Sir Edward Alleyn, baronet, of Essex, and died in October, 1693.

Thompson, Sir John (1648-1710), baronet, of Haversham, Buckinghamshire, sheriff of Buckinghamshire; lord of the admiralty, 1699-1701; and Member of Parliament (Whig) for Gatton Borough, Surrey, 1685-87, and 1689-96. The son and heir of Maurice Thompson of Lee, Kent, a London merchant, who had been an influential member of Cromwell's government, he was educated at Lee School, Sidney College, Cambridge, and Lincoln's Inn. After serving as sheriff, he was created baronet in 1673. Because he followed his father's political and religious views, he became a spirited opponent of James II's policies, and he was one of the early supporters of William of Orange and the Revolution. After the settlement he was appointed a commissioner of public accounts and a lord of the admiralty. In 1696 he was created Baron of Haversham. Later he resigned from his appointments and allied himself with the Tory party. Thompson married Martha, the daughter of the first Earl of Anglesey, and Martha Graham and died in November, 1710.

Thompson, William (1630-c. 1691), esquire, Member of Parliament from Scarborough Borough, Yorkshire, 1660-91. The son of Stephen Thompson, esquire, he was educated at Merchant

Taylors' School and Jesus College, Cambridge, which granted him an A.B. degree in 1651 and an M.A. degree in 1655. As a Member of Parliament, he took an active part in debates.

Thornagh, John (1648-1723), esquire, of Osherton, Lincolnshire, sheriff of Nottinghamshire, 1688-89, and Member of Parliament for East Retford Borough, Nottinghamshire, 1689-1701, and for Nottingham County, 1704-10. The son and heir of Francis Thornagh, esquire, of Fenton, Nottingham, he was educated at Jesus College, Cambridge. He married Elizabeth, the daughter of Sir Richard Earle, baronet, and died in May, 1723.

Thurbarne, John (b. 1635), esquire, of Sandwich, Kent, Member of Parliament for Sandwich (Cinque Port) Borough, Kent, 1678-95 and 1698-1700. The son of James Thurbarne, he was educated at Wadham College, Oxford, where he was granted a B.A. degree in 1655 and at Gray's Inn. He was called to the Bar and became a king's serjeant in 1689.

Tichborne, White (1638-1700), esquire, of Aldershot, Member of Parliament (Tory) for Haslemere Borough, Surrey County, 1689-90. The son of Francis Tichborne, he was educated at Winchester School. Tichborne married Elizabeth Shudd and Ann Supple and died in August, 1700.

Tipping, Thomas (1653-1718), esquire, of Wheatfield, Oxford County, Member of Parliament (Whig) for Oxfordshire, 1685-87, and for Wallingford Borough, Berkshire, 1689-90, 1695-1700. He was the eldest son of Sir Thomas Tipping, knight, and was educated at Trinity College, Oxford, and Lincoln's Inn. During the reign of James II, he was outlawed and exempt from the general pardon of 1688. He was created first baronet in 1698. Tipping was an overt supporter of William of Orange in the Convention Parliament speaking on the vacancy of the throne. When the Lords refused to accept the vacancy resolution, he urged rejection of the upper House action and expressed indignation that many would re-establish James on the throne because this action would be a threat to Protestantism even though the administration would be shared by William of Orange. He urged that the vacancy be speedily filled. After the Revolution the proscription against Tipping was removed, and he was created a baronet. He married Anne Checke and died in July, 1718.

Tollemache, Thomas (1651-1694), of Surrey, army officer; governor of Portsmouth; and a Member of Parliament for Malmesbury Borough, Wiltshire, 1689-90, and Chippenham Borough, Wiltshire, 1692-94. He was the second son of Elizabeth, the countess of Dysart (later the Duchess of Lauderdale) by Sir Lionel Tollemache, baronet, of Helmingham, Suffolk. A rumor hinted that he was Oliver Cromwell's son since his mother was allegedly Cromwell's mistress when he was in Scotland. He was educated at Queen's College, Oxford, and the Inner Temple as well as abroad. Choosing the army as his career, he entered the service in 1678 as a captain in the Coldstream Guards. After a tour of duty in Flanders, he was ordered to Tangier where he helped expel the Moors. Following a duel with Captain John Parker, he was relieved of the Coldstream commission but was later assigned as lieutenant colonel in a regiment of fusiliers in June, 1685. He soon gave up his command because he saw "that the army was to be used to set up an arbitrary power." After his assignment as colonel in a Dutch regiment sent to England in July, 1685, he went to Holland in the fall and refused to leave his assignment upon the king's order in March, 1688. His regiment was a part of William's expeditionary force in November, 1688. Later he became governor of Portsmouth and a colonel in the Coldstream Guards. Tollemache served in the Convention Parliament as a member for Malmesbury. Although none of his speeches were recorded, he was said to have "asserted with utmost vigor the rights of his countrymen." After the Revolution, he served in Ireland as second in command to Marlborough and in Flanders as lieutenant general in place of Marlborough. Following duty at Steinkirk and Neerwinden, he was appointed commander-in-chief of an expedition against Brent in 1694 and was mortally wounded in the operation probably through foul play. He died of his wounds at Plymouth, unmarried, in June, 1694.

Trafford, Sigismund (1653-1723), esquire, of Walthamstow, Essex, and Duton Hall, sheriff of Lincolnshire, 1674, and Member of Parliament for King's Lynn Borough, Norfolk County, in 1689-90. The son of John Trafford, he was educated at Trinity College, Cambridge. Trafford married Susanna Orme and Anne, the daughter of Sir Edward Morris, baronet, and died July, 1723.

Treby, Sir George (1644-1700), knight, of Plympton, Devonshire, recorder of Plympton, 1678, and London, 1680-85; a commissioner of peace for London, 1681; and Member of Parliament (Whig) from Plympton, 1677-81, and 1689-92. The son and heir of Peter Treby of Plympton, he was educated at Exeter College, Oxford, and the Middle Temple. Although he left Oxford without a degree, he was called to the Bar in 1671 and became a bencher ten years later. Entering Parliament from Plympton, he was active as politician and lawyer during the reigns of Charles II and James II. After participation in the investigation of the Popish Plot and the impeachment of the Catholic lords, he became a champion of rights and freedom in the perjury trial of Sir Patience Ward, in the London *quo warranto* proceedings, in the Sandy's Case, in the Exeter College Case, and in the trial of the seven bishops. Treby was one of the most active proponents of the Whig proposals in the Convention Parliament, speaking six times before the House or in the conference with the Lords committee. He, along with the majority, accepted the compact idea of government and assumed that because the king had violated the contract, he was no longer the sovereign. Treby asserted that a ruler who "cannot, or will not, administer the government, is no longer king." [74] He interpreted James's action as a "manifest declaration of his will, no longer to retain the exercise of his kingly office, thus limited, thus restrained." [75] He believed that the action of James had effected a renunciation of the crown and that the throne was vacant. He said "We have found the crown vacant . . . we have not made it so." [76] Treby believed that since the nation could provide for the crown in case a lunatic or infant were in line for the succession, it had authority to act where a renunciation occurred, and it was now the duty of the nation to fill the void. [77] But the Lords in a conference asked legal precedence for the vacancy. Treby referred to the statutory enactment of Henry VII's reign. By the provisions of this law, the statute of Edward IV which had declared the vacancy of the throne during Richard II's reign null and void was repealed. This act thus restored the measure of Henry IV as it referred to the vacancy, and as the law remained on the statute books, the measure was still valid. Thus, the first and last precedent supported the ideas of the Whigs in the Convention.[78] The similarity of the situations in 1399 and in 1688 provided the Convention with legal principles that could be applied in charging James II with the responsibility for creating the vacancy. Furthermore, Treby favored religious limitations on the Crown because of the implications of the king's pro-Catholic policies. He pointed out that after dispensing with the Statute of Provisors, James had appointed an ambassador to Rome, and the Pope had sent a nuncio to England.[79] These developments implied submission to foreign jurisdiction, with the further worse implication that the nation would be subjected to the Pope. After William landed in England, Treby was restored to his post as recorder of London and later was appointed solicitor general and, then, attorney-general. In April, 1692, he became chief justice of the Court of Common Pleas. During the illness of Lord Somers, he served as speaker of the House of Lords. He was married four times and died in December, 1700.

Trelawney, Charles (1654-1731), esquire, of Trelawne, Cornwall, army officer and Member of Parliament (Tory) from East Looe Borough, Cornwall, 1685-87, and 1689. He was the fourth son of Sir Jonathan Trelawney, baronet, and the brother of Sir Jonathan Trelawney, the Bishop of Winchester. The family owned about 6,000 acres of land in Cornwall and Flint counties. Choosing the army as a career, he was commissioned a captain in a regiment in the French service. He saw action at Maestricht, along the Rhine under Turenne and in Tangier where he succeeded Kirke as colonel of the Second Tangier Regiment. As this unit was returned to England in 1684, it was a part of the regular force that defeated the Duke of Monmouth at Sedgemoor in 1685. In November, 1688, he was stationed at Warminster as colonel of the Queen's Regiment of Foot with Colonel Kirke when the latter refused to lead his troops against William of Orange. Trelawney then led thirty of his soldiers and Charles Churchill to William's camp and became one of the first officers to desert James II. Although the king relieved Trelawney of command of the regiment, the unit was restored to him in December, 1688. After the Revolution he fought in

Ireland under William and Marlborough and served as governor of Dublin. Although he was appointed major general, he resigned his commission because of the agitation over William's preference for foreign officers. But he was made governor of Plymouth in 1696. He was married twice and died without children in 1731.

Trelawney, Henry (d. 1702), esquire, of Trelawne, Cornwall, army officer and Member of Parliament from West Looe Borough, Cornwall, 1681, 1685-87, East Looe Borough, Cornwall, 1689, and Plymouth Borough, Cornwall, 1702. He was the third son of Sir Jonathan Trelawney, baronet, a royalist during the Civil War and Member of Parliament during the Restoration. The manor of Trelawney, located outside Looe, had been purchased from Queen Elizabeth in 1600. The family was noted for its loyalty to the Crown and its courage in arms. The fishermen of the area had a saying that "a Godolphin was never known to want wit, a Trelawney courage, or a Grenville loyalty." Entering the army as a lieutenant in 1678, Trelawney saw action in Flanders, in Tangier, and at Sedgemoor. After the Revolution he fought in Ireland as a regimental colonel and became a brigadier general in 1691. He married Mary, the daughter of Sir Edward Seymour, and died in 1702.

Trenchard, John (1640-1695), esquire, of Lytchett, Dorsetshire, Member of Parliament, Taunton Borough, Somersetshire, 1678-81, Thetford Borough, Norfolk County, 1689-90, and Poole Borough, Dorsetshire, 1690. The son of Thomas Trenchard, he was educated at Winchester School, New College, Oxford, and the Middle Temple. He was called to the Bar in 1674. After entering Parliament from Taunton, he associated with a group of revolutionaries which met at King's Head Tavern on Fleet Street among whom were Aaron Smith and the Spekes. Their discussions concerned anti-Catholic and anti-royal activities. In Parliament he supported William Sacheverell and Henry Powle. In the Exclusion Parliaments Trenchard spoke against the Duke of York and supported the Exclusion Bill. After the Oxford Parliament he associated with "the Six," a revolutionary committee later implicated with the Rye House Plot. Although he was arrested in June, 1683, he was released after questioning and fled abroad upon Monmouth's landing. Granted a pardon by James upon the advice of William Penn, he conferred with the king on the character of Whig feelings. Because of his advice, James considered abandoning the Catholics and sending for the Whig leaders to work out a compromise. Although he played no part in the parliamentary settlement because of his late election, he was knighted in October, 1689, and appointed secretary of state in 1692 as well as privy councilor. Trenchard married Phillippa, the daughter of George Speke and a sister of Hugh Speke. He died in April, 1695.

Trenchard, Thomas (1640-1694), esquire, of Wolverton, Dorsetshire, Member of Parliament (Whig) for Poole Borough, Dorsetshire, 1670-79 and Dorchester Borough, Dorsetshire, 1689. He was the son of Sir Thomas Trenchard, who had been Member of Parliament for Dorsetshire in the Long Parliament, and the brother of Sir John Trenchard who served as secretary of state under William III. The family had come from the Isle of Wight to Dorsetshire where it acquired the manor of Wolfeton during the reign of Edward IV and added to the estates in the time of Henry VIII. Trenchard was educated at St. John's College, Cambridge, and the Middle Temple. He married Anne, the daughter of Thomas Erle, and died in 1694.

Trendenham, John (1668-1710), of St. Tew, Cornwall, Member of Parliament for Turo Borough, Cornwall County, 1689 (until election made void in May), and St. Mames Borough, Cornwall County, 1690-1705. The eldest son of Joseph Trendenham, he was educated at Christ Church College, Oxford, and the Inner Temple. He died in December, 1710.

Trendenham, Sir Joseph (d. 1707), knight, of Tregonan, Cornwall County, governor of the fort at Dartmouth, 1686; and Member of Parliament (Tory) for St. Mames Borough, Cornwall County, 1665-79, 1679-81, 1685-87, 1689, and Grampound Borough, Cornwall County, 1679. He was the fourth son of John Trendenham, of Philleigh, Cornwall. In the reign of Charles II he was granted a pension of £500 a year and in 1686 was appointed governor of the fort at Dartmouth. After the Revolution he was appointed commander of the garrison at St. Mames and comptroller of army accounts. He died in April, 1707.

Trevor, Sir John (1637-1716), knight, of Brynkinalt, Denbighshire, king's counsel; speaker of the House of Commons; master of the rolls; privy councilor; and Member of Parliament for Castle Rising, Norfolk County, 1673-79, Beeralston Borough, Devonshire, 1679; 1689-90, Denbigh County, Wales, 1681; and Monmouth Borough, 1690-95. He was the second son of John Trevor, a Member of the Long Parliament and judge on the North Wales circuit, and a cousin of Baron George Jeffreys. His father owned estates in Salop, Flint, and Denbigh counties as well as a share in a coal mine at Newcastle. Although a supporter of Cromwell, he favored the restoration of Charles II. After studying at St. Paul's School, his son read law under his cousin, Arthur Trevor, and entered the Inner Temple in 1654. After being called to the Bar, he was knighted and elected to the Cavalier Parliament from Castle Rising in 1673. In his early parliamentary career, he allied himself with the County party and served on committees dealing with the growth of Catholicism and the five popish lords. He was apparently one of the managers in the impeachment proceedings of these lords. However, after his protest against the removal of Jeffreys as recorder of London, he was appointed king's counsel and elected speaker of the Commons in 1685. Under James II he was, too, appointed as master of the rolls and a privy councilor. He was present at the meeting of the council which certified the birth of the Prince of Wales and responded to James's summons to a council meeting on December 16. After the Revolution he was elected speaker of the Commons in 1690 and was appointed commissioner of the great seal and master of the rolls. He was expelled from the Commons for accepting a bribe in 1695. Trevor married Jane Rogers, the widow of Roger Puleston, and died in May, 1716.

Turgis, Thomas, esquire, Member of Parliament from Gatton Borough, Surrey County, 1660, 1661-79, 1679, 1679-81, 1685-87, and 1689.

Turner, Sir John (d. 1712), knight, of Lynn, Norfolk County, army officer; mayor of Lynn, 1691; and Member of Parliament (Tory) for King's Lynn Borough, Norfolk County, 1679, 1685-87, 1689-98, and 1701. The son of Charles Turner of North Eland, an attorney, he followed a career as a merchant and was knighted in 1684. He married Jane Syms, the widow of Allen

Syms, a vintner at the "Rose" in Cambridge where he had earlier served as a waiter. He died in 1712.

Twisden, Sir Roger (1640-1703), baronet, of East Malling, Kent, Member of Parliament (Tory) for Rochester City, Kent, 1689. He was the son of Sir Thomas Twisden, Member of the Long Parliament and serjeant-of-law, who was knighted and created a baronet by Charles and who was appointed a justice of the King's Bench. He was educated at the Inner Temple and succeeded to the baronetcy and the estate of Brodbourn in 1683. Besides his estate interests, he was involved in a variety of London and local trading activity. He was proposed by William of Orange as a candidate for Member of Parliament in 1689. Twisden married Margaret, the daughter of Sir John Marsham, and died in 1703.

Vane, Sir Christopher (1653-1723), knight of Roby Castle, Durham County, privy councilor under James II and Member of Parliament (Whig) for Durham County, 1675-79, and Boroughbridge Borough, Yorkshire, 1689. The fourth son of Sir Henry Vane, who was executed for treason as a regicide in 1662, he succeeded his brother, Thomas Vane, to the family estates in 1673. He entered Parliament in 1675 as a Whig and, although an Anglican, he favored a liberal policy toward the dissenters and was zealous in his support of the constitution and individual liberties. He was knighted by Charles II and, as a reward for his father's suffering in the cause of liberty, was created Baron Barnard in 1699. As a lord he supported the Tory party. Vane married Elizabeth, the daughter of Gilbert Holles, Earl of Clare, and died in October, 1723.

Vaughan, Edward (d. 1718), esquire, of Llandiarth, Montgomery County, sheriff of Montgomery County, 1688, and Member of Parliament for Montgomery County, 1679-81, 1685-87, 1689-1718. The son of Edward Vaughan, who was a member of the Long Parliament until secluded by Pride's Purge and imprisoned, he inherited the estates in 1661. Under Queen Anne, he was created custos rotulorum of Merioneth. He died in 1718.

Vaughan, Richard (1654-1724), esquire, of Court Derllis, Carnarvon County, a Member of Parliament for Camarthen Borough, Carnarvon County, 1685-87, and 1689-1724. The eldest son of John Vaughan, who owned over 4,000 acres of land in Brecon and Carmarthen counties, he was educated at Gloucester Hall, Oxford, and Gray's Inn from which he was called to the Bar in 1686. In 1714 he was appointed chief justice of the Great Sessions for the counties of Carmarthen, Cardigan, and Pembroke. He married a relative, Miss Vaughan, and died in 1724.

Ventris, Peyton (1645-1691), esquire, of Wenham Hall, Suffolk, Member of Parliament (Whig) for Ipswich Borough, Suffolk County, 1689. The son of Edward Ventris, a barrister-at-law, he was educated at Bury School, Suffolk, Jesus College, Cambridge, and the Middle Temple from which he was called to the Bar in 1671. Unable to develop a legal position, he did court reporting. The reports, published posthumously, are noted for their accuracy. During the reign of James, he was annoyed by the increase in royal prerogative and was overjoyed when William of Orange invaded England. After his appointment as privy councilor, he was knighted in October, 1689. After the Revolution, he was appointed serjeant-at-law, and justice of the Court of Common Pleas. He was knighted in October, 1689. Ventris married Margaret, the daughter of Henry Whiting, and died April, 1691.

Verney, Sir Ralph (1613-1696), baronet, of Middle Claydon, Buckinghamshire, justice of peace, 1685, and Member of Parliament (Tory) from Aylesbury Borough, Buckinghamshire, 1640 (April-May), 1640-45 (disabled), Great Bedwyn, Wiltshire, 1660, Buckingham Borough, Buckinghamshire, 1681, 1685-87, and 1689-90. The eldest son of Sir Edmund Verney, knight, marshal and standard bearer to Charles I, he succeeded his father in 1642 when he was killed at Edgehill, and was created baronet in 1661. After attending Magdalen Hall, Oxford, he entered politics as a royalist Member of the Short Parliament. Opposed to Strafford and Laud although a loyal Anglican, he supported Parliament in the Civil War. When he refused to sign the Covenant, he was disabled to sit and went into exile. His estates were sequestered although the action was reversed through the efforts of his wife. Upon his return to England, he was imprisoned and fined for his alleged role in royalist plots. While he hated dictatorships, he would not take action against

Cromwell, and he refused to entertain General Monck. Accepting the Restoration he attended the coronation and received a baronetcy. In the reign of Charles II he opposed the extension of royal power and was removed from his position of justice of peace by James II for his opposition to Jeffrey's policies. Verney married Mary, the daughter of John Blackwell, and died in 1696.

Verney, Sir Richard (1621-1711), knight, of Belton, Rutland County, sheriff of Rutland County, 1682, and Member of Parliament (Tory) for Warwickshire, 1685-87, and 1689-90. He was the third son of Sir Grenville Verney and the grandson of Sir Richard Verney, who had acquired estates in six counties. Educated at Jesus College, Cambridge, Sir Richard, the grandson, inherited the Verney properties upon the death of his brother in 1683. He was appointed sheriff of Rutland in 1682 and was knighted in 1685 after he presented an address of congratulations from the constituents of Warwick to the king at his accession. After the Revolution he petitioned for the title Baron Willoughly de Broke and took his seat in the House of Lords in 1695. He wrote "A Poem on the Safe Arrival of the Prince of Orange in England," and "In Honorem Legis Oratio." Verney was married twice and died in July, 1711.

Vincent, Henry (1653-1717), esquire, of Trelevan, Cornwall, Member of Parliament for Michael Borough, Cornwall County, 1681, and Turo Borough, Cornwall County, 1685-87, and 1689-1713. The son of Walter Vincent, baronet, he was educated at Exeter College, Oxford, and the Inner Temple. He was called to the Bar in 1672. Vincent married Rebecca Serle and died in December, 1717.

Vincent, Shadrack, esquire, of Turo, Cornwall County, Member of Parliament from Fowey Zorough, Cornwall County, 1689-95. He was the son of Walter Vincent and the brother of Henry, Member of Parliament from Turo. An army officer, he served under the Earl of Ossory and in Flanders under Sir John Fenwick. When 10,000 tinners of Cornwall drafted a declaration of allegiance to the king in 1690, Vincent presented it to William III.

Vincent, Thomas (1660-1700), esquire, of Fetcham, Surrey, Member of Parliament for Reigate Borough, Surrey County,

1689-90. The son of Francis Vincent, baronet, of Stoke D'Alieron, Surrey, he attended Christ Church, Oxford and died in 1700.

Vincent, Walter, esquire, of Turo, Cornwall, army officer and Member of Parliament for Turo Borough, Cornwall, 1660, Michael Borough, Cornwall County, 1679-81, and St. Ives Borough, Cornwall County, 1689. He was made captain of an independent company of troops raised in November, 1688, to support William of Orange upon his landing in England. After the settlement, he was assigned as captain in Luttrell's regiment.

Vivian, Francis, esquire, a large landowner in Cornwall County, Member of Parliament (Tory) from Michael Borough, Cornwall County, 1689.

Waller, Edmund (1651-1699), esquire, of Beaconsfield, Buckinghamshire, Member of Parliament (Whig) from Saltash Borough, Cornwall County, 1685-87 and Agmondesham Borough, Buckinghamshire, 1689-95. The son of Edmund Waller and the brother of Stephen Waller, he was educated at Christ Church College, Oxford, and was called to the Bar from the Middle Temple in 1675. The family had long opposed the policies of royal tyranny. He died in 1699.

Wallop, Henry (1658-1691), esquire, of Farleigh Wallop, Southampton County, Member of Parilament (Whig) from Whitechurch Borough, Southampton County, 1678-81, 1685-87, and 1689-91. He was the son of Henry Wallop, Member of the Cavalier Parliament, and the grandson of Robert Wallop, an outspoken republican in the Civil War and a member of the regicide court who was imprisoned for life and had his estates confiscated in the Restoration. Wallop attended Trinity College, Oxford, and inherited his father's extensive western estates. He died unmarried in December, 1691.

Walpole, Robert (1650-1700), esquire, of Houghton, Norfolk, colonel of militia; deputy lieutenant; and Member of Parliament (Whig) from Castle Rising Borough, Norfolk County, 1689-1700. The eldest son of Sir Edward Walpole, knight, a royalist during the Civil War, he was granted an M.A. degree by Trinity College, Cambridge, and was incorporated at Oxford University in 1669. In politics he was in influential Whig leader and was highly esteemed because of his consistent support of party policies. Walpole married Mary, the daughter of Sir Jeffrey Burwell, and to the union were born nineteen children, the fifth being Sir Robert Walpole, the prime minister. He died in November, 1700.

Walrond, Edmond, esquire, of Boney, Devonshire, Member of Parliament from Honiton Borough, Devonshire, 1689.

Ward, Sir Patience (1629-1696), knight, of London, alderman, 1670; mayor, 1680; sheriff of London, 1670; colonel of trained bands, 1689; and Member of Parliament (Whig) from Pontefract Borough, 1679-81, and London, 1689-90. The son of Thomas Ward of Tonshelf, Yorkshire, he was prepared for the ministry by his mother after his father died. After studying at a university, he became interested in business and became an apprentice to a merchant taylor in 1646. By 1671 he became a master merchant taylor. Entering politics as a London alderman, he was knighted at the lord mayor's banquet in 1675 and was elected mayor in 1680. As chief executive of London, Ward was an exponent of the Protestant elements in London. After Charles dismissed the Oxford Parliament, the London council voted to ask the king to continue Parliament in session until measures were enacted to provide the succession and the security of the nation. Ward was the leader of the committee designated to present Charles with the address. The king expressed his displeasure at Ward's activities and, after he charged that the London fire had been started by Catholics, Ward was removed from his command of the trained bands. In the subsequent mayoralty election Sir John Moore was elected through irregularities at the polls. Ward was later charged of perjury for his testimony in the trial of Sir Thomas Pilkington when the Duke of York charged him with *scandalum magnatum*. Ward's denial that he heard the remark was proven false, and he was found guilty of perjury. After fleeing to Holland he asked James II for a pardon through an attorney. Upon the invasion of William of Orange, he was restored to favor and was elected to represent London in the Convention Parliament. In the debates he spoke in support of Birch's resolution against a popish ruler. In his opinion, all of the plots against Charles II and the Protestant religion were inspired by the prospect of the accession of a Catholic king. After the settlement, he was appointed colonel of a regiment of London militia and a commissioner for managing customs. He married Mary Hobson and died in July, 1696.

Warden, John, esquire, Member of Parliament for Saltash Borough, Cornwall County, 1689.

Wareing, Walter, esquire, of Owlebury, Salop County, Member of Parliament for Bishop's Castle Borough, Salop, 1679 and 1689.

Warnford, Sir Edward, knight, Member of Parliament (Tory) for Great Bedwin Borough, Wiltshire, 1689.

Warre, Sir Francis (1659-1718), baronet, of Hestercombe, Somerset, recorder of Bridgewater, army officer, vice-admiral of Somerset and Bristol and Member of Parliament (Tory) for Bridgewater Borough, Somersetshire, 1685-87, 1689-95, 1699-1700, and Taunton, Somersetshire, 1701-15. The son of Sir John Warre, knight, he attended Oriel College, Oxford, and was created a baronet in 1673. Commissioned a captain in the Duke of Monmouth's regiment, he rose to the rank of colonel. Warre married Anne Cuffe and Margaret, the daughter of John Harbin, a London merchant, and died in December, 1718.

Warton, Sir Michael (1649-1725), knight, of Beverley, Yorkshire, deputy lieutenant for East Riding and Member of Parliament for Kingston-on-the-Hull, Yorkshire, 1681, and for Beverly Borough, 1689-95, and 1700-02. The son of Michael Warton, esquire, Member of Parliament who was killed at the siege of Scarborough Castle, he was educated at Cheam School, Surrey, St. John's College, Cambridge, and Gray's Inn. Warton died unmarried in March, 1725.

Wattson, Lewis (1655-1724), baron, Member of Parliament (Whig) for Canterbury Borough, Kent, 1681, and Higham Ferrers Borough, Northamptonshire, 1689. The eldest son of Edward Wattson, Baron Rockingham, he succeeded his father in the barony and was seated in the House of Lords in November, 1689. His political fortunes rose after the accession of Anne when he received appointments as vice-admiral and lord lieutenant of Kent, master of the bloodhounds, and deputy warden of the Cinque Ports. He married Catherine, the daughter and heiress of the Earl of Feversham. After the lapse of his father-in-law's titles, Wattson was created Earl of Rockingham in 1714. He died in 1724.

Weld, George (b. 1637), esquire, of Willey, Salop, army officer and Member of Parliament (Tory) for Much Wenlock Borough, Salop, 1661-79, 1685-87, and 1689-1705. The fourth son of Sir John Weld, knight, he was educated at Balliol College, Oxford, and Gray's Inn. In 1685 he was commissioned captain in an infantry regiment at Berwick garrison.

Wenman, Richard (1657-1690), viscount, of Carswell, Oxfordshire, Member of Parliament (Tory) for Brackley Borough, Northamptonshire, 1679-81, 1685-87, and 1689-90. The fourth son and heir of Sir Wenman, baronet, he was educated at Oriel College, Oxford, and, after succeeding to the baronetcy, he became Viscount Wenman of Tarum (Ireland) upon the death of his uncle Philip, third Viscount Wenman in 1686. He married Catherine, the daughter of Sir Thomas Chamberlayne, with a fortune of £15,000. Wenman died in March, 1690.

Wentworth, Sir Michael (1654-1696), knight, of Woolley, Yorkshire, justice of peace; army officer; and Member of Parliament for Aldborough Borough, Yorkshire, 1685-87, and 1689-95. He was the son Sir John Wentworth, nephew of the Earl of Strafford, by Anne, the daughter of Thomas, first Baron of Fairfax of Cameron. Wentworth was educated at Wakefield School and St. John's College, Cambridge. He was knighted in 1681 and succeeded his father in 1683. After receiving a commission as captain in a cavalry troop in 1685, he rose to the rank of lieutenant colonel. He married Dorothy, the daughter of Sir Godfrey Copley, and died in September, 1696.

Weston, John (1651-1712), esquire, of Ockham, Surrey, sheriff and receiver general for Surrey County and Member of Parliament (Tory) for Guildford Borough, Surrey County, 1689-90, and Surrey County, 1698-1702. A member of an old landed and political family, Weston was the son of Henry Weston, sheriff of Surrey and Sussex, 1661, and attended Christ Church College, Oxford, and the Inner Temple. He married Elizabeth Hall and died in 1712.

Weston, Samuel, esquire, Member of Parliament from Winchelsea, a Cinque Port, 1689.

Wharton, Goodwin (d. 1704), esquire, army officer, and Member of Parliament (Whig) for the East Grinstead Borough, Sussex County, 1679 and Westmorland County, 1689. The second son of Philip, Baron Wharton by his second wife and a brother of Thomas Wharton, he was commissioned a captain in the Earl of Macclesfield's cavalry regiment. In 1688 he was apprehended and sent to the Tower for irregular activities at Portsmouth. After his release following the Revolution, he was a military courier between London and army headquarters in Flanders. Later, he participated in operations at Brest, Dieppe, and La Havre and served as a lord of the Admiralty. In 1703 he resigned his commission as lieutenant colonel of cavalry because of ill health and died unmarried in 1704.

Wharton, Henry (c. 1656-1689), esquire, soldier, of Westmorland County, army officer and Member of Parliament for Westmorland County, 1689. He was the son of Philip, fourth Baron of Wharton, and the brother of Thomas Wharton. After entering Gray's Inn, he was commissioned an ensign in the Earl of Craven's regiment in 1674 and rose to the rank of colonel by 1688. Wharton commanded an infantry regiment in the Irish campaign which participated in the sieges of Carrickfergus and Dundalk. He died at Dundalk of the sickness that killed a large portion of the Duke of Schomberg's army in October, 1689.

Wharton, Thomas (1648-1716), esquire, Member of Parliament (Whig) for Wendover Borough, Buckinghamshire, 1673-79, and for Buckingham County, 1679-96. He was the son and heir of Philip, the fourth Baron of Wharton, who had been a Presbyterian member of the House of Lords during the Protectorate and lord lieutenant of the counties of Lancaster, Buckingham, and Westmorland. Although Baron Wharton met Charles II upon his landing in 1660, he was later engaged in many plots and was among the first to lend his support to William of Orange at the Revolution. Educated by a tutor at Caen, Normandy, and by a two-year tour of Europe, Thomas Wharton modified his early Puritan outlook and developed a reputation as the greatest rake in England principally through his activities at Newmarket. Swift wrote that he was "an atheist grafted upon a dissenter." Entering politics as Member of Parliament from Wendover, he became one of the most skillful politicians of his generation. With his great wealth, he developed electioneering techniques that enabled him to return twenty to thirty members to Parliament although his activities cost him an estimated

£80,000 of his own fortune. During the Exclusion struggle, he joined Lords Russell, Cavendish, and Colchester in support of the Exclusion Bill. His opposition to the Crown was intensified in 1680 when he signed a presentment to the grand jury of Middlesex, urging the indictment of James for failure to attend church. Upon the accession of the Duke of York, he opposed granting the king an income for life on the grounds that a portion might be used to support a standing army. Because of his suspected implication in Monmouth's Rebellion, his house at Winchester was thoroughly searched. His opposition to James II won wide support through his composition of the song, "Lili Borlero" set to music by Purcell. Later, Wharton bragged that he had sung James out of Great Britain. He cooperated with William of Orange during 1688 and joined him at Exeter in November of that year. In the Convention Parliament Wharton was staunch in his opposition to James II and vigorous in his support of William and Mary. In the state of the nation debate he asserted that James "is not our king" and opposed any arrangement "to let in the king; for I believe not myself nor any Protestant in England safe, if you admit him." [80] He, furthermore, favored the vacancy of the throne and urged that William and Mary be selected to rule England immediately with a settlement "as near the ancient government as can be." [81] After the settlement was made he was appointed privy councilor, comptroller of the household, a commissioner to reform abuses in the army and for prizes, but he never advanced far during William III's reign and was dismissed from his offices under Anne. He succeeded his father in 1696 and was created Earl of Wharton in 1706. He became the Marquis of Wharton in 1715. Wharton married Anne, the daughter of Sir Henry Lee, and Lucy, the daughter of Adam Loftus, Viscount Lisburne. He died in April, 1716.

White, John (d. 1704), esquire, of Tuxford, army officer and Member of Parliament for Nottingham County, 1679-98. He was elected to the Convention Parliament in May, 1689, to replace John, Lord Houghton, who was called to the House of Lords. The son of Thomas White, he entered Colonel Fitzgerald's regiment in Tangier in 1664 and had risen to the rank of lieutenant colonel by 1692. White married June Williamson. After fighting at Steinkirk and Schellenberg, he was killed at Blenheim in 1704.

Whitelock, Sir William, knight, Member of Parliament for Great Marlow Borough, Buckinghamshire, 1689. The son of Bulstrode Whitelock, keeper of the great seal, he entertained William of Orange on his march from Exeter to London and was knighted April, 1689.

Whithed, Richard (b. 1630), esquire, Member of Parliament for Stockbridge Borough, Southampton County, 1658-60, and 1689-95. The second son of Richard Whithed, he entered the Inner Temple in 1646 and was called to the Bar in 1656.

Whitley, Roger (1618-1697), esquire, of Hawarden Castle, Flint County, army officer; governor of Aberystwith Castle; and Member of Parliament (Whig) for Flint Borough, Flint County, 1660-81, Chester City, 1681, 1689-90, and 1695-97. The son of Thomas Whitley, he attended Christ Church College, Oxford, and Gray's Inn. As a colonel in the royal army, he had served as quartermaster general and governor of Aberystwith Castle. During the Exclusion crisis he was aligned with the Country party. After the Revolution he was elected mayor of Chester. Whitley married the sister of Charles, Lord Gerard of Brandon, in whose militia regiment he had served as a major and died in July, 1697.

Whitmore, Sir William (1627-1699), baronet, of Apley, Shropshire, Member of Parliament from Bridgenorth, Shropshire, 1661- 99. He was the eldest son of Sir Thomas Whitmore, an Oxford graduate, and a barrister-at-law from the Middle Temple, who owned considerable land in Cheshire and Worcestershire. He succeeded to the baronetcy in 1653. Whitmore married Mary, the daughter of Eliab Harvey of London, a Levant merchant, and died in March, 1699.

Wildman, John, Jr. (1646-1710), esquire, of Becket, Berkshire, army officer and Member of Parliament (Whig) for Wootton Bassett, Wiltshire, 1689-95. The son of John Wildman, "postmaster and plotter," he was educated at University College, Oxford, and Lincoln's Inn and participated in numerous schemes and plots with his father. During the reign of Charles II, he served a prison term with Major Wildman and received a captaincy when he joined his father upon the invasion of William of Orange. He raised an infantry company to support William and, later, was engaged as a spy to get information about Jacobite activities. After the Revolution, he was elected alderman of London and was knighted in October, 1692. Wildman married Eleanor Chute, the daughter of a Kentish gentleman, and, after accumulating considerable wealth, died in 1710.

Wildman, John, Sr. (1621-1693), esquire, of London, army officer during the Civil War; London alderman; and Member of Parliament (Whig) for Scarborough Borough, Yorkshire, 1654, Great Bedwin Borough, Wiltshire, 1681, and 1689. Of unknown ancestry, he was educated at Cambridge University and studied law in London. During the Civil War he served with Sir Thomas Fairfax and Colonel John Reynolds, and for the remainder of his life he was known by his associates as Major Wildman. Yet, he preferred intrigue and money-making above fighting and participated in the army debates leading to the foundation of the "Agreement of the People." Although imprisoned on two occasions for his republican intrigues, he continued his activities against the Protectorate government. In spite of his efforts to effect the return of Charles, he became involved in anti-royalist plots and was imprisoned for six years. After his return from European travels, he cooperated in the resistance movement to Charles II and was committed to the Tower for his involvement in the Rye House Plot. Released in 1684, he negotiated with Monmouth after the accession of James II but refused to join the Duke after his landing in England. Fleeing to Holland, he identified himself with William's cause and, along with Lord Macclesfield, accompanied the Prince on his invasion of England. Wildman was elected to represent Great Bedwin in the Convention Parliament. For a time he and other republicans favored a regency since it would give Parliament greater power over the king. When the question of the religion of the sovereign arose, he urged that rigid limitations be imposed to make "it against our law" to be governed by a Catholic ruler.[82] When the settlement was under consideration he favored making William and Mary joint sovereigns. After the Revolution he was postmaster general, 1689-91. Wildman married Frances, the daughter of Lord Teynham, and Lucy, the daughter of Lord Lovelace, and died in June, 1693.

Wilkinson, Christopher, esquire, of Clitheroe, Lancashire, served as justice of peace for West Riding and Member of Parliament for Clitheroe Borough, Lancashire, in 1689. He had been enrolled as a foreign burgess of the Preston Guild in 1682.

Williams, John (1656-1704), esquire, of Langibly Castle, Monmouth County, army officer and Member of Parliament for Monmouth Borough, Monmouth County, 1689-90, and for Monmouth County, 1698-1704. The son of Sir Trevor Williams, first baronet, he was educated at Jesus College, Oxford, and Gray's Inn from which he was called to the Bar in 1680. Entering the army as an infantry ensign, he rose to the rank of lieutenant colonel in the Queen's Regiment and saw active duty in Ireland and Flanders. After succeeding to the baronetcy in 1692, he acted as lord of the manor of several estates in Hereford and Monmouth counties. The cost of his political activities required him to sell the manor of Caerwent to liquidate his debts. Williams married Catherine Baskerville, and Catherine, the daughter of the Earl of Pembroke. He died in November, 1704.

Williams, Richard (1652-1692), esquire, of Cabalna, Radnor County, Member of Parliament for Radnor County, 1677-78, 1685-87, 1689-92, and for Brecknock, 1678-81. The son of Henry Williams, he was educated at Pembroke College, Oxford. He died in 1692.

Williams, Sir Trevor (1623-1692), knight and baronet, of Llangebby Castle, Monmouth County, commissioner of array for Monmouth County, 1642; governor of Monmouth during the Civil War; justice of peace in Monmouth County; and Member of Parliament for Monmouth Borough, Monmouth County, 1660-79, and Monmouth County, 1667-79, 1679-81, 1689-90. He was the eldest son of Sir Charles Williams, knight, who had served as Member of Parliament and sheriff of Monmouthshire in 1627. After studying law at Gray's Inn, he succeeded his father in 1642 and was created a baronet for valuable service to the royal cause. In the same year he was appointed as commissioner of array for Monmouth County. When he was captured near Gloucester in 1643, he seemed to change his allegiance and was arrested, but later released, on the order of the king. When he captured Monmouth in 1645, he was appointed its governor, but he apparently changed sides again. Although

Williams was a member of the landed gentry, valuable lead deposits were discovered and worked on his property. He married Elizabeth, the daughter and sole heiress of Thomas Morgan, and died in 1692.

Williams, Sir William (1634-1700), knight and baronet, of Chester, alderman and recorder of Chester, 1667-84, 1687-1700; speaker of the House of Commons, 1679-81; solicitor general, 1687-89; and Member of Parliament (Whig) for Chester City, Chester County, 1675-81; Montgomery Borough, Montgomery County, 1685; and Beaumoris Borough, Anglesey County, 1689-90, 1695-98. The eldest son of Reverend Hugh Williams, rector of Llantrisent, Anglesey County, he was educated at Shrewsbury School, Jesus College, Oxford, and Gray's Inn from which he was called to the Bar in 1658. In a few years he had developed an extensive legal practice and became engaged in politics. After his appointment as clerk of the crown, he was chosen as recorder of Chester and was elected Member of Parliament from Chester City in 1675. An ardent member of the Country party he supported parliamentary privilege and individual rights against the growth of royal prerogative. After his vigorous stand in defense of parliamentary power on important issues, he was chosen speaker of the House of Commons on the nomination of Lord Russell. Following the dissolution of the Oxford Parliament he returned to his legal practice and served as chief counsel in several cases involving individual rights among which were those of Edmund Fitzharris, Thomas Pilkington, Sir Patience Ward, Thomas Papillon, Algernon Sidney, John Hampden, Jr., Hugh Speke, and Richard Baxter. Action was taken against Williams for licensing the publication of Dangerfield's libelous "Narrative" in 1684 and, later, for scandalum magnatum by the Earl of Peterborough. In the settlement of the cases, he had made his submission to the king, and he was restored as alderman and recorder of Chester as well as appointed solicitor general and knighted in December, 1687. In 1688 he was created a baronet. As solicitor he aided in the prosecution of the seven bishops and became the most hated man in England besides Jeffreys. His break with James came when he realized that the king did not plan to dismiss Jeffreys or to call Parliament. Although his attempt to welcome

William of Orange was unsuccessful, he entered the Convention Parliament from Beaumaris and supported the Whig position in the Convention. Agreeing with other lawyers, William asserted that James had voluntarily left England without provisions for the exercise of government and proposed that the Convention declare "That James II by withdrawing himself from England, has deprived the kingdom of England of the exercise of kingly dignity."[83] After the motion against a Catholic king was approved, Williams advocated that action should be taken to protect the laws before the throne was filled. This decision could be reached by using William's Declaration as a foundation for the settlement and by nullifying the arbitrary power assigned to the king by the judges as well as the corporation charters. Serving on the Somers Committee which drafted the Declaration of Rights, he urged formulating a comprehensive arrangement for guaranteeing rights and liberties. Using the old constitution as a basis, he recommended that detailed conditions for preserving laws be worked out before the successor to James was selected.[84] After the Revolution the House of Commons resolved that the action against Williams for the authorization of the publication of the pamphlet was "illegal and subversive of the freedom of parliament" and the prosecution was condemned by the Somers Committee. He was appointed king's counsel and lord lieutenant of Merionethshire as well as commissioner of taxes for Flint County. He married Margaret Kyffin in 1664 and died in July, 1700.

Williams, Sir William (d. 1696), baronet, of Vaynal, Carnarvon County, Wales, Member of Parliament (Whig) for Carnarvonshire, Wales, 1689-96. He was the younger son of Sir Griffith Williams, fourth baronet, and the brother of Sir Thomas Williams whom he succeeded as sixth baronet. Williams married Ellen, daughter of Viscount Bulkley, and died in 1696.

Willoughby, Sir George, knight, served as a privy councilor, under treasurer of the Exchequer, and Member of Parliament (Tory) for Marlborough Borough, 1685-87, and 1689. He lived at Bishopston in Wiltshire and was knighted in 1689.

Winchcombe, Sir Henry (1659-1703), baronet, of Bricklebury, Berkshire, Member of Parliament (Whig) for Berkshire, 1689-90, and 1690-95. He was the son and heir of Sir Henry Winchcombe, first baronet, and succeeded his father in 1667. He married Elizabeth Hungerford and Elizabeth Rolle and died in November, 1703.

Wogan, William (1647-1708), esquire, of Richardstone, Pembroke County, Member of Parliament (Tory) for Pembroke County, 1681, and for Haverfordwest Borough, Pembroke County, 1679, 1685-87, and 1689-1701. The second son of Thomas Wogan, he was trained for the law at Gray's Inn where he was called to the Bar. After the Revolution, Wogan was knighted and appointed king's serjeant as well as chief justice of the Great Sessions for Carmarthen, Cardigan, and Pembroke counties. He married Elizabeth, the daughter of Sir John Ashburnham, and died in 1708.

Wortley, (Montagu), Sidney (d. 1727), esquire, of Hinchingbrooke, Huntingdon County, Member of Parliament (Whig) for Huntingdon Borough, Huntingdon County, 1679-81, and 1689. He was the second son of Edward Montagu, the first Earl of Sandwich, who supported the parliamentary party in the Civil War and played an important role in public life during the Protectorate and the Restoration. Sidney married Anne, the daughter and heiress of Francis, Baronet of Wortley, of Yorkshire and, then, assumed the name of Wortley. He died in November, 1727.

Wren, Sir Christopher (1632-1723), knight, of London, surveyor general of all public works, 1669-1719, and Member of Parliament for Plympton Borough, Devonshire, Windsor Borough, Berkshire, 1689, 1690 and Weymouth Borough, Dorsetshire, 1701-02. The son of Christopher Wren, rector of East Knoyle, he was educated at Westminister School under Dr. Busby and Wadham College, Oxford, where he received a B.A. degree in 1651 and an M.A. in 1653. In the same year he was elected Fellow of All Souls College and later received a D.C.L. from Oxford and an LL.D. from Cambridge where he was incorporated in 1664. Wren served as professor of astronomy at Gresham College, 1657-71, and Savilian professor of astronomy at Oxford, 1661-73. While at Gresham College, he was instrumental in the establishment of the Royal Society of which he was president, 1680-82, and he presided at its meetings for over twenty years. Although he was a brilliant scientist, his reputation was derived from his architectural accomplishments. Already the virtual surveyor of public works at the time of the London fire, he submitted a plan for rebuilding the city. After the death of Sir John Denham, the surveyor, in 1669, Wren held the office of surveyor general of all public works until 1719. Not only did he rebuild St. Paul's Cathedral but also fifty parish churches, thirty-six company halls, many private houses and several provincial structures. For his achievements he was knighted in 1672. Entering politics during the reign of James II as a Member of Parliament from Plympton, he was returned to three additional Parliaments including the Convention Parliament of 1689. He married Faith Coghill and Jane Fitzwilliam and died in February, 1723.

Wrey, Sir Bourchier (1653-1696), knight and baronet, of Tavistock Court, Devonshire, army officer; governor of Sheerness; and Member of Parliament (Tory) for Liskeard Borough, Cornwall County, 1678-79, 1689-96, and for Devon County, 1685-87. The son and heir of Sir Chichester Wrey, third baronet, he was knighted in 1661 and succeeded his father in 1668. Entering the army as a lieutenant in 1666, he rose to the rank of colonel and, after serving under the Duke of Monmouth at Maestrich, he commanded a cavalry regiment at Torbay. A famous duelist, he fought Thomas Bulkeley and James Praed, Members of Parliament, and died from wounds received in a fight with James Pound. He married Florence, the daughter of Sir John Rolle, and died in 1696.

Wroth, John, esquire, army officer and Member of Parliament from Essex County in 1689.

Wyndham, Sir Charles, knight, army officer during the reigns of Charles II and James II and Member of Parliament for Southampton Borough, Southampton County, 1689. The son of Sir Francis Wyndham, he entered his older brother's regiment of horse in 1661 and rose to the rank of captain by 1685 when he commanded his own cavalry troop at the Battle of Sedgemoor.

Wyndham, Sir Edward (1667-1695), baronet, of Orchard Wyndham, Somerset County, Member of Parliament (Tory) for Somerset County, 1685-87, 1689-90, and 1690-95. The son and heir of Sir William Wyndham, created baronet by Charles II, he succeeded to the baronetcy in 1683. He married Catherine, the daughter of Sir William Levison Gower, and died in 1695.

Wyndham, Sir Thomas, second baronet, of Trent, army officer and Member of Parliament for Monmouth Borough, Southampton, 1679-87, and for Wilton Borough, Wiltshire, 1689. He was the son of Sir Francis Wyndham, baronet, who owned over 8,000 acres of land in the counties of Wilts and Somerset.

Wyndham, Thomas (b. 1644), esquire, of Witham Friary, Somersetshire, recorder of Wells and Member of Parliament for Minehead Borough, Somersetshire, 1673-78, and Wells City, Somersetshire, 1685-87, and 1689-90. The third son of John Orchard Wyndham, he studied at Wadham College, Oxford, where he received an M.A. degree in 1673 and at Middle Temple. He owned 8,600 acres of land in the counties of Wilts and Somerset.

Wynn, Sir John (1628-1719), knight and baronet, of Watslay, Denbigh County, custos rotulorum of Merioneth, 1685-88; sheriff of Carnarvon, 1674, Denbigh, 1675, and Merioneth, 1676, counties; and Member of Parliament for Merioneth County, Wales, 1679-81, 1685-87, 1689-90, and 1690-95. He was the son of Henry Wynn, the tenth son of the first baronet, and succeeded his relative, Sir Richard Wynn, as fifth baronet in 1675. He married Jane, the daughter of Eyton Evans, from whom he secured an estate at Gwydir worth £7,000 a year. After taking possession, he rebuilt the mansion and renamed it Wynnstay. Wynn died childless in 1719.

Yarburgh, Sir Thomas (1637-1708), knight, of Snaith, Yorkshire, justice of peace for West Riding; sheriff of Yorkshire, 1676; and Member of Parliament for Pontefract Borough, Yorkshire, 1685-89. The first son of Sir Nicholas Yarburgh, knight, he attended Jesus College, Cambridge, and the Inner Temple and was knighted in 1663. He married Henrietta Maria, the daughter of Colonel Thomas Blague of Suffolk, and died in 1708.

Yonge, Sir Walter (1653-1731), baronet, of Colyton, Devonshire, Member of Parliament (Whig) for Honiton Borough, Devonshire, 1678-81, 1690-1711, and for Ashburton Borough, Devonshire, 1689-90. The son and heir of Sir Walter Yonge, second baronet, he attended Exeter College, Oxford, and succeeded to the baronetcy in 1670. In 1689 he purchased an estate at Escott, Devonshire, and built Escott House. After the Revolution, he served on two occasions as a commissioner of customs. Yonge married Gertrude, the daughter of Sir William Morice, and Gwen Williams and died in July, 1731.

Yorke, Thomas, esquire, Member of Parliament for Richmond Borough, Yorkshire, 1689-90, 1695-1710, and 1713-16. He was the eldest son of Sir John Yorke, who was knighted in 1660.

Yorke, Sir William, knight, of Burton, Pedwardyn, Lincolnshire, Member of Parliament (Whig) for Boston Borough, Lincolnshire, 1679-81, and 1689. He was knighted in 1674 and was married twice.

Young, John, esquire, army officer in Sir Edward Breet's regiment of horse and Member of Parliament for Old Sarum Borough, Wiltshire, 1679-81, and 1689. His election to the Convention Parliament was declared void.

REFERENCES

1. William Cobbett, *The Parliamentary History of England*, London, 1806, V, 38.
2. D. C. Coleman, *Sir John Banks: Baronet and Businessman*, Oxford, 1963, p. 115.
3. Charles Dalton, ed. *English Army Lists and Commission Registers, 1661-1714*, London, 1960, III, 138.
4. *The Dictionary of National Biography*, London, 1937-38, II, 524, 526.
5. Cobbett, V, 530, 1127; Great Britain, *A Collection of Parliamentary Debates in England*, London, 1741, I, 342; Great Britain, *An Exact Collection of the Debates of the House of Commons, Held at Westminster, October 21, 1680*, London, 1689, p. 36; James Ralph, *The History of England*, London, 1744, I, 521.
6. Cobbett, V, 33, 51; Philip Yorke, Second Earl of Hardwicke, *Miscellaneous State Papers*, London, 1778, II, 413.
7. Cobbett, V, 51; Architell Grey, *Debates of the House of Commons*, London, 1763, IX, 26, 27.
8. Great Britain, *Journals of the House of Commons*, London, 1803, X, 15.
9. Great Britain, *Journals of the House of Lords*, London, N. D., XIV, 10.
10. Cobbett, V, 57.
11. Cobbett, V, 49.
12. *Ibid.*, p. 54.
13. *D.N.B.*, II, 1018.
14. Alexander Chalmers, *The General Biographical Dictionary*, New Ed. London, 1812, VI, 374.
15. Duncan Warrand, ed. *Hertfordshire Families*, London, 1907, p. 95.
16. Cobbett, V, 34.
17. *Ibid.*, p. 47.
18. Cobbett, V, 53, 55.
19. *Ibid.*, 52, 53, 62.
20. *D.N.B.*, IV, 314.
21. Cobbett, V, 42, 61.

22. *Ibid.*, pp. 34, 35, 42.
23. John Burke, A *Genealogical and Heraldic History of the Commoners of Great Britain and Ireland,* London, 1938, IV, 271.
24. W. R. Williams *The Parliamentary History of the County of Hereford, 1213-1896,* Brecknock, 1898, p. 133.
25. Cobbett, V, 36.
26. *Ibid.*, p. 37.
27. Hardwicke, II, 401.
28. Cobbett, V, 51.
29. *Ibid.*, p. 62.
30. Cobbett, V, 108-09.
31. *Ibid.*, p. 108.
32. *Ibid.*, p. 50.
33. *Ibid.*, p. 45.
34. *Ibid.*, p. 49.
35. *Ibid.*, p. 107.
36. *Ibid.*, pp. 33, 53, 54.
37. *D.N.B.,* VIII, 726.
38. *D.N.B.,* VIII, 832.
39. W. R. Williams, *The Parliamentary History of the Principality of Wales,* Brecknock, 1895, p. 174.
40. Cobbett, V, 57.
41. *Ibid.*, pp. 33, 34.
42. *Ibid.*, p. 67.
43. *Ibid.*, p. 68.
44. Grey, IX, 28-29.
45. *D.N.B.,* VIII, 1150.
46. Dalton, III, 111.
47. Cobbett, V, 70-72.
48. *Ibid.*, 46.
49. Grey, IX, 19-20.
50. Cobbett, V, 33.
51. Collins, *Peerage,* VIII, 142.
52. Cobbett, V, 100.
53. *D.N.B.,* XI, 1255.
54. *Ibid.*, XIII, 160.
55. Cobbett, V, 36, 40, 45, 54, 65, 73, 73, 89, 90.
56. Grey, IX, 10-11.
57. Hardwicke, II, 406.
58. Cobbett, V, 50, 88.
59. Dalton, I, 87.
60. Cobbett, V, 48.

61. *Ibid.*, p. 47.
62. Grey, IX, 30.
63. Cobbett, V, 55.
64. *D.N.B.*, XIV, 63.
65. Cobbett, V, 49.
66. *Ibid.*, pp. 48, 51.
67. *Parliamentary Debates*, II, 213.
68. *Ibid.*, p. 190.
69. *Commons Journals*, X, 15; Hardwicke, II, 416.
70. Grey, IX, 9.
71. Hardwicke, II, 407, 416.
72. Cobbett, V, 38.
73. Hardwicke, II, 416.
74. Cobbett, V, 41.
75. *Parliamentary Debates*, II, 213.
76. Cobbett, V, 40.
77. Grey, X, 10.
78. *Parliamentary Debates*, II, 234.
79. Cobbett, V, 41.
80. *Ibid.*, p. 40.
81. *Ibid.*, pp. 52, 53.
82. *Ibid.*, p. 52.
83. *Ibid.*, p. 42.
84. Hardwicke, II, 415.

BIBLIOGRAPHY

I. *PRINTED SOURCES*

Admissions to the College of St. John the Evangelist in the University of Cambridge. Cambridge, 1893-1903. Parts I, II, III.

Ball, W. W., and Venn, J. A. *Admissions to Trinity College.* London, 1911-16. Vols. I-V.

Boyd, Percival. *Roll of the Drapers' Company of London.* Croydon, 1934.

Cobbett, William. *The Parliamentary History of England.* London, 1806. Vols. IV, V.

Dalton, Charles, ed. *English Army Lists and Commission Registers, 1661-1714.* London, 1960. Vols. I-III.

Fletcher, Reginald J., ed. *The Pension Book of Gray's Inn (Records of the Honourable Society) 1569-1669.* London, 1901. Vol. I.

Foster, Joseph. *The Register of Admissions to Gray's Inn, 1521-1889.* London, 1889.

Great Britain, Parliament, *A Collection of Parliamentary Debates in England.* London, 1741. Vols. I, II.

Great Britain, Parliament, *An Exact Collection of Debates of the House of Commons, Held at Westminster, October 21, 1680.* London, 1689.

Great Britain, *Flagellum Parliamentum.* London, 1827.

Great Britain, Parliament, *Journals of the House of Commons.* London, 1803. Vols. IX, X.

Great Britain, Parliament, *Journals of the House of Lords.* London, N. D., Vols. XIII, XIV.

Great Britain, Parliament, House of Commons, *Members of Parliament.* London, 1878. Part I.

Great Britain, Parliament, 1680, *The Oxford Parliament.* Oxford, 1680-81.

Grey, Anchitell. *Debates of the House of Commons.* London, 1763, Vols. IX, X.

Gun, W. T. J. *The Harrow School Register, 1571-1800*. London, 1934.

Lincoln's Inn. *The Records of the Honorable Society of Lincoln's Inn*. London, 1898. Vols. II, III.

Newman, A. N., ed. *The Parliamentary Diary of Sir Edward Knatchbull, 1722-1730*. London, 1963.

Petyt, William. *Miscellanea Parliamentaria*. London, 1680.

Robinson, Charles J. *A Register of the Scholars Admitted into Merchant Taylors' School*. Lewes, 1882, Vol. I.

Sturgess, H. A. C., comp. *Register of Admissions to the Honourable Society of the Middle Temple*. London, 1949. Vol. I.

Venn, John, and Venn, J. A. *The Books of Matriculations and Degrees: A Catalogue of Those Who Have Been Matriculated or Have Been Admitted to Any Degree in the University of Cambridge from 1544 to 1659*. Cambridge, 1913.

Walker, J. Douglas, ed. *The Records of the Honorable Society of Lincoln's Inn*. London, 1897. Vol. II.

Yorke, Philip, Second Earl of Hardwicke, *Miscellaneous State Papers*. London, 1778. Vol. II.

II. SECONDARY WORKS

Acres, W. Marston. *The Bank of England from Within, 1694-1900*. London, 1931. Vol. I.

Alberry, William. *A Parliamentary History of the Ancient Borough of Horsham, 1295-1885*. London, 1927.

Ashley, Maurice P. *John Wildman*. New Haven, 1947.

Aspinall, A., *et al. Parliament Through Seven Centuries: Reading and Its M. P.'s*. London, 1962.

Barron, Oswald. *Northamptonshire Families*. London, 1906.

Bateman, John. *The Acre-Ocracy of England*. London, 1876.

Bateman, John. *The Great Landowners of Great Britain and Ireland*. London, 1878.

Bates-Harbin, S. W. "Members of Parliament for the County of Somerset," *Somersetshire Archaeological and Natural History Society Proceedings*, LXXXIV (1938), Taunton, 1939.

Bayne, Peter. *The Chief Actors in the Puritan Revolution*. London, 1879, 2nd ed.

Bean, William W. *The Parliamentary Representation of the Six Northern Counties of England, 1603-1886*. Hull, 1890.

Beaven, Alfred B. *The Aldermen of the City of London.* London, 1908-13. Vols. I, II.

Benham, Charles E. *Colchester Worthies.* London, 1892.

Benson, Arthur C. *Fasti Etonenses.* Eton, 1899.

Birch, Thomas. *General Dictionary.* London, 1734-41. Vols. I-X.

Blomefield, Francis. *An Essay Toward a Topographical History of the County of Norfolk.* Fersfield, 1739-75. Vols. I-V.

Bolton, Soloman. *The Extinct Peerage of England.* London, 1759. 1st ed.

Borlase, William C. *The Descent, Name, and Arms of Borlase of Borlase.* London, 1888.

Browning, Andrew. *Thomas Osborne Earl of Danby and Duke of Leeds, 1632-1712.* Glasgow, 1944-51. Vol. III.

Browning, Andrew, and Milne, Doreen J. "An Exclusion Division List," *Bulletin of the Institute of Historical Research,* XXIII (1950).

Brunton, Douglas. *Members of the Long Parliament.* Cambridge, 1954.

Burke, Sir Bernard. *Dormant, Abeyant, Forfeited, and Extinct Peerages of the British Empire.* London, 1866.

Burke, Sir Bernard. *A Genealogical and Heraldic History of the Landed Gentry of Great Britain and Ireland.* London, 1894. 8th ed. Vols. I, II.

Burke, John. *A Genealogical and Heraldic History of the Commoners of Great Britain and Ireland.* London, 1836-38. Vols. I-IV.

Burke, John. *A Genealogical and Heraldic History of the Extinct and Dormant Baronetcies of England.* London, 1838.

Burke, John. *A Genealogical and Heraldic History of the Peerage, Baronetage, and Knightage.* London, 1956. 101st ed.

Burke, John. *A General and Heraldic Dictionary of the Peerage and Baronetage of the British Empire.* London, 1837. 5th ed.

Burke, John B. *The Extinct and Dormant Baronetcies of England.* London, 1838.

Burtchaell, G. D., and Sadleir, T. V. *Alumni Dublinenses.* London, 1924.

Campbell, John, Lord. *The Lives of the Chief Justices of England.* New York, 1878.

Campbell, John, Lord. *The Lives of the Lord Chancellors.* London, 1846-47. 2nd ed. Vols. I-VII.

Carswell, John. *The Old Cause: Three Biographical Studies in Whiggism.* London, 1955.

Cave-Brown, J. "Knights of the Shire from Kent from A.D. 1275-to A.D. 1831," *Archaeological Cantiana*, XXI (1895). London. 1895.

Chalmers, Alexander. *The General Biographical Dictionary*. London, 1812-17. New Edition. Vols. I-XXXII.

Charnock, John. *Biographia Navalis*. London, 1794. Vols. I, II.

Chauncy, Sir Henry. *The Historical Antiquities of Hertfordshire*. London, 1826. Vols. I, II.

Christie, James. *Northumberland*. Carlisle, 1904.

Clapham, Sir John. *The Bank of England*. Cambridge, 1945. Vol. I.

Clark, G. N. *The Later Stuarts, 1660-1714*. Oxford, 1934.

Cokayne, George Edward. *Complete Baronetage*. Exeter, 1900-06. Vols. I-V.

Cokayne, George Edward. *The Complete Peerage of England, Scotland, Ireland, Great Britain, and the United Kingdom*. London, 1910-59. New Edition Revised. Vols. I-XII.

Coleman, D. C. *Sir John Banks: Baronet and Businessman*. Oxford, 1963.

Collins, Arthur. *The English Baronage*. London, 1727.

Collins, Arthur. *Historical Collections of the Noble Families of Cavendish, Holles, Harley, and Ogle*. London, 1752.

Collins, Arthur. *Peerage of England*. London, 1812. Vols. I-IX.

Collinson, John. *The History and Antiquities of the County of Somerset*. London, 1791. Vols. I-III.

Courthope, William. *Synopsis of the Extinct Baronetage of England*. London, 1835.

Courtney, William P. *The Parliamentary Representation of Cornwall to 1832*. London, 1889.

Cox, Hamersham. *Ancient Parliamentary Elections*. London, 1868.

Dasent, Arthur I. *The Speakers of the House of Commons*. London, 1911.

Davies, Godfrey. "Election of Richard Cromwell's Parliament, 1658-59," *English Historical Review*, LXIII (1948).

De Beer, E. S. "Division Lists of 1688-1715: Some Addenda," *Bulletin of the Institute of Historical Research*, XVIII (1940-1941).

De Beer, E. S. "Members of the Court Party in the House of Commons, 1670-78," *Bulletin of the Institute of Historical Research*, XI (1933-34).

Denne, Samuel. *The History and Antiquities of Rochester*. Rochester, 1772.

Dictionary of National Biography. London, 1937-38. Vols. I-XXII.

Dictionary of Welsh Biography. London, 1939.

Ditchfield, P. H. *The Story of the City Companies.* Boston, 1926.

Ditchfield, P. H. *The Victoria History of Berkshire.* London, 1907. Vol. II.

Doyle, James E. *The Official Baronage of England.* London, 1886, Vols. I-III.

Drummond, Henry. *Histories of Noble British Families.* London, 1846. Vols. I, II.

Dugdale, Sir William. *The Baronage of England.* London, 1675-76. Vols. I, II.

Edmondson, Joseph. *An Historical and Genealogical Account of the Noble Family of Grenville.* London, 1776.

Emerson, William R. *Monmouth's Rebellion.* New Haven, 1950.

Feiling, Keith. *A History of the Tory Party, 1640-1740.* Oxford, 1924.

Ferguson, Richard S. *Cumberland and Westmorland M. P.'s.* London, 1871.

Firth, J. D. E. *Winchester College.* London, 1949.

Fisher, George W. *Annals of Shrewsbury School.* London, 1899.

Forrester, Eric G. *Northamptonshire County Elections and Electioneering, 1695-1832.* London, 1941.

Foss, Edward. *Biographia Juridica: A Biographical Dictionary of the Judges of England.* London, 1870.

Foster, Joseph. *Alumni Oxonienses.* Oxford and London, 1891. Vols. I-IV.

Foster, Joseph, ed. *Collectanea Genealogica.* London, 1881. Vols. I-IV.

Foster, Joseph, ed. *Collectanea Genealogica.* London, 1882. Part 7.

Gooder, Arthur. "The Parliamentary Representation of the County of York, 1258-1832," *Yorkshire Archaeological Society, Record Series,* XCVI (1937), Wakefield, 1937.

Granger, James. *Biographical History of England,* London, 1824. Vols. I-VI.

Grantham, W. W. *List of the Wardens of the Grocers' Company.* London, 1907.

Great Britain, Treasury, *Interim Report of the Committee on House of Commons Personnel and Politics, 1264-1838.* London, 1932.

Grego, Joseph. *A History of Parliamentary Elections.* London, 1892.

Hardy, Rear Admiral John. *A Chronological List of the Captains of His Majesty's Royal Navy.* London, 1784.

Harwood, Thomas. *Alumni Etonenses.* Birmingham, 1797.

Hasted, Edward. *The History of the County of Kent.* Canterbury, 1797. Vols. I-XII.

Heath, Baron. *Some Account of the Worshipful Company of Grocers*. London, 1869. 2nd ed.

Herbert, William. *The History of the Twelve Great Livery Companies of London*. London, 1836-37. Vol. I.

Hoskins, W. G. *The Victoria History of the County of Leicester*. London, 1954. Vol. II.

Hutchins, John. *The History of the County of Dorset*. Westminster, 1861-70. Vols. I-IV.

Hutchinson, William. *The History and Antiquities of the County Palatine of Durham*. Newcastle, 1785-87. Vols. I, II.

Hutchinson, William. *The History of Cumberland*. Carlisle, 1794. Vols. I, II.

Inner Temple, London. *Students Admitted to the Inner Temple, 1547-1660*. London, 1877.

Johnson, A. H. *The History of the Worshipful Company of Drapers*. Oxford, 1914-15. Vol. I.

Jones, J. R. *The First Whigs: The Politics of the Exclusion Crisis, 1678-1683*. London, 1961.

Jones, J. R. "Shaftesbury's 'Worthy Men!' A Whig View of Parliament of 1679," *Bulletin of the Institute of Historical Research*, XXX (1957).

Jones, Theophilis. *A History of the County of Brecknockshire*. Brecknock, 1909.

Keeler, Mary F. *The Long Parliament, 1640-41*. Philadelphia, 1959.

Kimber, Edward. *An Extinct Peerage of England*. London, 1769.

Kippis, Andrew, ed. *Biographia Britannica*. London, 1778-93. Vols. I-VI.

Kirby, Thomas F. *Winchester Scholars*. London, 1888.

Knight, Charles B. *A History of the City of York*. York, 1944.

Leach, Arthur F. *A History of Winchester College*. London, 1899.

Le Neve, Peter. *Pedigrees of the Knights*, Publications of the Harleian Society, Vol. VIII, London, 1873.

Lloyd, Sir John E. *A History of Carmarthenshire*. Cardiff, 1935-39. Vols. I, II.

Lodge, Edmund. *The Peerage and Baronetage of the British Empire*. London, 1873.

Lodge, Richard. *The Political History of England, 1660-1702*. London, 1910.

Macaulay, T. B. *The History of England* (C. H. Firth edition). London, 1913. Vol. III.

McDonnell, Sir Michael. *The Annals of St. Paul's School*. Cambridge, 1959.

Maddison, Arthur R. *Lincolnshire Pedigrees, 1902-06.* Vols. I-IV.

Maitland, William. *The History of London from Its Foundation to the Present Time.* London, 1775. New ed. Vol. I.

Maning, James A. *The Lives of the Speakers of the House of Commons.* London, 1850.

Martin, Geoffrey. *The Story of Colchester from Roman Times to the Present Day.* Colchester, 1959.

Merz, Teresa. *The Junto.* Newcastle, 1907.

Meyrick, Samuel R. *The History and Antiquities of the County of Cardigan.* Brecon, 1907.

Michell, A. T. *Rugby School Register, 1675-1842.* Rugby, 1901. Vol. I.

Morley, Iris. *A Thousand Lives: An Account of the English Revolutionary Movement, 1660-1685.* London, 1954.

Moss, W. G. *The History and Antiquities of the Town and Ports of Hastings.* London, 1824.

Musgrave, Sir William. *Obituary Prior to 1800.* London, 1899-1901. Vols. I-VI.

Nash, T. R. *Collections for the History of Worcestershire.* London, 1799, 2nd ed. Vols. I, II.

Neale, C. M. *The Early Honours Lists (1498-9 to 1746-7) of the University of Cambridge.* London, 1909.

Nichols, John. *The History of the County of Leicester.* London, 1795-1815. Vols. I-IV.

Noble, T. C. *A Brief History of the Worshipful Company of Ironmongers, 1351-1889.* London, 1899.

Norfolk Records Society. "The Visitation of Norfolk," *Norfolk Record Society Publications.* London, 1931. Vol. IV.

Ogg, David. *England in the Reigns of James II and William III.* Oxford, 1955.

Oldfield, T. H. B. *An Entire and Complete History, Political and Personal, of the Boroughs of Great Britain.* London, 1792. Vols. I, II.

Oldfield, T. H. B. *The Representative History of Great Britain and Ireland.* London, 1816. Vols. I-VI.

Oldham, J. Basil. *A History of Shrewsbury School, 1552-1952.* Oxford, 1952.

Oldmixon, John. *The History of England.* London, 1739.

Ormerod, George. *The History of the County Palatine and the City of Chester.* London, 1882. 2nd ed. Vols. I-III.

Page, William. *The Victoria History of the County of Bedford.* London, 1908. Vol. II.

Page, William, ed. *The Victoria History of the County of Buckingham.* London, 1927. Vol. IV.

Page, William, Proby, Granville, and Ladds, S. I., ed. *The Victorian History of the County of Huntingdon.* London, 1932. Vol. II.

Park, Godfrey R. *Parliamentary Representation of Yorkshire.* Hull, 1886. Vols. I, II.

Peile, John. *Biographical Register of Christ's College, 1505-1905.* Cambridge 1910-13. Vol I.

Pink, W. D., and Beaven, A. B. *The Parliamentary Representation of the County and Borough Constituencies of Lancaster, 1258-1885.* Manchester [1889].

Pinkham, Lucile. *William III and the Respectable Revolution.* Cambridge, 1954.

Plumb, J. H. "Elections to the Convention Parliament of 1688-89," *The Cambridge Historical Journal.* V (1937).

Pugh, R. B., and Critall, Elizabeth, ed. *A History of Wiltshire (The Victoria History of the Counties of England).* London, 1957. Vol. V.

Ralph, James. *The History of England.* London, 1744. Vol. I.

Ranke, Leopold Von. *A History of England.* Oxford, 1875. Vols. IV, V.

Rees, J. Aubry. *The Worshipful Company of Grocers, 1345-1903.* London, 1923.

Rees, T. Mardy. *Notable Welshmen, 1700-1900.* Carnarvon, 1908.

Rex, M. B. *University Representation in England, 1604-1690.* New York, 1954.

Ronalds, Francis S. *The Attempted Whig Revolution of 1678-81.* Urbana, 1937.

Rouse, W. H. D. *The History of Rugby School.* London, 1898.

Russell-Barker, G. F., and Stenning, Alan. *The Records of Old Westminsters.* London, 1928. Vol. I.

Rye, Walter. *Norfolk Families.* Norwich, 1913.

Saltzman, L. F., ed. *The Victoria History of the County of Cambridge and the Isle of Ely.* London, 1948-59. Vols. II, III.

Saltzman, L. F., ed. *The Victoria History of the County of Oxford.* London, 1939. Vol. I.

Sanford, J. L., and Townsend, Meredith. *The Great Governing Families of England.* London, 1865. Vols. I, II.

Sargeaunt, John. *Annals of Westminster School.* London, 1898.

Schubert, H. R. *History of the British Iron and Steel Industry, 450 B.C. to A.D. 1775.* London, 1957.

Shaw, William A. *The Knights of England.* London, 1906. Vols. I, II.

Simmonds, Mark J. *Merchant Taylor Fellows of St. John's College, Oxford.* London, 1930.

Smith, Frederick F. *Rochester in Parliament, 1295-1933.* London, 1933.

Smith, John E. *The Parliamentary Representation of Surrey from 1290-1924.* London, 1927.

Sterry, Sir Wasey. *The Eton College Register, 1441-1698.* Eton, 1948.

Stuckey, Robert G. "An Analysis of the Parliamentary Representation of Wiltshire, 1688-1714," *The Wiltshire Archaelogical and Natural History Magazine.* LIV (1952), No. CXCVI.

Tickell, John. *History of the Town and County of Kingston-upon-Hull.* Hull, 1796.

Trevelyan, G. M. *The English Revolution.* New York, 1939.

Venn, John, and Venn, J. A., comp. *Alumni Cantabrigienses.* Cambridge, 1922-54. Part I.

Venn, John. *Biographical History of Gonville and Caius College, 1349-1897.* Cambridge, 1897. Vol. I.

Walcott, Robert. *English Politics in the Early Eighteenth Century.* Cambridge, 1956.

Walcott, Robert. "Division Lists of the House of Commons, 1689-1715," *Bulletin of the Institute of Historical Research,* XIV (1936-37).

Walford, Edward. *Tales of Our Great Families.* London, 1890.

Walker, Patrick. *Biographia Presbyteriana.* Edinburg, 1837. Vols. I, II.

Warrand, Duncan, ed. *Hertfordshire Families.* London, 1907.

Watney, Sir John. *An Account of the Mistery of Mercers of the City of London.* London, 1914.

Wedgwood, Josiah C. "Staffordshire Parliamentary History," *The William William Salt Archaeological Society* (1920), Vol. II, Part 1, 1920.

Welch, Joseph, ed. *The List of the Queen's Scholars of St. Peter's College, Westminster.* London, 1852.

Whitley, T. W. *The Parliamentary Representation of the City of Coventry.* Coventry, 1894.

Williams, J. Fisher. *Harrow.* London, 1901.

Williams, W. R. *The History of the Great Sessions in Wales, 1542-1830.* Brecknock, 1899.

Williams, W. R. *The Parliamentary History of Gloucester, 1213-1898.* Hereford, 1898.

Williams, W. R. *The Parliamentary History of the County of Hereford, 1213-1896.* Brecknock, 1898.

Williams, W. R. *The Parliamentary History of the County of Oxford, 1213-1899.* Brecknock, 1899.

Williams, W. R. *The Parliamentary History of the County of Worcester, 1213-1897.* Hereford, 1897.

Williams, W. R. *The Parliamentary History of the Principality of Wales.* Brecknock, 1895.

Willis, Browne. *Notitia Parliamentaria,* London, 1715-50. 2nd ed. Vols. I, II.

Wilson, H. B. *The History of the Merchant-Taylors' School, London, 1812-14.* Vol. I.

Wood, A. C., ed. *The Continuation of the History of the Willoughby Family by Cassandra, Duchess of Chandos.* Eton, 1958.

Woods, Anthony. *Athenae Oxonienses.* London, 1721.

Wotton, Thomas. *The Baronage of England.* London, 1771. Vols. I-III.

Wyndham, H. A. *A Family History, 1410-1688: The Wyndhams of Norfolk and Somerset.* London, 1939.

INDEX